SOCIAL ORDER AND AUTHORITY IN DISNEY AND PIXAR FILMS

STUDIES IN DISNEY AND CULTURE
Series Editor
Priscilla Hobbs-Penn,
Southern New Hampshire University

The Disney Studies series is a home for critical research related to Disney and its relationship with culture and global society. This series welcomes a mixture of monographs and edited collections exploring the large network of Disney offerings, from animation and film to theme parks, from corporate leadership studies to urban planning. The goal of this series is to turn an interdisciplinary lens onto Disney across all theoretical approaches to track the evolution of imagination and magic that, to paraphrase Walt Disney, "all started with a mouse." This series also welcomes explorations of the intersections between Disney and acquired franchises, such as Star Wars, Marvel, Fox, etc.

Titles in the Series

Social Order and Authority in Disney and Pixar Films, edited by Kellie Deys and Denise F. Parrillo

SOCIAL ORDER AND AUTHORITY IN DISNEY AND PIXAR FILMS

Edited by Kellie Deys and Denise F. Parrillo

LEXINGTON BOOKS
Lanham • Boulder • New York • London

Published by Lexington Books
An imprint of The Rowman & Littlefield Publishing Group, Inc.
4501 Forbes Boulevard, Suite 200, Lanham, Maryland 20706
www.rowman.com

86-90 Paul Street, London EC2A 4NE

Copyright © 2022 by The Rowman & Littlefield Publishing Group, Inc.

All rights reserved. No part of this book may be reproduced in any form or by any electronic or mechanical means, including information storage and retrieval systems, without written permission from the publisher, except by a reviewer who may quote passages in a review.

British Library Cataloguing in Publication Information Available

Library of Congress Cataloging-in-Publication Data

Names: Deys, Kellie, 1980- editor. | Parrillo, Denise F., 1974- editor.
Title: Social order and authority in Disney and Pixar films / edited by Kellie Deys and Denise F. Parrillo.
Description: Lanham : Lexington Books, [2022] | Series: Studies in Disney and culture | Includes bibliographical references and index.
Identifiers: LCCN 2021039020 (print) | LCCN 2021039021 (ebook) | ISBN 9781793622105 (cloth) | ISBN 9781793622129 (paperback) | ISBN 9781793622112 (epub)
Subjects: LCSH: Walt Disney Productions. | Pixar (Firm) | Motion pictures—Social aspects. | Motion pictures—Political aspects. | Motion pictures—United States—History and criticism. | Animated films—United States—History and criticism.
Classification: LCC PN1999.W27 S66 2022 (print) | LCC PN1999.W27 (ebook)
| DDC 791.43/6552—dc23
LC record available at https://lccn.loc.gov/2021039020
LC ebook record available at https://lccn.loc.gov/2021039021

To Jim, Charlotte, and Emmy,
the best research assistants I could ask for. –K.D.

For Jeff, Sam, my parents, and in memory of Papa. –D.F.P.

CONTENTS

Introduction by Kellie Deys and Denise F. Parrillo   1

SECTION I   MAINTAINING SOCIAL ORDERS

1. "We Don't Like What We Don't Understand":
   Mob Mentality and Individualism in *Beauty and the Beast*
   and *The Hunchback of Notre Dame*   9
   by Kellie Deys

2. Animated Fantasy and Isolation: The Asian Identity
   Vacuum in Disney's Constructed Universe   25
   by Christopher Maiytt

3. The Magic Island of Seabrook High: Disney Retcons the Civil
   Rights Movement in *High School Musical* Descendant *Zombies*   53
   by Aaron Clayton

SECTION II   REGULATED WORLDS OF (RESISTING) CHILDREN

4. Do You Want to Build a Childhood Trauma?:
   Parental Agency and Authority in Disney's *Frozen*   75
   by Denise A. Ayo

5 "Because My World Would Be a Wonderland":
Fantasy Circumscription & Adult Constructions of Girlhood
in *Alice in Wonderland* (1951) and *Peter Pan* (1953) 93
by Joseph V. Giunta

6 It Isn't Just His Nose That Grows: Disney's *Pinocchio* and
the Erotic Afterlives of Errant Boys 115
by Vincent A. Lankewish

SECTION III   CHALLENGING SOCIAL CONSTRUCTS

7 Who Can Be Super?: Examining the Shifted Ability Spectrum
in *The Incredibles* 139
by Ethan Faust

8 Risk and Reflexivity in Pixar's *The Incredibles* 157
by Francine Rochford

9 Out There: Science Fiction and Surveillance in Pixar's
WALL-E and *Up* 175
by Farisa Khalid

10 Pixar's *Coco*: The Power of Celebrity and Its Impact on
the Adolescent Mind 193
by Susan Ray

Index 211

About the Editors 221

About the Contributors 223

INTRODUCTION

Kellie Deys and Denise F. Parrillo

When the Walt Disney Corporation launched Disney+ in November 2019, the conglomerate could not have anticipated the vital financial role its streaming service would play in the COVID-19 world. The virus initially brought billion-dollar losses to Disney following the closures of its theme parks and delays in filming. But by August 2020, Disney+ had amassed over 60 million subscribers, meeting its five-year goal in just eight months, and topped over 100 million by March 2021 (Hayes and Hipes 2020; Alexander 2021). After drawing in pandemic-weary families with early releases of big-name films such as *Frozen II* and *The Rise of Skywalker* and redirected theatrical releases like *Hamilton*, the Disney catalogue has never been more widely accessible to audiences. Therefore, the eyes turned upon screens should be analytical.

It's not that the Mouse giant hasn't already garnered its share of attention. Both film critics and Disney scholars alike have looked at representations of race, class, gender, sexuality, and place extensively, and rightfully so. Films featuring traditional and rebellious princesses, princes, "paupers," and/or diverse but often still-problematic portrayals of people from places like Africa, Mexico, and Polynesia call on us to explore them. Important works such as *From Mouse to Mermaid* (1995), *Diversity in Disney Films* (2013), *Debating Disney* (2016), and the groundbreaking *The Mouse That Roared* (1999) certainly influenced *Social Order and Authority in Disney and Pixar Films*. Our book builds upon all of these but shifts perspective toward cinematic representations of power relations and their connections to contemporary issues, movements, and critiques. These types of analyses have never been more necessary.

The 2020s have already been turbulent. A pandemic unlike anything seen in over a century, a nation bruised by a president who stretched his powers toward authoritarianism, attempts at voter suppression, and ongoing protests against racist police brutality paint a picture of a world in which power, control, and order are pressing concerns. Blatant disavowals of science and climate change paired with a virulent anti-intellectualism impact policy at the national and global levels. Members of the dominant culture typically wield power, leading to questions about who is valued and heard. But fortunately, power is not always exerted from the top down, since fissures, ruptures, and light-filled cracks occasionally appear. However, despite great resistance, conventional modes of authority may nevertheless still win out.

Social Order and Authority in Disney and Pixar Films asks how power dynamics are questioned, reinforced, and disrupted in Disney productions. These questions address ways of approaching and seeing the world, and we should broach them with children. Applying the lenses of various theoretical approaches, including ecofeminism, critiques of American/Euro exceptionalism, and gender, queer, and disability studies, allows us to review movies as cultural texts, as well as opportunities to face challenging topics. For example, *Frozen* helps us to interrogate parental authority, *Beauty and the Beast* opens up a dialogue about difference, and *Zombies* probes the myth of American identity. Storytellers often oversimplify or mischaracterize complex issues, but by unpacking the films, the narratives' unspoken and sometimes unintended meanings and thus underlying ideologies are revealed.

We hope that the following chapters provide avenues for further analysis of the films and the larger contexts that shape them. Some concentrate on recent movies with little scholarship, while others resee older ones with attention to overlooked power structures. Given that Disney+ interweaves newer releases with the earliest classics, putting them in conversation with one another, we too consider works from all

INTRODUCTION

periods. By incorporating films across decades, this collection allows readers to note shifts, waves, and continuities in manifestations of social order and authority. We can look for those cracks and fissures, see who resists, and challenge harmful ideologies that persist. The wide scope of chapters and their foci easily demonstrates the far-reaching realm of the Disneyverse, which includes theatrical releases, as well as Disney Channel and Disney+ programming.

Although Pixar Animation Studios has a distinctly different approach to storytelling, it is nonetheless still a subsidiary of the Walt Disney Company. Including discussions of several Pixar films helps us think about Disney and Pixar individually and relationally. For example, while Disney often prioritizes a few select protagonists made distinct by circumstance or birth, Pixar crafts worlds in which all supporting characters are unique and could star in their own fully fleshed-out stories. Viewers can imagine or long to hear the tale of one of the other scarers in *Monsters, Inc.*, dolls in the *Toy Story* franchise, or Mind Workers in *Inside Out*. Disney champions the power of the individual, whereas Pixar stresses mutuality. While both Disney and Pixar characters confront challenging situations, those in Pixar movies experience a broader range of powerful and messy emotions possibly deemed too much for children. However, by addressing them, Pixar affords greater opportunities for emotional growth and questioning. We can recognize patterns within the two animation studios, and how, arguably, Pixar has pushed Disney through its more curious and inquisitive approach to filmmaking. The distinctions between the two styles become clear as readers move through the book and conclude with the final section and its focus on Pixar.

The book's first section, Maintaining Social Orders, explores how dominant social paradigms are upheld. In "'We Don't Like What We Don't Understand': Mob Mentality and Individualism in *Beauty and the Beast* and *The Hunchback of Notre Dame*," Kellie Deys argues that these two 1990s films show the harms of othering, groupthink, and a preoccupation with individualism but minimize their critiques and ultimately reinforce traditional modes of power. The following two chapters consider how governmental and ideological apparatuses work together to manage and marginalize difference. Christopher Maiytt and Aaron Clayton investigate some ways that EuroAmerican exceptionalism leads to the suppression of racial identities. Maiytt contends that Disney relies on racist tropes to describe Asians and Asian locales as both inferior to and separate from the West in "Animated Fantasy and Isolation: The Asian Identity Vacuum in Disney's Constructed Universe," an underexplored topic in Disney scholarship. These representations reflect and influence popular attitudes about Asians from the Yellow Power movement through today. Aaron Clayton's semiological analysis deconstructs American myth. His chapter, "The Magic Island of Seabrook High: Disney Retcons the Civil Rights Movement in *High School Musical* Descendant *Zombies*," demonstrates how town and school officials and the community at large control and segregate zombies, who represent racially marked citizens in the fictional town of Seabrook.

Section II, Regulated Worlds of (Resisting) Children, focuses on childhood. Denise A. Ayo and Joseph V. Giunta point out that adults curtail and even outright suppress youthful wonder and expression in the Disneyverse. In "Do You Want to Build a Childhood Trauma?: Parental Agency and Authority in Disney's *Frozen*," Denise A. Ayo unpacks the harmful consequences of the king and queen's decision to lock Elsa up and deny her powers. Addressing an overlooked aspect of the film, she shows us that when societal fears and norms motivate parenting, kids suffer. Parents limiting their children's potential has a long history in Disney's oeuvre. Giunta points to similar messaging in two older films in "'Because My World Would Be a Wonderland': Fantasy Circumscription and Adult Constructions of Girlhood in *Alice in Wonderland* (1951) and *Peter Pan* (1953)." Even when girls rebel, their actions still get reinscribed by parental anxieties and sociocultural forces. In the end, they leave worlds of fantasy and exploration and return to safe, closed home environments, ready to step into gendered positions. While the films attempt to teach viewers "the way," Giunta points out that, fortunately, young viewers do not necessarily read them as intended. Vincent A. Lankewish offers hope for countering heteronormative limitations imposed on youth in his queer reading of *Pinocchio*. His chapter, "It Isn't Just His Nose That Grows: Disney's *Pinocchio* and the Erotic Afterlives of Errant Boys," like Giunta's, emphasizes that children can experience Disney films in unintended and subversive ways. It provides a good transition to the next section, which looks at films that overtly contest the status quo.

INTRODUCTION

The chapters in the final section, Challenging Social Constructs, explore four Pixar films that critique limiting societal mandates. They do so more fully than their Disney counterparts—even if not always completely or perfectly. "Who Can Be Super?: Examining the Shifted Ability Spectrum in *The Incredibles*" by Ethan Faust scrutinizes the maligning of people perceived to have disabilities, including those who rely on prosthetics. Though the film's message can be problematic at times, the overall representation of disability can still inspire viewers and has led subsequent movies to feature more progressive disabled characters. Francine Rochford also provides an analysis of *The Incredibles* in "Risk and Reflexivity in Pixar's *The Incredibles*." According to Rochford, when superheroes are held legally liable for the implications of rescues, the government pulls its support for them, thereby forcing citizens to fend for themselves. The film offers a progressive criticism of individualism. Farisa Khalid's "Out There: Science Fiction and Surveillance in Pixar's *WALL-E* and *Up*" illustrates how protagonists take courageous stands against environmental degradation and abuses of surveillance. In the end, they even use surveillance technology against disciplining forces. Finally, Susan Ray offers a compelling look at the dismantling of celebrity worship in "Pixar's *Coco*: The Power of Celebrity and Its Impact on the Adolescent Mind." She shows us the perils of looking to stars for moral guidance but also how the character of Miguel eventually grows beyond it.

We do not have clear-cut, uncomplicated happy endings in in any of these films, but the resistance seen in some, especially those explored at the end of this book, give us pause and room for a bit of promise, even in light of great onslaughts. Whether films challenge or perpetuate traditional power dynamics (or do both), their considerable influence requires us to look carefully at them. Disney goes to great lengths to provide entertainment that audiences will enjoy and pay to experience. From polls about who viewers are and what they want to see to teams hired to help portray places Americans perceive as far flung, the corporation works tirelessly to stay relevant and maintain its sway over both children and adults. After pushback about the limited number of diverse voices included in its canon, Disney recently unveiled Launchpad, a well-received series of short films created by Chinese, Mexican, and Muslim filmmakers (Kim 2021). This movement is a work in progress, though, as Disney's popular programming still includes old and limiting ideas about gender and sexuality, what constitutes ability, and how racial and ethnic identities need containment. Even Disney recognizes the need to contextualize much of its earlier fare. Disney+ now includes a disclaimer about racist stereotypes in its content.

This book initiates a lively and ongoing conversation about the interplay of social orders and authorities and those resisting them in Disney and Pixar films. These discussions help us understand how Disney's output both reflects and impacts cultural conditions. Depictions of surveillance, racial segregation, othering, and ableism represent real issues that impact people and their lived experiences. In exploring these themes, we hope to unpack the films and their power, while contextualizing them within larger dialogues about social order and authority. Children, often the targeted demographic for these films, need such conversations. And if we want them to question, challenge, and subvert these power dynamics, we must jump in. We're ready.

REFERENCES

Alexander, Julia. "Disney Plus surpasses 100 million subscribers." *The Verge*, March 9, 2021. https://www.theverge.com/2021/3/9/22320332/disney-plus-100-million-subscribers-marvel-star-wars-wandavision

Hayes, Dade and Patrick Hipes. "Disney+ Passes 60.5M Subscribers, Reaches 5-Year Streaming Goal In First Eight Months—Update." *Deadline*, August 4, 2020. https://deadline.com/2020/08/disney-nears-5-year-streaming-goal-in-first-eight-months-with-57-5m-subscribers-1203003841/

Kim, Kristen Yoonsoo. "Disney Creates a 'Launchpad' for Underrepresented Filmmakers." *The New York Times*, June 2, 2021, updated June 3, 2021. https://www.nytimes.com/2021/06/02/movies/launchpad-review-disney-plus.html

I

MAINTAINING SOCIAL ORDERS

1

"WE DON'T LIKE WHAT WE DON'T UNDERSTAND"

Mob Mentality and Individualism in *Beauty and the Beast* and *The Hunchback of Notre Dame*
Kellie Deys

INTRODUCTION

On January 6, 2021, as armed insurrectionists stormed the US Capitol chanting "Stop the Steal," (of the 2020 presidential election), they hunted, with clear intentions of murder, for Speaker of the House Nancy Pelosi, then Vice President Mike Pence, and members of Congress they deemed traitors. As I watched, what struck me was how, despite the surrealness of it, it was also utterly unsurprising. Donald Trump's presidency had been leading toward this moment for four years and reflected something intrinsic to American identity: a fervent individualism ironically wrapped in the paradox of strong group identities based upon us/them labels. Fingers can—and should—be pointed at Trump himself for the role he played not just in the insurrection itself when he encouraged his followers to rally and fight in protest of the election results, but also in his relentless spreading of conspiracy theories. I am more focused, here, though, on the insurrectionists and what they represent. The storming, violent crowd embraced oppositional binary logic, casting themselves as free-thinking anti-sheep, all while shouting the same mantra—parroting the words of Trump himself. While Pape and Ruby argue, in their February 2021 study of the insurrectionists, that "What's clear is that the Capitol riot revealed a new force in American politics—

not merely a mix of right-wing organizations, but a broader mass political movement that has violence at its core," I see the root cause as the same twisted application of American ideals.

Sometime during the hours I spent fixed to my television on January 6, fear and disbelief mingling, I saw in the chaos the climactic battle scene of *Beauty and the Beast*: a dimwitted blowhard with delusions of grandeur empowered and emboldened by followers attacking those perceived as Others. In another flash, my mind flickered to multiple moments in *The Hunchback of Notre Dame* when crowds become crazed, fueled by a feeling of superiority. Reading the insurrection through the lens of these films is an admittedly imperfect comparison, not one I claim offers perfect parallels. What I do suggest, though, digs at an underlying ideology—one which obviously warrants (and has garnered) attention. Exploring pop culture's fictional images of this ideology helps us to recognize its normalized insidiousness. While I could point to a number of films, animated or live action, Disney or not, that depict this amalgam of forceful adherence to groupthink and devotion to individualism, I focus on *Beauty and the Beast* (1991) and its fellow Disney Renaissance Era film *The Hunchback of Notre Dame* (1996) because of their depictions of more complex acts of evildoing than most of Disney's canon.

Of course, we see wickedness in other films, from the Evil Queen in the debut *Snow White and the Seven Dwarfs* (1937) during the Classical Disney Era to Ursula in the Renaissance Era's *The Little Mermaid* (1989) to the Revivalist Era's Shadow Man in *The Princess and the Frog* (2009). Traditionally, Disney has relied upon clearly marked villains with sinister expressions, less attractive appearances, or some other nonconforming quality, using their physical traits to simplistically emphasize notions of good and bad. "Disney's idealised worlds rest largely on the artifice of animation: Good characters . . . exhibit juvenile traits such as big eyes and round cheeks and are drawn in curves, smooth, round, soft, bright and with European features; villains . . . are drawn with sharp angles, oversized, and often darkly" (Artz 2004, 118). *Beauty and the Beast* and *The Hunchback of Notre Dame* complicate these usually simple demarcations of good/bad through physically "grotesque" heroes with whom viewers sympathize, which gives us a more complex vision of horror. Ridiculed and attacked, the protagonists, the Beast and Quasimodo, are marked by their difference. Resultingly, both films demonstrate that mob mentality and adherence to an ideology of Othering through fearmongering represent the true horror. However, the films minimize this moral lesson by depicting the relative ease with which the mob is overcome. Though they purport a message of acceptance, the tales reinforce traditional power structures: *Beauty and the Beast* argues for the restoration of a social order predicated upon royal authority and *The Hunchback of Notre Dame* elevates a Person with Disability (PWD) as a "Sweet Innocent" (Norden 2013, 169), thereby replicating stereotyped images of PWDs. The critique of Othering also seems narrowly focused on the treatment the heroes themselves face and not upon the ideology itself. Therefore, the films espouse that this type of Othering, though wrong, is easily righted by the power of an individual (or pair), rather than requiring action or accountability on the part of society as a whole. The films imply, then, that change does not arise from social activism but through the heroics of singularly unique characters, reflecting the paradoxical vision of American individualism.

THE OTHERING OF HEROES AND MOB MENTALITY

The titular characters, the Beast and Quasimodo, are regarded as freakish creatures by many of the secondary personalities; the Beast is considered an animalistic threat and Quasimodo a deformed simpleton. Both films focus on the Othering that impacts the two, but the differences in how they are regarded determine the treatment that each faces. The Beast is never even given a name and Quasimodo, whose name means "half-formed," is labeled "The Hunchback." Norden explains that PWDs face two paradigms: the Moral model, which views disability as a moral punishment for evilness, and the Medical model, which sees it as a problem to overcome and thus privileges medical fields (2013, 164). The Beast fits into the former, Quasimodo, the latter. We must ask if the films critique or actually reinforce these paradigms by presenting sympathetic characters considered different.

Beauty and the Beast opens with a prologue establishing the Beast's backstory: once a spoiled prince, the Beast finds himself on the receiving end of a sorceress's curse after he turns her away based on her appearance. Transformed into a "hideous beast," he must give and receive love to break the spell. Tammy Berberi and Viktor Berberi argue:

> The Disney acculturation process follows the same trajectory as what Paul Longmore terms a "drama of adjustment," the stock depiction *par excellence* among stereotypical portrayals of disability. In a drama of adjustment, a central character copes with anger and resentment about his impairment. Non-disabled characters in the film condemn a "bad attitude" and encourage his emotional adjustment and self-acceptance, proffering advice as if they understand better than he the issues at hand . . . [D]ramas of adjustment never engage issues of prejudice or social injustice; the responsibility for conformity falls squarely on the shoulders of the individual. (2013, 204)

The Beast's appearance thus acts as a type of moral punishment, and the central narrative of his reformation commences through Belle's teaching and love. Belle, a beautiful outsider and avid reader, yearns for more than her "poor provincial town" (Trousdale and Wise 1991). Though all admire her looks, the villagers eye her strangely, chorusing that there's "No denying she's a funny girl, that Belle" (Trousdale and Wise 1991). At her home, physically separated from the community, Belle expresses her dissatisfaction with the "quiet village" to her father Maurice, an eccentric inventor widely regarded as "crazy" (Trousdale and Wise 1991). When Maurice leaves to enter his newest creation in a fair, he becomes lost in the woods and finds himself at the Beast's castle. Her father's horse brings Belle there, and understanding her father's predicament, she quickly sacrifices herself, exchanging her father's imprisonment for her own. The Beast seeks to punish Maurice, and then Belle, for penetrating his bubble of confinement and forcing him to face his own altered humanity. Having spent years locked away, the Beast has seemingly accepted his station because he understands how he will be seen and "isolates himself from others, having internalized the stigma of its [his impairment's] difference" (Berberi and Berberi 2013, 204). In this way, the film hints early on at the villainy in Othering. Belle's presence painfully reminds the Beast of the outer world's potential perception of him, so he can barely muster a flicker of hope of finding true love, even as Belle resides in his home.

Like the Beast, Quasimodo is considered different, though the latter's physical disability defines him as such from birth. Early in the film, Quasi refers to himself as "ugly" and "deformed," parroting the words of his adopted master, Judge Frollo, as they sing a duet. Frollo only assumes the role because the Archdeacon makes him accept responsibility after catching him in the act of killing a young "Gypsy"[1] woman and attempting to drown Quasimodo, her disabled baby. For twenty years, Quasimodo remains locked away in the bell tower, allowed to watch the life down below, his only friends the stone gargoyles who come alive in his imagination. Norden, arguing that Disney sanitized and simplified Victor Hugo's original novel to a *Beauty and the Beast* level," maintains that the film falls back "on one of the most enduring beliefs about 'good' PWDs: that they possess an inner beauty that compensates for their less-than-perfect exteriors" (2013, 166), evidenced by Quasimodo's steadfast kindness in the face of malevolent treatment. Through Quasi's conversations with the gargoyles, we hear his internalized self-hatred, created by Frollo's fictional tales of Parisians' horrified reactions to his disability. On the advice of his gargoyle friends, he finally ventures down from the bell tower during the Feast of Fools. From that point on Quasimodo begins to question his master as he falls in love with Esmeralda, a beautiful Roma woman.

While their physical differences could signify monstrosity in both the Disneyverse and our culture, the Beast and Quasimodo are not the villains and do not represent the true horrors in the films. The first villain, Gaston, the blowhard of Belle's town, struts and clomps around, knocks over his sidekick LeFou (fool), and believes that he will have Belle, the most beautiful girl in all the land. Gaston appears more physically heroic than the usual wicked prototype, acting as a caricature of the hypermasculinity of the 1980s action hero (Davis 2013, 235). He "eats five dozen eggs" every morning, so he's "roughly the size of a barge" and "every last inch of him's covered in hair" (Trousdale and Wise 1991). "Drawn as a caricature of the macho hero, Gaston still attracts the rest of the women in the film who swoon over him, comically faint when in his presence, and become a parody of traditional femininity" (Zarranz 2007, 57). And Lefou, just to associate himself with the sexual prowess and force of Gaston, falls into line, playing the punching bag who does the dirty work.[2] In taking society's values to ridiculous extremes, the film both shows Gaston as a product of his culture while also critiquing it and him.

While some critics argue that Gaston is merely a bully and not a villain, using that term underscores how aggressive male behavior is normalized and excused; he treats Belle as a possession, threatens to rape her, and often uses violence without a second thought. He is a villain, but his caricatured personality emphasizes the source of his hypermasculinity, so that rather than seeing him in isolation, we grasp a larger social critique. "The Disney film, like so many of its 1991 companions, pinpointed men's problems in the very place that their successes had been located earlier—in the muscular bodies that made them heroes" (Jeffords 1995, 171).[3] Thus, Gaston fits the definition of a villain, a comic villain, perhaps, because the audience is asked to laugh at his simple-minded flamboyancy and, at times, comedic one-liners, but a villain nonetheless.

Gaston recognizes his evilness and revels in sharing his manipulative plans to ensnare Belle. In developing his plot to have Maurice imprisoned in an asylum on the grounds of insanity, Gaston imagines Belle agreeing to marriage to earn her father's release. As this scheme unfolds, an unanticipated hurdle interrupts his plan: Belle's feelings for another. The Beast may keep him from winning Belle and remaining alpha male, so Gaston fabricates baseless and illogical fears to convince the townspeople that the Beast will destroy the village. Oblivious to Gaston's wrongdoing, these nameless people focus only on his physical strength and brute confidence, just as earlier they applaud him for his boorish and selfish behavior.[4] Gaston turns the crowd into an irrational mob, "telling them that the Beast will come for their children if he is not killed, and the villagers go to attack the castle. . . . [T]here is still an element of horror in the way the villagers describe the Beast. They make him their scapegoat out of fear and prejudice, even though he constitutes no real danger to them" (Fruzinska 2014, 109). Using his machismo and social sway, Gaston easily and immediately whips them up into a frenzy. Riled by his narrative, they sing in "Kill the Beast," "We're not safe until he's dead/He'll come stalking us at night" (Trousdale and Wise 1991). These followers then propel this hatred and fear themselves. They continue, "Set to sacrifice our children to his monstrous appetite/He'll wreak havoc on our village if we let him wander free" (Trousdale and Wise 1991). Embracing their ignorance, they persist, "We don't like what we don't understand, in fact it scares us/And this monster is mysterious at least" (Trousdale and Wise 1991). They soon advocate violence: "Bring your guns bring your knives/ . . . /We'll kill the Beast" (Trousdale and Wise 1991). Thus, Gaston attacks the Beast out of selfish motives, but the villagers, caught up in Gaston's physical presence, easily slip into a mob mentality, following him as before, but now, toward violent ends. They unthinkingly adopt a position of Othering based on simplistic notions of difference and unsubstantiated fears.

The Hunchback of Notre Dame offers an elevated critique of this Othering. For one, it is less comical and cartoonish (despite being an animated film). Frollo is no comic villain, and Quasimodo has not experienced a magical spell; he simply is a PWD. Frollo, physically similar to other Disney villains, with sharp features cast in heavy shadows (unlike Gaston), is a megalomaniac judge in fifteenth century Paris, who isolates, dehumanizes, and lies to Quasimodo for twenty years, making Quasi totally dependent upon him. When Quasimodo finally leaves the bell tower during the Feast of Fools, he is awarded the title of "The King of the Fools" for having the "ugliest face" because it is a topsy-turvy world (Trousdale and Wise 1996). But his momentary joy at being applauded—even for his differences—quickly turns. One of Frollo's two main soldiers, Oafish, leads the charge, throwing a tomato at Quasi. The Parisians, who cheer Quasi, quickly turn on him, and soon, they laugh and assault him with food. Quasimodo finds himself tied down, while Frollo watches on, hoping to teach him a lesson. Caught up in the topsy-turvy environment, the crowd revels in Quasimodo's pain. With nothing to gain, they cruelly attack his difference for simple enjoyment. Importantly, it just takes one person—the guard—to start the abuse, and the rest of the group follows. Like the villagers who regard Gaston as a type of authority figure, the Parisian crowd feels it has permission to hate and Other with the law on its side. Demonstrating how this scene sends conflicting meanings, Ward writes, "The overt messages of the film are strong: 'It is what's inside that matters,' but the subtext does not always support this idea. It is that conflict between the overt and the subtle that makes for a confusing and morally ineffective film; the subtext obfuscates the main theme by making it more complex and, in some instances, working against it" (2002, 77). While *Hunchback* attempts to deliver a moral, the violence and bullying Quasi endures at the hands of the Parisians weakens it. ". . . People are afraid of him and cheer when he is pilloried and subjected to cruel tauntings. . . . The film thus illustrates, right or wrong, that looks do matter—at least initially" (Ward 2002, 77).

Hunchback intensifies this portrayal of mob mentality, moving it past a single targeted individual. Frollo, and by extension his guards, show a cruelty not only directed at Quasimodo, but toward the Roma as an entire ethnic group. In addition to trying to kill Quasimodo as a baby, Frollo also attempts to commit genocide, repeatedly referring to Roma as "vermin," and likening them to insects to seek and squish (Trousdale and Wise 1996). Believing he follows God's will allows him to justify his actions and may explain his elevated level of hatred and violence. *Hunchback* begins with Frollo and his men chasing "Gypsies" (including Quasi's mom), and though viewers become most familiar with Quasimodo and his pain, his treatment is aligned with that of the Roma and establishes a strong background of discrimination for his story. When we meet Esmeralda, a beautiful Roma woman, she, too, is in danger and must hide from the soldiers while she busks. Esmeralda feels a kinship with Quasi and saves him during the Feast of Fools, which begins Frollo's focused desire to destroy her. A fiery and clever woman, Esmeralda sends Frollo into a breakdown because he views himself as above human desires but finds himself powerfully drawn to her. This forces him to confront the incompatibility of this attraction and his dehumanization of her people. With his ideological worldview at stake, Frollo turns his self-disgust at this desire outward onto Esmeralda, vengefully seeking her capture and destruction.

The film's end includes an even larger attack against perceived difference. When Frollo attempts to punish Esmeralda, he also aims to destroy her people's sanctuary in the city. In the climax, he captures the Roma, delivers Esmeralda's guilty sentence (for witchcraft), and ties her to a stake to burn her alive. Unlike in *Beauty and the Beast*, the citizens refuse to rally around this hatred. Only Frollo's soldiers unquestioningly support the sentencing and hold the protesting Parisians back. This raises some interesting questions: Are those fighting the guards on Esmeralda's behalf rejecting the severity of her "punishment" while also willingly humiliating Quasimodo because of his disability? The Parisians seem to feel that the Feast of Fools gives them a "pass" of sorts to behave horribly, but that pass also reflects their view of their target as lesser, whereas Esmeralda's beauty gains her compassion. Though

Frollo is unmistakably a villain, his power comes from the guards (except for Phoebus who switches sides once he understands Frollo's intentions), who surround him and act without question. So, the soldiers are responsible for attempted murder or genocide, not the average citizen. Thus, the film critiques groupthink in a somewhat different fashion here than in *Beauty and the Beast*.

Both *Beauty and the Beast* and *The Hunchback of Notre Dame* feature sharp distinctions between good and bad: protagonists who make one final effort to save their opponents, despite having nearly died at their hands moments earlier, and villains who, of course, try to destroy the heroes once last time but, instead, ultimately bring their own doom. Given that this plot construction repeats throughout many Disney films, this begs the question: how do these two films portray a different type of horror? I would argue that though Gaston and Frollo are certainly wicked and share characteristics with other of their ilk, unlike most Disney villains, they rely upon the complicity of the nameless members of their respective societies to embolden them. While the Evil Queen in *Snow White* (Cottrell and Hand 1937) uses her magic to singlehandedly attack her victim,[5] and *Aladdin*'s (Clements and Musker 1992) Jafar calls upon his hench-bird, Iago, to support his plans, Gaston and Frollo are powerless without the backing of those around them. Their strength comes from groups who act because instructed to—whether worked into a frenzy by Gaston or by orders from Frollo. Unlike the hyenas in *The Lion King* (1994), who help Scar take down Mufasa and Simba to serve their own self-interest, the mob in *Beauty and the Beast* and the guards in *The Hunchback of Notre Dame* obey the villains without reasonable motivations, representing an ideology of Othering, a vision of power dependent upon crowds riled up by unsubstantiated fears or a belief in hegemonic authority. And, here, the echoes of January 6, 2021 can be heard again: a powerful figure lies about imminent disaster and orders minions to fight anyone deemed Other.

The films, in creating nontraditional heroes (The Beast and Quasimodo) and one attractive villain (Gaston), shake up what "good" and "evil" look like. Othering, particularly when delivered by a mob whipped up by a blowhard and a demagogue, respectively, is shown as the films' true dangerous horrors. This criticism rings superficial, though, given the stereotypical tropes of PWDs at the foundation of the protagonists' characters. Furthermore, I will argue that the films insinuate that groupthink is problematic only in relation to the films' heroes and not as a practice generally.

THE QUESTION OF INDIVIDUALISM

As we know, "it is impossible to imagine what might be meant by 'pure' (apolitical) entertainment" as it cannot exist without context, ideology, or cultural meaning (Giroux and Pollock 2010, 6). Disney, in particular, has altered our understanding of fairy tales (Zipes 1995, 21) while creating dominant images of childhood and "innocence" (Giroux and Pollock 2010, 94). Zarranz asserts that "The dramatic transformation of literary fairy tales, nonetheless, has been problematic, since Disney's . . . adaptations have systematically undergone a process involving sanitization and Americanization, two distinctive features to compound the so-called 'Disneyfication' of folklore and popular culture" (2007, 55).[6] Tracey Mollett points out, though, that "there are no 'original' values inherent in these stories since they stem from a long-standing oral and literary tradition in which fables have been retold and rewritten, and hence constantly transformed over time" (2016, 56). Mollett, arguing for the malleability of fairy tales and turning a sympathetic eye toward Disney, interprets *Snow White* as "relay[ing] new ideas about the American dream of success to the American people" during the Great Depression (2016, 57).

Regardless of whether we see Disney sanitizing fairy tales of their original meanings or adopt Mollett's position on their constant evolution, Disney films clearly avow American ideals. As Brown explains, ". . . Disney strategically appropriat[es] stories from other cultures and purposely redeploy[s] and reconfigur[es] them, both to serve its own ideological ends and to ascribe to its preferred worldview" (2015, 199). Though Brown focuses on live-action Disney films of the 1950s–1960s set in Britain, I can apply his underlying contention to my argument. *Beauty and the Beast* and *The Hunchback of Notre Dame*, both undeniably American in their narratives, themes, and characterizations, despite being set in France, are intended for American audiences, and reflect imbedded American values. "National identity—a powerful arbiter of individual and group identity—becomes in Disney's hands a symbolic mode of expression through which wider, and specifically American, ideologies of freedom and individualism are articulated" (Brown 2015, 199–200). Justyna Fruzinska (2014) sees the Emersonian vision of individualism as one of "the defining traits of the American identity" visible throughout American culture (2). She writes, "The model of the Disney Company's films is strongly Emersonian, with the hero being different (and better) than his/her surroundings, listening to his/ her heart and striving at self-realisation whatever the cost . . . Emerson's self-reliance is one of the key constituents of American identity, which allows one to view the Disney Company as expressing a sort of national myth" (Fruzinska 2014, 2). Brown concurs: "The idea of individualism is everywhere in US political doctrine and cultural expression, and as several other critics have noted, these values are articulated time and again, in various guises and across a broad time span, in Disney's films" (2015, 191).

However, imbedded contradictions exist within America's vision of itself, such as the "belief in individual distinctiveness, freedom, and agency and, on the other hand, group commitment" (Fischer 2008, 369). Americans assume persons bear responsibility for their own fate, plight, and so on, and "cross-national polling suggests that Americans are likelier than other Westerners to understand the world in terms of independent, self-reliant individuals" (Fischer 2008, 365–66). But the World Values Survey and the International Social Survey Programme (ISSP) show Americans were "least likely [compared to other Western nations] to defend the individual against national interests" or to feel that matters of "right and wrong" are personal ethical questions (Fischer 2008, 366). In this sense, despite their beliefs about individualism, Americans actually obey authority and groupthink more stringently than other Western nations (Fischer 2008, 366). Rather than viewing American culture as individualistic, Fischer finds it more apt to describe it as voluntaristic:

> In contrast to societies based on corporate communities into which individuals are born and to which they are organically bound, American society defines groups—with the great exception of racial groups—as voluntary associations. A person is a member of a group—a married couple, family, neighborhood, church, club—voluntarily. He or she joins out of free will and stays or leaves as a matter of free will; the individual cannot be drafted into or obliged to stay in a group. (How realistic this notion

of free will may be is not especially relevant.) Unlike individualism, voluntarism incorporates, even celebrates, group affiliation. Indeed, in this worldview, individuals pursue their personal goals through the voluntary association. (2008, 368)

Of course, voluntarism is conceptual—in that many of the "freely chosen" groups are not actually equally open to all (i.e., carte blanche mixing of social classes)—but its importance lies within people's belief in their free will to join or leave. Central to American ideology is the idea of an individual's power, even when ensconced within a group. In applying voluntarism to *Beauty and the Beast* and *The Hunchback of Notre Dame*, we see that while the films critique the practice of othering on the surface, the groupthink or adherence to authority figures remains intact. Since the Beast and Quasimodo *are* the heroes, audiences are implicitly shown that maligning them is wrong and that they deserve acceptance.

In *Beauty and the Beast*, Gaston, as he turns the villagers into a violent mob, tries to shut down Belle's protest by telling her that, "If you're not with us, you're against us" (Trousdale and Wise 1991). In other words, the members of the community act as one, demonstrating the "important corollary to the voluntaristic principle [that] might be called contractualism or covenantalism. Implicitly, each member has made a 'contract': he or she is free to join, stay, or leave, but while belonging he or she owes fealty to the group. . . . One can join and one can leave, but when in the group one is expected to be committed: love it or leave it" (Fischer 2008, 368). When Gaston and the mob storm the castle, its Enchanted Objects stop them in comic fashion. So, from the audience's perspective, the assailers are defeated. But has their ideological perspective actually changed? Has *anything* really changed? Without Gaston, the townspeople lack a force to manipulate them, but the film does not suggest that they have learned from their experiences or renounced their adherence to the will of a strong force. Nothing indicates that they will no longer be swayed by another power-hungry blowhard (or worse) or that the overarching system will be altered. Only the beautiful Belle loves the Beast in his "hideousness"; when the Beast returns to his proper exterior and reclaims his privileged normate position, he seemingly "earns" it by gaining Belle's love. No real questioning of the power dynamics occurs. Order returns with royalty recouping power:

a handsome prince finds a happily ever after with a beautiful girl, and the Enchanted Objects joyfully embrace returning to human form and continuing their roles as servants.

In *Hunchback,* the ease with which the public celebrates Quasimodo at the film's end minimizes the critique of the mob mentality. Their swift reversal of perspective, driven by Frollo's cruelty toward Esmeralda, undercuts the lesson about the severity of their behavior. As Ward points out, the film has a "confused morality": the "tragic ending [of Hugo's novel] is gone, replaced by a different romance that leaves the involved parties optimistic about life" (2002, 58). Given the Parisians' earlier treatment of Quasimodo, we must ask ourselves if this change occurs because of the presence of Esmeralda, a beautiful and sexualized woman. She is not only on Quasi's side but also rescued by him from the burning stake. In this sense, the Parisians accept not Quasimodo himself, but Esmeralda's savior. When Esmeralda prompts Quasimodo to step out of Notre Dame and join her and Phoebus, the crowd freezes. A young girl approaches Quasi, touches his face in wonder, and then "accepts" him through a hug. After she leads him through the crowd, Quasimodo is hailed by cheers and lifted onto their shoulders in a clear mirroring and reversal of the earlier Feast of Fools scene. Has the film failed to question the underlying ideology of Othering by simply positioning Esmeralda as a beautiful exception worth caring about and Quasimodo as a privileged special case who should be cared *for* because of his disability? "[The film] seems to preach tolerance of society's Others while criticizing attempts to segregate and isolate them, yet it relies on age-old stereotypes and other forms of outdated thinking about PWDs to propel its narrative" (Norden 2013, 174). People can applaud Quasimodo and herald him as a hero, but he will never "win" the girl, for the romance is left to Esmeralda and Phoebus, the classically handsome former guard. Quasimodo, in assuming his fate happily, is "Too good to be true" (Ward 2002, 69).

In most Disney films, heroes and heroines are attractive and/or powerful, while villains actively try to destroy their beauty or capture this power, usually for personal gain. However, the Beast and Quasimodo physically bear signifiers that the villains wield against them with the help of mobs. Although the "good guys" win in *Beauty and the Beast* and *The Hunchback of Notre Dame,* these are shallow victories. The crowds, so easily swayed, show little growth or thoughtfulness as they unquestioningly change allegiances. In *Beauty and the Beast*, the cruel world order is not transformed, but rather replaced with familiar power structures: the Beast becomes a handsome prince again, and the castle returns to its glory. The world of Disney maintains royal authority. And while *The Hunchback of Notre Dame* proclaims to embrace a more open perspective on PWDs, it does so at the individual instead of structural level. Arguing for special exceptions for these glorified figures, Disney purportedly embraces difference but only by overtly marking marginalized characters as such. The films offer redemption for the Beast and Quasi, but the underlying hierarchies remain firmly ensconced. The riotous followers, so quickly forgotten in the heroes' moments of victory, are overlooked by the films' narratives and therefore audiences.

Many are also ready to forget the mob of January 6 insurrectionists. "Flouting all evidence and their own first-hand experience, a small but growing number of Republican lawmakers are propagating a false portrayal of the Jan. 6 attack on the Capitol, brazenly arguing that the rioters who used flagpoles as weapons, brutally beat police officers and chanted that they wanted to hang Vice President Mike Pence were somehow acting peacefully in their violent bid to overturn Joe Biden's election" (Jalonick 2021). Our job is to not follow suit. We should acknowledge how easily people can get caught up in a groundless and often self-defeating anger often directed at an Other and recognize that our world does not always crystallize clear heroes and villains.

NOTES

1. When I use the term "Gypsy," rather than the more accepted Roma, I do so not to be pejorative, but to reflect the film's attitudes and language.

2. The 2017 live-action version of *Beauty and the Beast* addresses Lefou's motivation by having him clearly infatuated with Gaston (Condon 2017).

3. In addition to looking at how Gaston's ultra-masculinity represents late 1980s/early 1990s gender stereotypes, Allison Craven argues that the film demonstrates the era of masculinity's place in a "postfeminist" world through an emphasis on the Beast and his narrative: "The Disney production . . . not only adapts the story for the early 1990s postfeminist audience but transforms it from Belle's story into Beast's—a story of his masculinity if the Beast is seen as an avatar of the crisis of masculinity during the film's era of production" (2016, 191).

4. We can also see the mob mentality earlier. Nielsen et al. point out, ". . . [I]n the fantastical time and place of *Beauty and the Beast*, the heckling villagers constitute the triers of fact, and their 'jury decision' solidifies Maurice's fate in the asylum. No one (except protagonist Belle) challenges Maurice's institutionalization. As a result, Belle is left on her own to be the sole champion of morality struggling against the rules of law, and moral resolution is not reached until the film plunges into violent conflict" (2017, 116).

5. Although the Evil Queen commands the huntsman to kill Snow White and steal her heart, he cannot follow through (Cottrell and Hand 1937).

6. According to Zipes, "[Disney's] revolutionary technical means capitalized on American innocence and utopianism to reinforce the social and political status quo" (1995, 21–22).

REFERENCES

Artz, Lee. 2004. "The Righteousness of Self-Centered Royals: The World According to Disney Animation." *Critical Arts* 18, no. 1: 116–46. https://doi: 10.1080/02560240485310071.

Berberi, Tammy and Viktor Berberi. 2013. "A Place at the Table: On Being Human in the *Beauty and the Beast* Tradition." In *Diversity in Disney Films: Critical Essays on Race, Ethnicity, Gender, Sexuality, and Disability*, edited by Johnson Cheu, 195–208. London: McFarland & Company, Inc.

Brode, Douglas and Shea T. Brode, eds. 2016. *Debating Disney: Pedagogical Perspectives on Commercial Cinema*. Lanham: Rowman & Littlefield.

Brown, Noel. 2015. "Individualism and National Identity in Disney's Early British Films." *Journal of Popular Film and Television* 43, no 4: 188–200.

Clements, Ron and John Musker, dir. *Aladdin*. 1992; Burbank, CA: Walt Disney Pictures, 1993. VHS.

Condon, Bill, dir. *Beauty and the Beast*. 2017; Burbank, CA: Walt Disney Pictures and Mandeville Films, 2017. *DisneyPlus.com*.

Cottrell, William and David Hand, dir. *Snow White and the Seven Dwarfs*. 1937; Burbank, CA: Walt Disney Productions, 1994. VHS.

Craven, Allison. 2016. "Upon a Dream Once More: Beauty Redacted in Disney's Readapted Classics." In *Debating Disney: Pedagogical Perspectives on Commercial Cinema*, edited by Douglas Brode and Shea T. Brode, 187–97. Lanham: Rowman & Littlefield.

Davis, Amy M. 2013. *Handsome Heroes and Vile Villains: Masculinity in Disney's Feature Films*. Bloomington: Indiana UP.

Fischer, Claude S. 2008. "Paradoxes of American Individualism." *Sociological Forum* 14, no. 2: 363–72. https://doi: 10.1111/j.1573–7861.2008.00066.x.

Fruzinska, Justyna. 2014. *Emerson Goes to the Movies: Individualism in Walt Disney Company's Post-1989 Animated Films*. Cambridge Scholars Publishers.

Giroux, Henry A., and Grace Pollock. 2010. *The Mouse That Roared: Disney and the End of Innocence*. Lanham: Rowman & Littlefield Publishers.

Jalonick, Mary Clare. "What Insurrection? Growing Number in GOP Downplay Jan. 6." *APNews*, May 13, 2021. https://apnews.com/article/politics-michael-pence-donald-trump-election-2020-capitol-siege-549829098c84b9b8de3012673a104a4c.

Jeffords, Susan. 1995. "The Curse of Masculinity: Disney's *Beauty and the Beast*." In *From Mouse to Mermaid: The Politics of Film, Gender, and Culture*, edited by Elizabeth Bell, Lynda Haas, and Laura Sells, 161–72. Bloomington, Indiana UP.

Mollett, Tracey. 2016. "'With a Smile and a Song': Disney and the Birth of the American Fairy Tale." In *Debating Disney: Pedagogical Perspectives on Commercial Cinema*, edited by Douglas Brode and Shea T. Brode, 55–64. Lanham: Rowman & Littlefield.

Nielsen, Laura Beth, et al. 2017. "'Ahead of the Lawmen': Law and Morality in Disney Animated Films 1960–1998." *Law, Culture, and The Humanities* 13, no. 1: 104–22.

Norden, Martin F. 2013. "'You're a Surprise from Every Angle': Disability, Identity, and Otherness in *The Hunchback of Notre Dame*." In *Diversity in Disney Films: Critical Essays on Race, Ethnicity, Gender, Sexuality, and Disability*, edited by Johnson Cheu, 163–78. London: McFarland & Company, Inc.

Pape, Robert A. and Keven Ruby. "Capitol Rioters Aren't Like Other Extremists." *The Atlantic*, February 2, 2021. https://www.theatlantic.com/ideas/archive/2021/02/the-capitol-rioters-arent-like-other-extremists/617895/.

Trousdale, Gary and Kirk Wise, dir. *Beauty and the Beast*. 1991; Burbank, CA: Walt Disney Pictures, 1991. VHS.

———. *The Hunchback of Notre Dame*. 1996; Burbank, CA: Walt Disney Animation Studios, 1996. VHS.

Ward, Annalee R. 2002. *Mouse Morality: The Rhetoric of Disney Animated Film*. Austin: University of Texas Press.

Zarranz, Libe Garcia. 2007. "Diswomen Strike Back? The Evolution of Disney's Femmes in the 1990s." *Atenea* 27, no. 2: 55–65.

Zipes, Jack. 1995. "Breaking the Disney Spell." In *From Mouse to Mermaid: The Politics of Film, Gender, and Culture*, edited by Elizabeth Bell, Lynda Haas, and Laura Sells, 21–42. Bloomington, Indiana UP.

2

ANIMATED FANTASY AND ISOLATION

The Asian Identity Vacuum in Disney's Constructed Universe

Christopher Maiytt

In August 2019, Disney released a trailer for its new on-demand streaming service, Disney+. The advertisement featured a montage of various media now owned and distributed by Disney Studios, including clips from their animated films, live-action remakes, television channel series, and copyright owned films to heighten the excitement. An excerpt of Danny DeVito as Max Medici in *Dumbo* (2019) promised the viewer "something authentic and true," and the titular protagonist of *Aladdin* (1992) asked, "Do you trust me?" (Disney Plus 2019). Ironically, both scenes showed the characters promoting an experience predicated on misleading self-representation. Medici Circus uses manipulation behind the scenes, and Aladdin is no prince. Disney's mass media empire similarly peddles its promises of magic and escapism in the shape of its unassuming mouse mascot. Still, the full might of the media conglomerate is more extensive than advertised.

Disney's ability to shape global culture through popular media, and thereby pass judgment on what is accepted socially, is the subject of this anthology. While this chapter does not intend to infer the intentions of any specific scriptwriters, animators, directors, or actors, I argue that Disney has not behaved as a reflective entity of contemporary American socio/cultural shifts. My examination of some of the company's animated films, from the Yellow Power movement forward, shows that Disney has acted as a restrictive agent of social change. Through the analysis of three films, namely *The Jungle Book* (1967), *Mulan* (1998), and *Moana* (2016), this chapter argues that even at its most progressive, Disney Studios introduces Asian protagonists in settings that limit their abilities to compete with assumptions of EuroAmerican supremacy. Unique to Disney's work is the consistent use of thematic isolation across these films, which symbolically dismisses Asian ethnic spaces to the periphery of American hierarchical social order.

During an age of economic global imperialism and nationalism, cinematography's birth made film a natural medium to immortalize social attitudes on race. Early motion pictures served a combination of academic and entertainment purposes, and filmmakers utilized this new technology to make arguments about the consequences of globalization for EuroAmerican dominance. Early examples, such as Edison Studios's *Bombardment of Taku Forts by the Allied Fleets* (1900) and the Lubin Company's *Chinese Massacring Christians* (1900), first introduced American audiences to moving image renditions of the meeting between East and West. These exaggerated and violent accounts reflected the deep-dyed ethnocentrism and Pacific contact anxieties that poisoned the twentieth-century Western imagination, prejudices known today as the Yellow Peril. Yellow Peril films incensed the public with their stereotypical images of the Orient, which implied that Chinese laborers and Eastern immigrants permeating the American border anteceded the fall of Western order and morality.

Furthermore, the existentialist dread that world power dynamics were shifting out of Western favor similarly influenced traditional academic scholarship. Early historical analyses of Asian cultures were scant. Even by the mid-twentieth century, amateurs, rather than scholars, primarily published research on the culture and peoples of the Asian continent with varying degrees of intentional or unintentional bias. The few available works were often disparaging and rife with racial stereotyping. Not until the social revolutions of the 1960s and 1970s did academics reconsider the narcissistic short-sightedness of EuroAmerican cultural anthropology and historical scholarship. Edward Said led this charge in East-West historiography. His postcolonial critique, *Orientalism* (1979), raised concerns about the validity of Orientalist scholarship.

At the time of *Orientalism*'s publication, "Oriental" referred to all peoples, cultures, and objects heralding from Central Europe, Asia, and a great deal of Muslim Africa. According to Said, EuroAmerican Orientalists typically construed the Orient in opposition to the West as diametric poles of civilization and morality (1979, 71–73). Interpretations of Orientalist topics employed pseudo-scientific philosophical analysis and imaginative vocabulary to describe the Orient as an exotic dimension of inescapable "Otherness." According to Said, twentieth-century EuroAmerican authorship wielded imperialistic authority over Asian history and identity through their domination of academic interpretation (1979, 3, 7–9). The objectification of a romantic and foreign Oriental paradigm, although unintended by Orientalists, created a distorted facsimile of the Asian world that existed only in the Western imagination.

Of course, historians published their work for others to consume and reinterpret. In *Orientalism*, Said expressed his concerns over the perpetuation of these falsified images beyond academics' strata. Popular television and film, according to Said, forced Orientalist "information into more and more standardized molds," and created cultural stereotypes of the Orient that "intensified the hold of the nineteenth-century academic and imaginative demonology of 'the mysterious Orient'" (1979, 26). As Said predicted, the staying power of stereotypes continued to influence media entertainment, and therefore dictated unfavorable popular attitudes toward Asian minorities for decades to come. Contemporary media historians, examining characters from the Disney franchise, frequently expressed dismay over the prevalence of Orientalist stereotypes present in the company's post-World War II films. For example, Dr. Kimiko Akita and Dr. Rick Kenney explored Si and Am of *Lady and the Tramp* (1955) in their research on Oriental villainy and Disney media diversity (2013). According to their article, Disney's depictions of Siamese cats precisely rendered the connections between the foreign, the unknown, malicious intent, and Asian stereotypes that Said criticized. In the analyzed scene, the authors point to the cats' Oriental inscrutability as a source of tension and a foil to Lady's more domestic Western benevolence. Using Said's theoretical framework to survey the film's dialogue, physical characteristics, and stereotypes, Akita and

Kenney argue that Disney presented Asian identity as a "legacy" of the villainous Orient in direct opposition to the West (2013, 61–62).

Akita and Kenney's article fits in among works by other contemporary scholars interested in trends in racial representation in Disney media. Daniel Goldmark and Utz McKnight's 2008 argument also drew on *Lady and the Tramp* and Said's 1970s-era conclusions to interpret twenty-first-century American ethnocentrism. The ahistorical reliance on *Orientalism* and the unjust emphasis on this singular film in a much larger franchise failed to account for variations in Asian stereotypes throughout Disney's extended filmography. Similarly, Yen-Rong Wong's editorial review of Disney's racist entertainment history sought evidence of "Orientalist undertones" to determine the presence of anti-Asian racism (2019, 3–4). Her critique of the imprecise "outdated cultural depictions" disclaimer before some films on the Disney+ platform questions if it had been faithfully applied to all appropriate works. Her short op-ed never reaches a conclusion on the matter, and therefore represents a missed opportunity to discuss Disney's role in shaping intercultural contact perceptions or their later characterizations of Asian identities in response to an increasingly self-aware multiethnic American public.

The trend of many media scholars, such as those previously mentioned, to fixate on Disney's earlier works discouraged consideration of how changing stereotypes shaped Disney's Asian protagonists over time. Reliance on Said's fledgling Orientalist critique was partially responsible for this oversight. Immediately after its publication, Orientalists and historians criticized *Orientalism*'s perspective of the West as simultaneously culturally homogeneous and singular in its approach to the East (Ma 2000, XII). Absent from Said's *Orientalism*, and subsequently from works that base their arguments upon it, was any meaningful investigation of blended East/West identities.

THE SILVER AGE (1950–1967): *THE JUNGLE BOOK* (1967) AND BLACK-ASIAN COOPERATION

Scholars of Walt Disney Studios's films have argued that the entertainment company remains stunted in the political atmosphere of the 1950s and 1960s (Burdick 2016, 47). Particularly prominent in this period of

Disney history, more often recognized as the Silver Age, was Disney's use of post-World War II racial stereotypes to create plot points driven by racial tension (such as the kidnapping of the Lost Boys by the "red men" in 1953's *Peter Pan*) (Giroux 1999, 103). As the Silver Age progressed, however, Disney abruptly shifted to a secondary presentation of Asian characters representative of an emerging mid-century model minority stereotype, which prospered by circulating narratives of submission, social awkwardness, and academic achievement as hallmarks of the race while simultaneously amalgamating dozens of different East Asian ethnic identities into a single group (Maiytt 2019, 54–55). Additionally, it specifically suggested that Asian peoples were more assimilable to EuroAmerican standards than other ethnic minorities. The stereotype emerged in response to changes in immigration policy, specifically the McCarran-Walter Act (1952). This reform ended the formal exclusion of Asian immigrants, in place since 1924, by introducing relaxed quotas that favored immigrants with exploitable skill sets. Pro-revisionist politicians, who adhered to the international relations theory that economic power imbalances preserved peace between nations, argued that the coalescence of these migrants into the American working class would undercut the competition of Japan's revitalized post-WWII economic boom.

Correspondingly, films that propagated images of the hardworking and servile East Asian migrant received accolades and generous box office returns. *The King and I* (1956), which presented a version of the Orient as docile and fertile to the civilizing influence of EuroAmerican mentorship, won numerous Academy and Golden Globe Awards (Lee 2004, 106–107). The first American film to feature a largely Asian cast, *Flower Drum Song* (1961), reversed the track of odious Yellow Peril social attitudes by celebrating the arrival of model minority Chinese immigrants eager to assimilate to the standards of American exceptionalism. It was nominated for five Academy Awards and was a rousing fiscal success (Maiytt 2019, 55–57). Media's formulaic construct of a supplicant race intent on appeasing a white majority temporarily soothed an American public already deeply divided by civil rights-era federal desegregation of the military and public education.

Filmmakers' praise for model minority images belied the American racial tensions of the mid-twentieth-century civil rights movement and its effect on Asiatic progressives. Initially, the "positive" influence of the model minority archetype, along with the absence of a shared pan-ethnic identity among Asian immigrants and their descendants, undermined demonstrative efforts by Asian minorities. Though they responded to the civil rights movement spearheaded by black reformers and its resistance to racial discrimination and colonialism, these early Yellow Power radicals struggled to make a substantive impact in the 1950s and 1960s. However, collaborations by individual Japanese, Filipino, and Chinese radicals with the Black Panthers and civil rights advocates demonstrated the shared frustrations between them and other American ethnic minorities. A nervous white American majority digested these messages and interpreted them as symptoms of a threatening new social order.

In this atmosphere, Disney released its animated version of Rudyard Kipling's *The Jungle Book* in 1967. The choice to reinvigorate Kipling's work was logical to Disney filmmakers. Kipling had also lived through a period of racial unrest when the Filipino colonies demanded independence from American imperial rule in the 1890s, which inspired his famous "White Man's Burden" poem. The collection of fables that Kipling called *The Jungle Book* features a number of anthropomorphized animal characters whose moralistic narratives lauded conformity to existing social hierarchy. Mowgli, a human child from central India, appears in several of the stories. Adopted by a wolf pack, young Mowgli learns the laws of the jungle (a metaphor for the expectations of social stratification) from his brown bear teacher, Baloo. He also befriends Bagheera, a panther already familiar with the behaviors of "man" after growing up in captivity. The disgraced manhunting tiger, Shere Khan, who first fails to kill Mowgli when he chases away the infant's parents, frequently interrupts Mowgli's idyllic boyhood with attempts on his life. Mowgli's animal custodians protect him as he grows to adulthood, after which he leaves the jungle to rejoin Indian civilization and kill Shere Khan.

Disney's animated film took liberties with its adaptation of Kipling's *Jungle Book*. Rather than Kipling's "bold" toddler (1910) who woos the wolves into adopting him or the young man who slays the pursuing tiger, Disney's reimagining of Mowgli traps him in the eternal childhood of the guileless, unsophisticated model minority stereotype. The film concentrates specifically on stories about Mowgli and his relationship with Baloo and Bagheera. These guardian animals, voiced by the American jazz musician Philip Harris and British actor Sebastian Cabot, respectively, escort young Mowgli to a nearby village before Shere Khan discovers that the wolf pack has harbored Mowgli. Along the way, Mowgli shrugs off Bagheera's social lectures ("You wouldn't marry a panther, would you?") meant to convince the boy to stick with his own kind (Reitherman 1967). Resistant to the news that the jungle is no place for him, Mowgli repeatedly tries to find acceptance among different animal groups. Some take advantage of his innocence for personal gains, and the boy is only spared by Bagheera and Baloo's interferences.

The premiere of Disney's version of *The Jungle Book* during a historic pushback by the opponents of the civil rights movement alludes to the lure of multiracial collaboration for Asiatic minorities and demonstrates an assumed need for EuroAmerican intervention and control. Disney reflected this paradigm through the invention of King Louie, the orangutan monkey-king. For example, Kipling's Baloo and Bagheera criticize the monkeys as lawless, and explicitly, leaderless jungle outcasts (1910). Conversely, the jive-talking, swing-dancing King Louie rules Disney's monkey kingdom. He kidnaps Mowgli in the hopes of learning the ways of "man" from him. King Louie wants nothing more than to "be like other men," a clearly ridiculous hope doomed to fail (Reitherman 1967). The exaggerated facial distortions of King Louie and his subjects and their stereotypical associations with jazz and play encouraged associations with black American populations. King Louie's appeals to his "cousin" Mowgli constitute a thinly veiled reference to cooperative social demonstrations between civil rights and Yellow Power activists.

The animated film also includes anamorphic representations of Caucasian supporters of these progressive movements via the vultures Buzzie, Flaps, Ziggy, and Dizzy. Moments after vowing to champion Mowgli in "That's What Friends Are For," the vultures prove themselves oafish and cowardly (Reitherman 1967). This critique of hippie counterculture, identifiable through their Liverpudlian accents (Disney stylized the buzzards after The Beatles), represents the student anti-Vietnam war protests, a favored subject of the early Yellow Power movement. Mowgli's abortive search for companionship among the jungle's various social groups ultimately unmasks a number of false allies, until the Americanized Baloo comes to his rescue.

Mowgli's total isolation from identifying with these other "ethnic"/ animal groups is complete. Now that Mowgli recognizes that he has no place in the "jungle," he reluctantly trails Baloo and Bagheera to the "Man-village." Before closing, Disney's *The Jungle Book* sneaks in one more historically significant morality lesson. As the group approaches the village, Mowgli sees an Indian girl gathering water at the jungle's edge and falls for her at first sight. Enraptured, he follows her into the village with a submissive shrug. This subtle allusion to Bagheera's earlier marriage lecture exposes Disney's unfavorable stance toward miscegenation.

Interracial relationships were hotly debated in America in the late 1960s. In fact, the Supreme Court struck down state laws banning interracial marriages only a few months before the release of *The Jungle Book*. Though this landmark decision (1967's *Loving v. Virginia*) found miscegenation laws unconstitutional, Disney's statements via *The Jungle Book* criticized interracial love and cooperation. The girl who finally woos Mowgli willingly from the jungle offers the audience little sense of what society Mowgli joins. He and his newfound beloved are the only human characters. In a final demonstration of Disney's construction of a model minority universe, the audience bids farewell to Mowgli on the riverbank, where he appears to enlist in an underdeveloped community composed only of children. The young couple exists on the periphery of Baloo and Bagheera's jungle, and once they exit, they disappear into their own social vacuum.

THE BIRTH OF ASIAN AMERICAN IDENTITY DURING THE DISNEY BRONZE/DARK AGES (1970–1988)

The Jungle Book did not reflect the social politics of civil rights-era Asiatic communities or those of the following decades. American student-led protest movements in the late 1960s rejected all the stereotypes associated with the common term "Oriental," along with the word as a descriptor of Asian heritage. Instead, Asiatics favored the new identifier "Asian American" (Ogbar 2011, 130). Yuji Ichioka and Emma Gee, then graduate students, first coined the modernized moniker when they founded the multiethnic Asian American Political Alliance (AAPA) at the University of California, Berkeley (Maeda 2012, 9–10). As a collective, these Asian American student cooperatives sparked the revolutionary Yellow Power movement. Their twofold message stressed the rejection of EuroAmerican stereotypes that celebrated Asian meekness and assimilation into a white social order and the determination to make lasting institutional changes both on and off instructional campuses (Ogbar 2011, 123–125).

By November of 1968, the AAPA collaborated with other minority student organizations, including the Black Student Union and the Latin American Student Organization, to form the Third World Liberation Front (twLF). Operating predominantly in California, the twLF demanded that academic institutions diversify their Eurocentric curriculums to represent the modern American collegiate student body's cosmopolitan nature ("twLF Demands" 1969). Together, these organizations shut down college campuses and physically rebuffed police efforts to halt the strike, thereby disrupting white authority over academic institutions and defying stereotypes of Asian American malleability to the reigning social order (Maeda 2012, 29). This first-wave Yellow Power demonstration continued for nearly six months, making it the longest student-led strike on an academic campus in American history. It resulted in the successful establishment of the first of many schools of Ethnic Studies in the United States.

The use of Orientalist language and Yellow-Peril imagery in modern American film largely evaporated after the twLF strikes and the establishment of academically recognized ethnic studies. Disney never created another character in the likes of Si or Am again. However, Disney continued to play a role in the mass consumption of Asian identity images in their children's animation films, specifically, *Aladdin* (1992), *Mulan* (1998), *Lilo and Stitch* (2002), and *Moana* (2016), all featuring the media giant's conceptualization of Asian protagonists. These films delineated the exploration of Asian identity to escapist fantasy environments, where their actions could be interpreted as equally imaginary. The confinement of Disney's Asian protagonists outside realistic worlds made up of complex social and cultural interactions simultaneously insulated its largely EuroAmerican viewership from comparing these characters to an assumed white, Western standard. The result of separating images of mystic Asian heroism from white heroism reinforced EuroAmerican ethnocentrism and gave it sustainability beyond the realm of childish fiction. Conversely, culturally inaccurate depictions, historical errors, mythic/cultural historical revisions, and alienating plot devices dissolved spectators' sense of intrepid and moralistic Asian characters as part of an increasingly multicultural modern reality.

The intentional or subconscious desires of popular entertainers to deny these changing Western realities, even if only within fictional plot devices, sets the stage for real world consequences far more inhumane than the actions of any children's fantasy villain. Despite the progress of the Yellow Power's first wave, international economic competition thrust racial conflict between Asian Americans and the EuroAmerican majority into the forefront of Americans' media consciousness in the 1980s. The export of inexpensive manufactured products from Asia into the United States aggravated an ongoing American economic recession, particularly in the automotive industry. Suppliers' increasing proclivity for import sales over domestic production prompted reactions as far-reaching as bans on foreign cars in marked parking lots and assaults of Japanese vehicle operators on public roadways (Koshiro 1999, 2–3). One politician publicly suggested a return to nuclear warfare with Japan as a means of reviving automotive sales (Zia 2000, 58).

As the use of anti-Asian slurs returned to popular media discourse, acts of racist violence increased. In Michigan, where Chrysler closed numerous assembly plants between 1980–1982, two white automotive workers brutally and publicly murdered a young Chinese American trade school graduate, Vincent Chin (Espiritu 1992, 155–57). Multiple witnesses reported the perpetrators used racial epithets during the beating, indicating that they mistook Chin's ethnicity as Japanese. Despite this, local advocacy groups and government litigators refused to recognize Chin's murder as a hate crime. Similarly, a white, unemployed welder armed with a semi-automatic rifle fired on a group of South Asian elementary school children on a playground in January 1989, killing five children between the ages of six and nine years old. Investigations into the shooter's background revealed a vocal animosity to Asian American populations and a fear of foreign economic competition. Public media coverage again dismissed accusations that white supremacist ideologies motivated these violent perpetrators (Zia 2000, 91).

These events incensed the Asian American civil rights community and triggered the second wave of the Yellow Power movement. Minority rights advocates organized professional legal associations, such as the Asian American Citizens for Justice (AACJ), which lobbied for more stringent consequences for racial discrimination and violence (Zia 2000, 58–81). The AACJ worked tirelessly to bring awareness to the connections between racial stereotyping and violence against Asian minorities. As a result, Asian American communities received increased national recognition and became progressively more outspoken. In this radically galvanized and vigilant atmosphere, the Disney Renaissance, which featured several ethnically diverse protagonists, was born.

THE DISNEY RENAISSANCE (1989–1999): MODEL MINORITY *MULAN* (1998) SAVES THE CHINESE "RACE"

Immediately following the second wave of the Yellow Power movement, Disney released *Aladdin* (1992), the first film of Disney's Renaissance period starring a character of color. It was followed by several more over the ten-year term. Though *Aladdin* was nominated for numerous awards, particularly for its musical score, Disney found itself embroiled in controversy when Arab and Asian American viewers protested the offensive lyrics in the opening number, "Arabian Nights." The American-Arab Anti-Discrimination Committee (ADC) argued that *Aladdin* promoted Orientalist stereotypes and successfully lobbied to have the lines, "Where they cut off your ear/ If they don't like your face" removed from the introductory musical sequence (Giroux 1999, 104–5). Critics further lambasted Disney for the recurrent moralistic distinctions made between Agrabah's native subjects and *Aladdin*'s more racially ambiguous protagonists (Wingfield and Karaman 1995, 132–36). In contrast to the vicious, dark-skinned royal guards, greedy merchants, and the lecherous, hook-nosed villain, Disney modeled Aladdin's visage after Tom Cruise and cast Scott Weinger, who offered his standard American English speech patterns to the performance (Giroux 1999, 105).

Unique to this film over others covered in this chapter is its recurrent emphasis on the foreignness of Agrabah to the protagonists (such as the scene in which Princess Jasmine is horrified to discover the violent punishment reserved for marketplace thieves), indicative of Disney's duplicitous execution of an Asian worldview or setting. Rather than explore a West Asian perspective, *Aladdin* instead limits its protagonists' challenges to navigating a fictitious topography articulated solely by West Asian stereotypes of third world poverty, political corruption, and depictions of traditional arranged marriage as a vehicle for female oppression. Disney's maligned rendering of a West Asian environment and its incongruous, and arguably yellow-faced protagonists, all prompted the decision to give this film less attention in this chapter than others.

More importantly, criticisms of *Aladdin* set a new benchmark for the creation of *Mulan* in 1998. Disney began the process of storyboarding for the film under pressure to improve their track on racial representation (Anjirbag 2019, 89). The studio struggled to adapt the legendary poem, "The Ballad of Mulan," to the Disney standard (Holt 2019, 296–97). Most scholars believe the poem, of unknown origin, originated in fifth or sixth century China. Victor H. Mair's edited collection of Chinese poetry attributes both the poem's and the title character's lineage to the formally nomadic Särbi (Xianbei) people who formed the Northern Wei dynasty (Mair 1994, 474–76).

Extant versions, the oldest dating back to the eleventh century, begin similarly to Disney's rendition. A young girl commiserates with an unnamed narrator after the emperor's guard calls her father to war. She joins the army in her father's place while her family mourns her absence. The poem indicates that Mulan partakes in hundreds of battles before earning the recognition of the emperor. When offered a reward, she asks only for permission to return to her family. Once home, Mulan abandons her military garb and reveals her gender to her former comrades-in-war. The short poem does not directly speak to any consequences of Mulan's actions, nor does it imply that the narrator expects any. Likewise, the ballad gives no mention of an ethnically specific antagonist (Mair 1994, 474–76). Disney took creative liberties to expand the poem into a full-length film, including the addition of a romantic subplot and Mulan's teenage conformity anxieties while eschewing her years of military service and the commendations she earns for her sacrifice. At the expense of historical integrity, the filmmakers altered the ballad to appeal to heteronormative, white, middle-class expectations of female heroism over the narrative's original message of female potential (at least within the sphere of filial piety).

Disney's early work adapting the poem replicated little in respect to the original story. Initial drafts for the film featured Mulan as a spoiled, depressed bride of a British prince who had lost her way after pushing back against cultural traditions (Holt 2019, 296–300). Filmmakers revised the storyline after consultations with Chinese-American screenwriter Rita Hsiao. Hsiao encouraged filmmakers to reorient Mulan's struggle to balancing familial and national obligations with her personal identity. Disney's Mulan, no longer the figure of the fifth/sixth-century legend, instead expressed twentieth-century Asian American experiences of straddling two different worlds' expectations. However, the limits of Disney's fictional rendition of imperial China circumscribed Hsiao's contributions to Mulan's characterization and identity. Intentional or unintentional, EuroAmerican assumptions of Otherness, Orientalism, and racial paradigms stifled Mulan's expression of social identity and directly inhibited viewers' sense of an ethnically diverse social synchronicity.

The American sanctification of the assimilation myth, colloquially called the "melting pot," hampered Disney's ability to imbue *Mulan* with the complexities of the Asian American experience. The abandonment of ancestral heritages and cultural histories through assimilation (historically enforced both socially and forcibly by EuroAmerican authorities) was an unadvertised expectation for arriving immigrants. How thoroughly they adopted white, Anglo-Saxon Protestant behaviors and values typically determined the success of Asian migrants and their children, singled out as the minority group deemed most capable of acculturating into the preexisting social structure. Disney's preferential attitude toward assimilation appears initially antithetical to the plot of *Mulan* and its cross-dressing protagonist. However, Disney's reimagining of the "Ballad of Mulan" avoided blatant hypocrisy by favoring a lack of historical specificity in their rendition.

The absence of the poem's historical origins in *Mulan* overlooks important cultural standards in China's Northern Wei dynasty. Most scholars agree that the "Ballad of Mulan" originated after the fall of the Han dynasty during a period of civil war and dramatic social change that punctuated the invading Xianbei's successive imperial rule. Unaccustomed to a vast empire's organization, Xianbei rulers often relied on ethnically Han Chinese bureaucrats to maintain the traditional institutions of imperial command. Members of the Xianbei elite also increasingly intermarried with Han royalty of the southern dynasties to establish positive relations with the kingdoms at their border. Though Victor H. Mair's rendition of the poem argued Mulan, too, was of Xianbei heritage, the film gives no indication of this. Instead, Mulan dresses in ethnic Han style robes and writes in (anachronistically simplified) Chinese characters. Mulan's invisible ethnic heritage suggests her ability to seamlessly diffuse into any reigning social order (Tian and Xiong 2013, 865). In this way, Mulan demonstrates her aptitude for the model minority's lionization for perseverance, self-reliance, and assimilative behavior as she transforms herself again and again throughout the film. Her efforts are recurrently celebrated in the musical numbers "Honor to Us All" and "Make a Man Out of You" (Cook and Bancroft 1998). Even if unintentional, the songs imply it is not Mulan's ethnic-social identity that has value, but rather her ability to put it on and remove it at will.

In addition to Mulan's flawed characterization, Disney further cheapened the film's overall representative quality by rendering an entirely fictitious version of imperial China. The ahistorical mismatch of Chinese inventions and locations, such as the explosive rocket (invented around the eleventh century) (Winter and Neufield 2013) used in the climactic battle in the Forbidden City palace (constructed in the fifteenth century) (Tian and Xiong 2013, 865), betrayed a disinterest in protecting cultural integrity. Instead, Disney favored the presentation of Orientalist symbols already familiar to most American viewers. Elements outside of Chinese culture were also used, such as the Japanese Samurai armor worn by the Chinese army (Zia 2000, 117). Disney's filmmakers likewise scrubbed out historical linguistic and cultural differences among Imperial-era Chinese. The film further eliminated any suggestions of cross-cultural contact through trade or religion, despite the extensive movement of Buddhist monks to and from India during this period, establishing the illusion that the Orient existed in an impermeable bubble of fantasy. In doing so, *Mulan* purported a chinoiserie setting for its racially transparent heroine to single-handedly rescue a fictitious, homogeneous Chinese "race." The concoction of exoticized Orientalism, historical cherry-picking, and ethnic bleaching all reinvented imperial Chinese culture to end at the limits of the white American imagination.

So too, Disney revised the narrative's source of unrest into a racially dichotomous conflict recognizable to American audiences.

Insert the aggressive "Huns," who were more familiar to modern Western audiences than other nomadic warrior clans of the northern Mongolian Steppe. In the fourth and fifth century, the Hunnic Empire was engaged in the conquest of eastern European territories, five thousand miles away from the ballad's setting (Barfield 1989, 122–24). Nevertheless, *Mulan* ahistorically depicts the Huns scaling the Great Wall and destroying Chinese villages on their way to the capital. Furthermore, the film's characterization of the Huns exaggerates ethnic differences irreflective of the Northern Wei dynasty's historical social politics. *Mulan* portrays Shanyu, chieftain and general of the invading army, and his fellow Huns as ashy-complected, stringy-haired brutes with Orientalized Fu Manchu facial hair and little respect for human life.

Filmmakers also gave the Huns specifically inhuman characteristics, including exaggerated canines, claws, and glowing eyes. These features, reinforced by actions ranging from the scaling of trees to Shanyu hanging upside-down from the imperial palace's roof, summoned images of menacing apes (Ma 2000, 141–43). Disney's fabricated framework of ethnic conflict between *Mulan*'s Chinese empire and the Huns is a heavy-handed transliteration of the American black/white racial dichotomy. The bizarre combination of Yellow Peril stereotypes and the vitriolic Jim-Crow-era black caricature in the Huns's design exercised the same social conditioning evident in *The Jungle Book*.

As the film approaches the final climactic battle with the Huns, Mulan is left to the elements in the mountains after her gender is exposed. Her imposed isolation from the rest of Chinese social order allows her to finally divorce herself from the ethnic trappings designed by the plot. No longer a Chinese bride or a kung fu wielding warrior, the transformed Mulan alone ascertains that the beast-like Huns escaped defeat in a previous battle and are situated to sack the imperial city from within. In a more insidious version of *The Jungle Book*'s King Louie, Shanyu and the Huns "walk like" the Chinese, and gain access to the Emperor's castle by disguising themselves as a costumed lion dance troupe.

The traditional Northern Lion Dance, which Disney's mishmash of Orientalized icons most closely resembles, was believed to expel evil and call forth auspicious tidings in the imperial era. The performance typically employs only two dancers who move together in a combination of choreography and martial arts (Wang 2019, 525–27). In willful ignorance of the lion dance's cultural significance, Disney's looming costume dragon containing the furtive Huns is both suggestively and physically threatening. The unorthodox performance by the handful of surviving Huns unrealistically earns them direct access to the Emperor while again reducing ethnic traditionalism to flimsy tokenism. Meanwhile, Mulan's interference in the Huns's scheme revives the tone of Kipling's "white man's burden." Only after refiguring herself as the proto-model minority and physically positioning herself between Shanyu and the Emperor does Mulan defeat the Huns. In the final conflict, Mulan's adopted EuroAmerican social standards of individuality and self-determinism allow for her heroic defeat of Shanyu.

Mulan's dragon familiar, Mushu, provides the only other example of ethnic diversity in the film. As the stock animal sidekick and source of comic relief, viewers assume Disney characterized Mushu to balance Mulan's serious personality. However, careful analysis suggests that Disney opted to reinforce the racialization of Eddie Murphy, who voiced Mushu, for an alternative purpose (Ma 2000, 127–30). Murphy's "blackness" concentrates the white middle-class audience's attention on the similarities between Mulan, who devotes the entire film to shrugging off symbols of Chinese social order, and themselves. Mushu's humor is predicated on Murphy's race, and the lines exaggerating his linguistic patterns dissolve the audience's sense of historical and geopolitical distance. Despite his "Chinese" body, Mushu cannot shed his ethnic heritage the way that Mulan can. In comparison, Mulan's racial transparency isolates her from her companions and supports EuroAmerican ownership of her character, and her heroism, as closer to "whiteness."

Simultaneously, Mushu's racialization disrupts the context of Disney's fictional "China" through the resuscitation of his predecessor: King Louie. In direct opposition to the rest of the film's protagonists' speaking patterns, Mushu and King Louie's uses of contextual black lingo code them as culturally inferior and potentially threatening (Giroux 1999, 105–6). In both examples, the characters' attempts to forward their self-interests are the sole premise for their presence in the protagonists' stories. While King Louie plays a limited role in Mowgli's narrative,

Mushu's insertion into Mulan's tale is arguably a more nefarious attempt to increase his social status with little effort on his part. What assistance he provides often raises additional problems for Mulan, who again takes up the "'better minority" mantle through her forced stewardship and intellectual problem-solving. In divorcing black/Asian cooperation in *The Jungle Book* and *Mulan* through ahistorical manipulation and the perpetuation of racial stereotypes, Disney filmmakers established a pattern of social control and ethnic isolation across both films.

Many Asian American viewers responded favorably to *Mulan* because Disney remained faithful to Hsiao's experience and avoided relying on the more vicious Asian stereotypes used in their previous works. While *Mulan* marked a progressive shift in racial representation, the change in the protagonist's ethnic identity also conveniently capitalized on a popular trend kickstarted by Asian American filmmakers in the 1990s (Maiytt 2019, 80–86). Alongside *Pushing Hands* (1991), *The Wedding Banquet* (1993), and *The Joy Luck Club* (1993), entertainment media that foregrounded Asian American subjects represented a promise of fiscal returns. Much like the 1950s expansion of immigrant quotas for Asian migrants, Disney's relaxation of white social dominance over entertainment had more to do with economic gains than progressivism.

THE DISNEY REVIVAL PERIOD (2009–PRESENT): *MOANA* (2016) WAYFINDS AN EMPTY PLANET

The trend of Asian film protagonism evaporated in the wake of the World Trade Center attacks in 2001. Already in production that fall, *Lilo and Stitch* (2002) was Disney's first foray into exploring Pacific Asian identity. A native inhabitant of modern Hawai'i, the film's bilingual, hula-dancing lead seems the perfect subject to express Disney's take on multiethnic Asian American social standards in a tumultuous new century. Audiences are introduced to Lilo Pelekai, the titular heroine, as a socially awkward child whose behavior threatens to destroy her fragile family dynamic following the death of her parents. Lilo's older sister unknowingly gifts her an alien fugitive posing as a dog, whom Lilo names Stitch.

Comedic mayhem ensues when outside forces threaten to tear their non-nuclear family apart. In production prior to the Twin Towers' attack, the film originally featured Lilo's mixed human and alien family hijacking a Boeing 747 and wreaking havoc on Honolulu in a dizzying rescue mission designed for the feature's climax. This scene, revised before *Lilo and Stitch*'s 2002 release, substitutes an alien spacecraft for the skyjacking to protect audiences sensitive to the image of people of color forcibly seizing a commercial aircraft (Sanders and DeBlois 2002). Disney's indulgence of white middle-class standards as the norm further limited *Lilo and Stitch*'s neoteric potential. The casting of a white, American actress (Daveigh Chase), à la *Aladdin* a decade prior, stripped Lilo of contemporary representative capacity. Filmmakers also overlooked the opportunity to explore more expansive traditional Hawai'ian ideas of the family as a storyline device (AFFECT). As representative as *Lilo and Stitch* was of the new American century, it provides decidedly less value to this study because it reorients Lilo and her Hawai'ian ethnicity to the background as it foregrounds Stitch's search for identity. As such, it is more valuable to investigate *Moana*, Disney's 2016 film featuring a Pacific Islander protagonist.

In the decade and a half before Disney returned to the Pacific, the entertainment company struggled to shake off accusations of racism by audiences matured during the social media age. Disney's awkward attempts at progressivism, from the first black princess that spends the majority of her screen time in the body of a frog (2009's *The Princess and the Frog*) to the live-action *Beauty and the Beast*'s (2017) "exclusive" half-second of queer visibility, much was left to be desired (Harris 2019). *Moana*, equally part of this trend, similarly features a heroine of color in a setting intended to promote her history and culture. Disney Studios publicly committed to respectful representation in the production of *Moana* and cooperated with cultural authorities to create the Oceanic Story Trust (OST), which served as a creative guide during filmmaking (Anjirbag 2019, 89). The studio took several trips to various islands across Oceania (the geographic region comprising Polynesia, Micronesia, and Melanesia), studied native materials and colors for authenticity, and conducted interviews with natives to vet everything from character names to tattoos. The unadvertised existence of an additional, dominant, creative team, The Disney Story Trust (staffed primarily by white men), ultimately determined which information from the OST to use and what to ignore (Yoshinaga 2019, 201).

Disney's vision for *Moana* followed the familiar narrative employed in *Aladdin* and *Mulan*, in which their titular heroine struggles against the confines of tradition and familial expectations. The story takes place on the fictional island of Motunui, some two thousand years prior to the present era (Sciretta 2016). Moana's overprotective father, the island chieftain, bans his adventurous daughter from embracing the temptations of the open sea. The pressures of her looming cultural responsibilities encourage her to seek solace in her eccentric grandmother, Tala. She enraptures Moana with stories of the life-giving goddess Te Fiti, whose heart was stolen in the mythical world that exists beyond their circumscribed islet. When ecological ruin threatens the livelihood of Motunui's inhabitants, Tala confesses to witnessing evidence of Moana's destiny as part of Te Fiti's narrative, the resolution of which they believe will save them. Tala gives Moana the heart of Te Fiti, in the form of a Māorian greenstone, which she kept safe for her granddaughter. Moana defies her father and sails the open ocean, determined to garner the support of the disgraced demigod, Māui, to return the sacred object. Moana finds Māui marooned on a deserted island as punishment for his role in stealing, and subsequently losing, Te Fiti's heart. Much to Moana's dismay, Māui refuses to participate in her quest. Eventually, she convinces Māui to aid her after assurances that his support will restore his godly status. Together, the two team up against mystical Polynesian foes and traverse a vast Pacific to return the heart of Te Fiti.

Constructed from parts fiction and parts cultural resources, Disney's plot and setting relied heavily on support from the OST. To sidestep the pitfall of misrepresenting a subject of historical significance, Disney crafted a heroine of their own making instead of relying on a subject from Oceanic history. In interviews, Disney claimed that the title character's name was agreed upon by native authorities to mean a multilingual transliteration for "ocean." While perhaps true, it is the second film of the same title set in the South Pacific. The first, a docufiction created by Robert J. Flaherty in 1926, also intended to capture examples of traditional Polynesian culture and society. For his film, Flaherty hired Samoan locals to dress and perform discontinued cultural acts, which he then filmed on location to establish a false sense of authenticity for white American audiences (Trajkovski 2018, 988–89). While potentially coincidental, the similarities in the films' titles, settings, and subject matters betray an American fixation on the Pacific Islands as exotic destinations frozen in a primitive past.

Disney's *Moana* recalls this fascination with traditionalism by symbolically connecting her personal growth with the development of her ancestral wayfinding abilities. Before the technological innovations that made seafaring possible for Europeans, early pan-Polynesian wayfinders relied on observation of the stars and other natural signs to navigate the Pacific. They shared this knowledge with later generations through written accounts and oral traditions. Moana's story takes place during a specific period known as The Long Pause, when Pacific wayfinding exploration ceased for two thousand years (Thomas 2008, 98–102). While the reason for The Long Pause and what brought it to an end are both unknown, Disney's version implies that Moana's adventure reinvigorates Polynesian sea exploration and concludes this historical anomaly (Sciretta 2016). However, the lack of historical specificity makes the context and significance unclear. The film never directly discusses The Long Pause. Instead, it figures into Disney's narrative as an excuse for Moana's thematic isolation. None of her peers share her lifelong interest in oceanic exploration, nor does she meet any fellow islanders during her adventure. Even the urgency of her mission, to end the choking blight threatening all food sources on Motunui, suggests that her village does not participate in any kind of trade route. The premise that Pacific Island cultures each operated independently of one another denies a complex history of multicultural trade.

In addition to physical goods, cross-cultural exchanges in early Oceania spread various folk history traditions and origin stories, from which Disney liberally sampled characters. The anthropomorphized coconut Kakamora warriors are one such example. In *Moana*, the Kakamora, brandishing barbaric weapons, swarm and attack Moana at sea. Wielding ornamentally carved arrows and blow darts, they recall images of cannibalistic tropical pygmies. Disney's use of this stereotypical prototype again portrays their conservative mid-twentieth century mindset addressed previously in this chapter. The trope of the man-eating Pacific savage first surged into cult-cultural consciousness in the 1970s via the birth of the cannibal horror sub-genre in response to rapid Pacific decolonization during the same decade. The characterization of the Kakamora as "murderous little pirates" betrays Disney's reliance on dated stereotypes to create thematic drama and impart humor (Clements 2016).

It is equally important to note that the *kakamora* are not an invention of Disney. They are semi-legendary humanoids depicted in various Pacific Island cultures rendered anthropologically unrecognizable in *Moana*. Twentieth-century inhabitants across the Soloman and Melanesian islands believed the *kakamora* to be a now-extinct race of mischievous beings with long hair and nails who played tricks on island communities (Fox 1924, 138–39). Common lore accused them of stealing trinkets, only to abandon them close by, and of counting the fingers and toes of sleeping islanders. Emotionally sensitive, the *kakamora* could respond violently to teasing, but they were considered more of a nuisance than a threat. Amateur observers posited that the *kakamora* stories may have originated to distinguish between different Oceanic societies or record ancestral cultural communities' practices on islands they previously inhabited (Fox 1924, 141–42). Disney's choice to dehumanize the *kakamora* emphasized their ongoing intentions to isolate Asian protagonists from other supportive characters of color, as they similarly accomplished in their exaggerated racializing of Mushu in *Mulan*.

Regardless of these figures' cultural significance and the film's ancient setting, Moana expresses confusion when introduced to the *kakamora*. She frequently shows little historical or ancestral knowledge, despite Disney's pledge to craft a genuine role model of minority heritage. Moana's cultural illiteracy allows EuroAmerican viewership to explore "authentic" Polynesia in the spirit of the "It's a Small World" theme park ride. The elements of pan-Polynesian traditionalism that Disney deemed most appropriate for white middle-class viewers are spoon-fed to Moana through increasingly exotic settings, from the dangers of the open sea to Lalotai (a fictionalized version of a pan-Polynesian underworld). No depiction makes this more evident than the mischaracterization of Māui. Like the *kakamora*, the demigod Māui is of pan-Polynesian legendary/ethnohistorical significance. He is a trickster character who appears in, among others, Māori, Samoan, and Hawai'ian creationism narratives. Through a combination of intellect and brawn, regional interpretations of Māui celebrate his provisions for humanity by way of outwitting the gods of their prized possessions. However, filmmakers created *Moana*'s Māui by melding many versions into a single entity, and in doing so, erased important distinctions between divergent Oceanic populations.

Contemporary historians have already devoted a great deal of research to exploring the consequences of adulterating Māui. Vilsoni Hereniko's review of *Moana* in *The Contemporary Pacific* lambasts Disney's antithetical desexualization of Māui (2018, 219–21). Māui's reproductive prowess, for which Polynesian tradition reveres him as a regional ancestor, constitutes an essential part of his legendary identity. Disney's choice to promote a sexually demure and homely Māui, despite misgivings by the OST, indicates the filmmakers' discomfort in exploring authentic Asian masculinity. Conversely, the preference for young, single, female Asian protagonists in American films is a hallmark of the post-World War II reimagining of the Orient as an Eden of fiscal and sexual delights. The nymphetic island native who increasingly frequented the silver screen after the admission of Hawai'i to statehood in 1959, typically inhabited paradises entirely devoid of adult men, where she awaited her "discovery" by EuroAmerican adventurers. If present, Asiatic men were often characterized by crippling awkwardness or childlike demeanors that stripped them of their sexual potency. I coined this peculiarly gendered binary in American film as the Exotic Conquest stereotype in 2019 (Maiytt, 44–47).

Moana's use of the Exotic Conquest stereotype again demonstrates Disney's archaic approach to Asian identities. The film replaces Māui's traditional prowess, deemed inappropriate for middle-class EuroAmerican consideration, with impulsive arrogance and juvenile bathroom humor. The absence of romantic potential between the male and female protagonists (a Disney first) simultaneously preserves imaginary white male sexual dominion over the Pacific. The appropriation of Māui from Polynesian oral tradition, stripped of his virility, grants Disney's rendition a damaging and undeserved authenticity. A Mārata Ketekiri Tamaira and Dionne Fonoti's 2018 article "Beyond Paradise?" further argues that Disney's modifications both conserve Moana for more deserving suitors, while also absolving EuroAmerican audiences of historical wrongdoing by redefining Māui as a colonial scapegoat (303–5). Channeling Eve's betrayal in the Garden of Eden, Māui's theft of Te Fiti's heart in pursuit of immortality (a fictional story device invented by Disney) leads to both his exile and the inexorable decay of the entire Pacific. Refiguring Māui as the source of Motunui's blight minimizes the contemporary reality of tourists' abuse of the Pacific environment and excuses destructive change brought by EuroAmerican consumption of culture and ethnic memory.

More so than Māui, Moana's responsibility for preserving her people's ethnohistorical heritage as future chief makes her the most damning colonial icon of the film. Examining *Moana*'s ironically recurrent, if unintentional, coconut motif demonstrates her colonial identity. The overexaggeration of the tropical fruit as an object of cultural significance unknowingly coincides with the common use of "coconut" as a racial slur for dark-skinned Asians deemed "inauthentic" (brown on the outside, white on the inside) (Zia 2000, 15–16). The coconut first appears as a central aspect of Moana's childhood environment in the introductory musical number "Where You Are." The lyrics paint the island setting as a slice of a stagnant exoticism with lines such as "They dance to an ancient song (Who needs a new song? This old one's all we need)" (Clements and Musker 2016). The chorus celebrates the coconut as the only food source and building tool of the islanders, symbolically justifying their isolation from all other Pacific traders and explorers. As the film progresses, Moana's consistent cultural ignorance and her unquestioning acceptance of historical distortions gives Disney's embarrassing coconut *faux pas* footing. Much like Mulan, Moana's heritage gives the setting flavor but holds no sway over her choices.

"Where You Are" immediately prepares audiences to expect little more from pan-Polynesian societies beyond the consumable aesthetics of color and music. The song's apparent message is that the peoples of Motunui are culturally stale and Moana is meant for bigger and better things than the inert traditional role of her birthright. Like Mulan, Moana is the exception rather than the rule, and she can only become the heroic protagonist by eschewing her place in the traditional social structure. Furthermore, the complete absence of any other Oceanic societies provides no alternative for this introductory message of Polynesian primitive backwardness. The isolation of Motunui also offers moviegoers no other option but to imagine that wayfinding Moana will spend the rest of her days pioneering the uncharted islands of an unoccupied Pacific. *Moana*'s glorified fantasy of a boundless Oceania to discover dismisses the historical reality of conquest, exploitation, and the resulting generations of EuroAmerican social control that shaped the region. For all the authenticity granted by the OST, the viewer leaves having learned nothing about the EuroAmerican seizure and colonization of Oceania territories, but instead, with a sense of satisfaction in assuming that their "Polynesian" heroine lauds the opportunity to claim the Pacific for herself.

CONCLUSIONS

When the credits roll and audiences file from the theater, does Disney's spell come to an end? Certainly not if the takeaway is viewers' perceptions of ethnic identities, social/global politics, standards of civil organization, or the historical significance of artificially contrived barriers to diversity in popular American media. Persistent stereotypes have all the power of a wicked enchantment, capable of cursing generations to replicate static patterns of untenably unjust social orders year after year. Major media entertainment industries, of which Disney Studios is one of the largest, are responsible for depicting ethnic minorities and their histories with equitable candor. They must confront the reality that children's media companies have thrived despite their racist pasts and strive to be actively anti-racist in the present.

The reliance on thematically isolative plots and fictive, generalized regional settings by Disney filmmakers have continuously limited audiences' comprehension of global ethnic social diversity since the civil rights era. Accusations that Disney's approach to race stalled in the 1950s and 1960s remain accurate with each successive film age. In its Silver Age, *The Jungle Book* discouraged black-Asian cooperation at the height of the civil rights movement and condemned miscegenation. As growing public interest in Asian American stories promised financial returns in the post-Yellow Power Disney Renaissance, *Mulan* stressed Asian ethnic erasure and racial transparency as virtues of laudable model minorities. And for all the things Disney got right by their collaboration with cultural authorities during *Moana*'s making, the result exploited cultural-historical figures as spokespeople for colonial revisionism. Their treatment of Asian protagonists over these three films betrayed a preference for forestalling changes in social order to preserve EuroAmerican civil dominion.

The specter of Asian stereotypes, unintended or otherwise, over six decades of Disney's animated films have set a dismal tone for ethnic representation in popular media. What remains to be seen is if the entertainment giant can improve upon their fledgling efforts to participate in twenty-first-century progressivism. Disney's newest film, *Raya and the Last Dragon* (2021), once again features an Asian protagonist. Early marketing for the production indicates that it will be set in another invented Asiatic universe of an indeterminate past. Despite this, Disney has been quick to market *Raya*'s titular heroine as their first (ethnically non-specific) South Asian princess, a claim they've buttressed by again assembling a team of ethnic consultants Disney coined the "Raya Southeast Asia Story Trust" (Sirikul 2021). The teaser trailers' unpromising theme of overcoming ethnic strife and historical sociocultural distrust to produce a new era of unity also treads uncomfortably close to implications of Asiatic backwardness in wait for another heroine uniquely imbued with EuroAmerican virtues (Walt Disney Animation Studios 2021). Early popular and scholarly interpretations of *Raya* do not bode well for Disney's promises to divest from a white ethnocentric worldview and introduce audiences to places they haven't yet seen (Bui 2021; Ketsiri 2021). Until then, Disney will continue to fall short of performing magic.

REFERENCES

AFFECT. n.d. "Native Hawaiian Families." University of Hawaii College of Education. Accessed November 19, 2020. https://affect.coe.hawaii.edu/lessons/homelesstransitory/.

Akita, Kimiko, and Rick Kenney. 2013. "A 'Vexing Implication': Siamese Cats and the Orientalist Mischief-Making." In *Diversity in Disney Films: Critical Essays on Race, Ethnicity, Gender, Sexuality and Disability*, edited by Johnson Cheu, 50–66. Jefferson: McFarland & Company Inc.

Anjirbag, Michelle Anya. 2019. "Mulan and Moana: Embedded Coloniality and the Search for Authenticity in Disney Animated Film." In *The Psychosocial Implications of Disney Movies*, Social Sciences, edited by Lauren Dundes, 88–102. https://doi.org/10.3390/books978-3-03897-849-7.

Barfield, Thomas J. 1989. *The Perilous Frontier: Nomadic Empires and China, 221 BC to AD 1757*. Studies in Social Discontinuity. Cambridge: Blackwell Publishers.

Bui, Hoai-Tran. *Morning Edition*. By Rachel Martin. *NPR*, March 9, 2021. https://www.npr.org/2021/03/09/975125820/raya-and-the-last-dragon-criticized-for-lack-of-southeast-asian-actors.

Burdick, Jake. 2016. "Practical Pigs and Other Instrumental Animals." In *Disney, Culture, and Curriculum*, Studies in Curriculum Theory, edited by Jennifer A. Sandlin and Julie C. Garlen, 47–58. New York: Routledge.

Clements, Ronald and John Musker, dir. *Aladdin*. 1992; United States: Walt Disney Feature Animation, VHS.

———, dir. *Moana*. 2016; United States: Walt Disney Animation Studios, DVD.

Cook, Barry and Tony Bancroft, dir. *Mulan*. 1998; United States: Walt Disney Feature Animation, VHS.

Disney Plus. 2019. "Disney+ Announcement Advertisement." YouTube video, 1:56. Posted August 23, 2019. https://www.youtube.com/watch?v=P7zW53OuvMg.

Espiritu, Yen Le. 1992. *Asian American Panethnicity: Bridging Institutions and Identities*. Philadelphia: Temple University Press.

Flaherty, Robert J, dir. *Moana*. 1926; Samoa: Paramount Pictures.

Fox, C. E. 1924. *The Threshold of the Pacific: An Account of the Social Organization, Magic and Religion of the People of San Cristoval in the Solomon Islands*. New York: Alfred A. Knopf.

Giroux, Henry A. 1999. *The Mouse That Roared: Disney and the End of Innocence*. Lanham: Rowman & Littlefield Publishers.

Goldmark, Daniel and Utz McKnight. 2008. "Locating America: Revisiting Disney's *Lady and the Tramp*." *Social Identities* 14, no. 1: 101–20. https://doi.org/10.1080/13504630701848705.

Harris, Aisha. 2019. "Rewriting the Past Won't Make Disney More Progressive." *New York Times*, May 27, 2019. https://www.nytimes.com/2019/05/27/movies/aladdin-disney-diversity.html.

Hereniko, Vilsoni. 2018. Untitled review of *Moana* (2016), by Walt Disney Animation Studios. *The Contemporary Pacific* 30, no. 1: 216–24.

Holt, Nathalia. 2019. *The Queens of Animation: The Untold Story of the Women Who Transformed the World of Disney and Made Cinematic History*. 1st ed. New York: Little, Brown and Company.

Ketsiri, Andy. "An Open Letter to Disney: The Amalgamation of Asian Identities in 'Raya and the Last Dragon' Is Not Real Representation." *New University, University of California, Irving Newspaper*, February 24, 2021.

https://www.newuniversity.org/2021/02/24/an-open-letter-to-disney-the-amalgamation-of-asian-identities-in-raya-and-the-last-dragon-is-not-real-representation/.

Kipling, Rudyard. 1910. *The Jungle Book*. Project Gutenberg EBook. EBook #35997. New York: The Century Company. https://www.gutenberg.org/files/35997/35997-h/35997-h.htm.

Koshiro, Yukiko. 1999. *Trans-Pacific Racisms and the U.S. Occupation of Japan*. New York: Columbia University Press.

Lee, Josephine. 2004. "Asian America Is in the Heartland: Performing Korean Adoptee Experience." In *Asian North American Identities: Beyond the Hyphen*, edited by Eleanor Ty and Donald C. Goellnicht, 102–16. Bloomington: Indiana University Press.

Ma, Sheng-Mei. 2000. *The Deathly Embrace: Orientalism and Asian American Identity*. Minneapolis: University of Minnesota Press.

Maeda, Daryl Joji. 2012. *Rethinking the Asian American Movement*. American Social and Political Movements of the 20th Century. New York: Routledge.

Mair, Victor H., ed. 1994. *The Columbia Anthology of Traditional Chinese Literature*. New York: Columbia University Press.

Maiytt, Christopher. 2019. "Deep Imprints: 20th-Century Media Stereotypes Towards East Asian Immigrants and the Development of a Pan-Ethnic East-Asian-American Identity." *Master's Thesis*, 4728, https://scholarworks.wmich.edu/masters_theses/4728.

Ogbar, Jeffrey O. G. 2011. "The Formation of Asian American Nationalism in the Age of Black Power, 1966–75." In *The New Black History: Revisiting the Second Reconstruction*, Critical Black Studies Series, edited by Manning Marable and Elizabeth Kai Hinton, 1st ed., 123–34. New York: Palgrave Macmillan.

Reitherman, Wolfgang, dir. *The Jungle Book*. 1967; United States: Walt Disney Productions. Diamond ed., 2014, DVD.

Said, Edward W. 1979. *Orientalism*. Vintage Books edition. New York: Random House.

Sanders, Chris, and Dean DeBlois, dir. *Lilo and Stitch*. 2002; Walt Disney Feature animation, Big Wave ed., 2009, DVD.

Sciretta, Peter. 2016. "How Disney Formed the Oceanic Story Trust to Make 'Moana' More Authentic." Film: Blogging the Reel World, Accessed September 29, 2019. https://www.slashfilm.com/moana-oceanic-story-trust/.

Sirikul, Laura. 2021. "Disney's *Raya and the Last Dragon* Has a Bit of an East Asian Problem." whattowatch. February 1, 2021. https://www.whattowatch.com/features/disneys-raya-and-the-last-dragon-has-an-east-asian-problem.

Tamaira, A Mārata Ketekiri and Dionne Fonoti. 2018. "Beyond Paradise? Retelling Pacific Stories in Disney's *Moana*." *The Contemporary Pacific* 30, no. 2: 297–327.

Thomas, Tim. 2008. "The Long Pause and the Last Pulse: Mapping East Polynesian Colonisation." In *Islands of Inquiry: Colonisation, Seafaring and the Archaeology of Maritime Landscapes*, Terra Australis, 29, ed. Geoffrey Clark, Foss Leach, and Sue O'Connor, 97–112. Canberra: Australian University Press.

Tian, Chuanmao, and Caixia Xiong. 2013. "A Cultural Analysis of Disney's *Mulan* with Respect to Translation." *Continuum: Journal of Media & Cultural Studies* 27, no. 6: 862–74.

Trajkovski, Igor. 2018. "Chronological Development of Non-Fiction/Documentary Film, Main Developments and Subdivisions." *KNOWLEDGE-International Journal, Humanities* 26, no. 3 (September): 985–92. http://www.ikm.mk/ojs/index.php/KIJ/article/view/528/996.

"twLF Demands." 1969. Ethnic Studies Library, University of California, Berkeley. 1:2 twLF box 1 Folder 2. CES ARC 2015/1. http://revolution.berkeley.edu/assets/demands.pdf.

Walt Disney Animation Studios. 2021. "Disney's Raya and the Last Dragon | Official Trailer." YouTube video, 2:28. Posted January 26, 2021. https://www.youtube.com/watch?v=1VIZ89FEjYI.

Wang, Ningning. 2019. *A History of Ancient Chinese Music and Dance*. Salt Lake City: American Academic Press.

Wingfield, Marvin, and Bushra Karaman. 1995. "Arab Stereotypes and American Educators." *Social Studies and the Young Learner*, (March/April): 132–36. https://web.archive.org/web/20060615010923/http://www.adc.org/arab_stereo.pdf.

Winter, Frank, and Michael Neufeld. 2013. "The First Fireworks: Origins of the Rocket." Smithsonian National Air and Space Museum. Accessed June 13th, 2020. https://airandspace.si.edu/stories/editorial/first-fireworks-origins-rocket.

Wong, Yen-Rong. 2019. "Engaging Thoughtfully with Racist Disney." *Eureka Street*, 29, November 23, 2019. file:///home/chronos/u-fa9cbe9b5c5fe974164aa484f854f0724f3bd114/MyFiles/Downloads/ContentServer.pdf.

Yoshinaga, Ida. 2019. "Disney's *Moana*, the Colonial Screenplay, and Indigenous Labor Extraction in Hollywood Fantasy Films." *Narrative Culture, Thinking with Stories in Times of Conflict* 6, no. 2 (Fall): 118–215.

Zia, Helen. 2000. *Asian American Dreams: The Emergence of an American People*. New York: Farrar, Straus and Giroux.

③

THE MAGIC ISLAND OF SEABROOK HIGH

Disney Retcons the Civil Rights Movement in
High School Musical Descendant *Zombies*
Aaron Clayton

Deconstructing the myth of American identity discloses the structure and content of the colonial violence that inhabits the nation's history. By understanding myth as historiography that narrativizes or emplots the events of the past to make sense of the present, the text of myth provides a window into national consciousness. Roland Barthes outlines a semiotic approach that utilizes synchronic and diachronic analysis to articulate the work of myth in his often-overlooked essay "Myth Today." As Barthes explains, analysis becomes possible because it is shared by the national consciousness and must therefore be readable or understandable by that people. According to Barthes, "*myth hides nothing*: its function is to distort, not to make disappear" (1972, 121). As such, semiological analysis can be applied to contemporary texts such as the Disney Channel's 2018 film *Zombies* to deconstruct American myth. Juxtaposing a close reading of the film alongside a genealogy of American myth discloses how the film re-enacts the ritual of constructing national identity.

NATIONAL CONSCIOUSNESS AND IDENTITY

When Benedict Anderson introduced the phrase "imagined communities," he acknowledged the emergence of a national consciousness that he attributed to print technology and capitalism (2006, 77). Eric Hobsbawm suggests that without such vocabulary American colonists' use of the term "the people" among others constitutes a particularized instantiation of what scholars now conceive of as national identity (2013, 18–20). Central to this analysis is recognizing the function of myth in establishing the homogenous character of national identity, homogenous in the sense that what it means to be American transcends time and space. This is not to say that the experience of an American in 1787 was the same as it is today. Rather, the present national consciousness constructs a continuity with the past. As Étienne Balibar writes, "the imaginary singularity of national formations is constructed daily, by moving back from the present into the past" (1991, 87). As such, national identity presents as monolithic and ahistorical, handed down invariably from generation to generation fulfilling a destiny only conceivable in the present moment. A year prior to delivering his seminal frontier thesis in 1893, Frederick Jackson Turner penned an essay titled "Problems in American History" that insists on this point. He argues, "American history needs a connected and unified account of the progress of civilization across this continent, with the attendant results. Until such a work is furnished we shall have no real national self-consciousness; when it is done, the significance of the discovery made by Columbus will begin to appear" (1938, 72). Turner's words distill the geographic and teleological historiography that underlie his Daedalian project of constructing an American identity. He measures history and the progress of civilization spatially across the topography of the continent, underscoring that the significance of the past can only be understood in terms of its uninterrupted and ineluctable advance toward the present. Moreover, he identifies national identity as the intended product of such a history. By constructing such a continuity, the past is flattened and transformed into what Walter Benjamin describes as "homogenous, empty time" (2007, 261). Thus, contradictions get written out of history or, borrowing from Michel-Rolph Trouillot, "silenced" (1995, 27), and those that cannot be silenced are reframed. For example, slavery and the 3/5ths compromise are perceived as aberrations, flaws that the founding fathers were too short-sighted or too limited by historical context to set right.

Following in the tradition of films like *Green Book* (2018) or Disney's *The Help* (2011), *Zombies* allows audiences, principally, although not exclusively white audiences, to reconcile their racist history by reenacting the past and giving them the opportunity to be on the right side of history by rooting for characters who oppose discrimination. Unpacking the "bundle of silences" in *Zombies* exposes the film's reduction of Indian removal and the civil rights movement into a single narrative (Trouillot 1995, 27). Building on the success of previous Disney Channel movies such as *High School Musical* (2006) and *Descendants* (2015), *Zombies* is a musical that centers on the lives of several suburban high school students who struggle with teenage angst, fitting in, identity, and so on. Set in the fictional planned community of Seabrook, the diegetic world of *Zombies* approximates contemporary society if contemporary society included the presence of zombies. Typical of the genre, the zombie functions as signifier for the other. While the community's name pays homage to William Seabrook's 1929 travelogue *The Magic Island*, the hubris of its residents and forced acculturation of zombies more closely resembles Turner's historiographic account of the frontier than Seabrook's Haiti. Where the frontier myth designates indigenous peoples as the racial other, *Zombies* substitutes blacks.[1] The protagonists are synecdochical signifiers of their community as it negotiates the problem of racial difference. As such, the "normal" female Addison and the zombie male Zed, star-crossed lovers, personate the civil rights movement upon entering high school, staying true to themselves and each other by confronting discrimination.[2] Throughout the film, Addison's individuation requires reconciling the fact of her own difference with the community norms.

The deployment of the romantic hero as synecdochical signifier is not unique to this film. Disney has a long history of producing romantic heroes like Addison who revolt against social norms only later to be recast as heroes (Fruzinska 2014, 43). Characters like Elsa of *Frozen* (2013), Merida of *Brave* (2012), and Ariel of *The Little Mermaid* (1989) illustrate heroes who reject or are rejected by civilization, conduct their errand into the wilderness, and return with knowledge to promote social change. Like Addison, the efficacy of their contributions is determined by consensus politics. Despite their sophomoric fervor, they never fundamentally threaten the society that they, albeit temporarily, disavow. Paradoxically, the ubiquity of these transgressive heroes suggests that this narrative structure has been institutionalized as a ritual act of identity formation. Justyna Fruzinska broadly observes how "Disney's production inscribes itself into a wider tradition." She continues, "It seems that Americans are particularly fond of making anti-imperialist films that should redeem them from their own imperialist foreign policy and guilt complex" (2014, 144). The wider tradition that Fruzinska points to but does not name is the "errand into the wilderness" mythologized in American colonial historiography.[3] The simultaneous rejection of the decadence of European civilization and the savagery of indigenous peoples defined the collective consciousness of the early colonists. The errand into the wilderness forged the American national identity by mediating those two opposing forces. The unique character of this ritual identifies the individual with the national. As Myra Jehlen observes, "To be born an American is simultaneously to be born again. Americans assume their national identity as the fulfillment of selfhood rather than as its point of origin, so that they travel their lives in a state of perpetual landing" (1986, 9). To be American is to continually become American; it is not only teleology but also entelechy. Paraphrasing Edward Said, it is a community of individuals acting for themselves in concert, whose music continually constructs the past (1994, 332). As represented in the film by Addison's rivals on the cheer team, the failure of society to adapt results in its eventual downfall. Therefore, the ritual of national identity produces transgressive heroes like Addison who are reinterpolated by consensus politics to ensure its continual renewal. Through her success, the other is colonized and assimilated.

ERRAND INTO ZOMBIETOWN

The ritual formation of American identity is composed of the dialectical forces of civilization and savagery. In *Zombies*, Addison and Zed occupy a liminal space that threatens the mutual exclusivity of these forces. The film opens with parallel monologues, simultaneously introducing their personal histories and the film's backstory. According to the monologues, an accident at Seabrook power plant fifty years earlier turned half of the town into brain-eating zombies. The unaffected residents built a wall, dividing the city into Seabrook and Zombietown and invoking comparison to the border wall between the United States and Mexico. During the fifty years of apartheid, the government of Seabrook developed a wristband, z-band, to ensure the safety of normals by inhibiting zombies' superhuman athletic prowess and brain-eating impulses, essentially transforming them into functional isomorphs with ashy skin and dye-resistant green hair. Although the film does not disclose when all zombies were fitted with z-bands, Zed attributes the success of their assimilation to the device. Now that the first zombies are invited to attend Seabrook High School, signifying the initial stages of desegregation, Zed observes that "things are changing" (Hoen 2018). Designating the school a "contact zone" for zombies and normals is the obvious choice (Pratt 1991, 34); it simultaneously draws on the popularity of *High School Musical* and the colonial logic of forced assimilation in Indian boarding schools.

The juxtaposed musical monologues reveal Addison's and Zed's preoccupations with pursuing their own desires while also meeting the expectations of family and peers. Both are conflicted about seeking recognition from a society that disavows them for their otherness and yearn for a future where they will be accepted. Zed wants to join the football team, and Addison wants to be a cheerleader. Fittingly, when in high school, Addison's father, Dale played on the football team, and her mother, Missy, was a cheerleader. As adults, they are chief of Zombie Patrol and mayor, respectively. The achievements and status of Addison's family mark her as the apogee of civilization, but the expectations weigh on her. She sings, "Mom's counting on me" and later "Cheer's in my family genes" (Hoen 2018). We then learn that her cousin Bucky is captain of the cheer team. The significance of Addison's reference to her genetics cannot be overstated; it is the first in the bundle of silences unveiled. Not only does it invoke uncomfortable associations with race identity theory, but it also exposes genetics as the dividing line between normal and zombie. As Zed introduces himself and his zombie family, the importance of genetics becomes clearer. Because the accident at the Seabrook power plant occurred fifty years prior and zombification does not inhibit aging, Zed and his younger sister Zoey must have been born after the accident. The only explanation for their existence as zombie children is that their father Zevon procreated and genetically passed on the zombie trait.

We also learn in this opening song that Addison's family has disguised the fact that she has white hair. She rationalizes her family's discretion: "People here hate anything that's different. If anyone outside my family found out I wore a wig, I would never be allowed to cheer. So, I've worn a wig for as long as I can remember" (Hoen 2018). Her admission discloses the jeremiad as the apparatus by which the community maintains the boundary between normals and zombies. Sacvan Bercovitch cites John Winthrop's hallmark address to the Massachusetts Bay colonists voyaging across the Atlantic as the inauguration of the American jeremiad, a common litany delivered by religious leaders on momentous political occasions that links the strife, tribulations, and depravity of the time with society's moral decay (2012, 3–7). Winthrop's sermon unites these themes of mourning current moral failures of society and simultaneously calls for the (re)building of a new city, alert from threats within and without.[4] Not unlike the whiteness of Herman Melville's whale, to the community of Seabrook, the whiteness of Addison's hair symbolizes the sublime and the savage. Its suppression is essential for maintaining the rigid boundary of civilization.

GENETIC HYBRIDS

From this homogenous melting pot of multiculturalism, each American is born ahistorical. Addison, the model American, enacts the myth of national identity and the film is her bildungsroman. With her noble pedigree and contact with the frontier, she conforms to other heroes of American fiction such as Edgar Rice Burroughs's Tarzan and James Fenimore Cooper's Natty Bumppo. Her errand into the wilderness begins with a serendipitous introduction to Zed. On the first day of school, she ironically ends up trapped, alone with him in a saferoom designed to isolate and protect normals from zombies during an outbreak. Because they meet in darkness, Addison fails to recognize the coded visual signifiers of Zed's identity as zombie. She is charmed by his wit but recoils in horror when she discovers he is a zombie. Actually, she punches him in the face. Her reaction is what Julia Kristeva defines as abjection, the response of disgust that occurs when the subject, or presubject, simultaneously loathes and desires a "'something' that I do not recognize as a thing" (1982, 2). The "something" or pre-object to which Kristeva refers is the substance that collects on the external boundary of the self. It is neither subject nor object. Kristeva writes, "It is something rejected from which one does not part, from which one does not protect oneself as from an object [. . .] It is thus not a lack of cleanliness or health that causes abjection but what disturbs identity, system, order" (1982, 4). If this happened to any other student who sufficiently interpellated Seabrook's notions of identity, the interaction would have been silenced as an aberration. But because Addison, a freshman with genetically anomalous white hair, has not yet established her subjectivity, the experience is formative.

Once Addison makes the cut as a Seabrook cheerleader, she must undergo the initiation that secures the hegemonic interpolation of all team members. Bucky, along with several of the other current cheerleaders, drives the two new recruits in a minivan after curfew into Zombietown. Bucky explains the situation: "Every year, for cheer initiation, we like to remind zombies that we don't accept freaks in this town. Egg that zombie house and you're both officially one of us." To maintain social order, cheerleaders perform this ritual of re-affirming the boundary between normals and zombies. Later, in a conversation with Bucky, Addison says, "Zombies are students at Seabrook too, Bucky. Picking on them isn't right." After some back and forth, Bucky silences Addison and concludes, "It's best if you don't question things. Pep rally today, cuz. You're gonna rock it" (Hoen 2018). Kristeva argues social rite provides the cultural machinery for dealing with unstable boundaries. She states, "On account of the flexibility at work in rites of defilement, the subjective economy of the speaking being who is involved abuts on both edges of the unnamable (the non-object, the off-limits) and the absolute (the relentless coherence of Prohibition, sole donor of Meaning)" (1982, 74). To preclude pathological narcissism, ritual instructs individuals to reify the boundary between subject and object. Addison's refusal to participate disrupts social equilibrium by drawing attention to the non-totalizing distinction between zombies and normals. While her refusal may upset Bucky, it's really only a problem if her abjection persists. Whether or not Addison properly observes every ceremonial practice matters less than her univocal attention to the threshold of her subjectivity. Therefore, Bucky ends the conversation by redirecting Addison's thoughts to the next upcoming ritual, the pep rally. A cheerleader must hold the line on identity by celebrating purity. They are the deputies who stand watch over the periphery of the city upon a hill.

Addison's sensitivity to zombies is more than mere coincidence. Her white hair, an aperture in the perimeter of normals' subjectivity, binds her to the zombies genetically. When Addison expresses sympathy for them, Bucky reminds her that a zombie bit their grandfather's ear off. Based on the youthful appearance of all the adults, we can assume Addison's parents, as well as Bucky's, were born after the zombie bit their grandfather. While there's never any mention that zombies can infect normals, the existence of zombie children like Zed and Zoey demonstrates that zombie characteristics are passed on genetically. When Addison explains the anomaly of her hair, she states that, "[Doctors] think it's some rare genetic thing," suggesting that her hair color, like zombies,' is inheritable. Thus, the bite her grandfather sustained likely synthesized human and zombie genetics, making Addison part zombie. Such a theory explains her family's famed athletic ability and recalls Addison's earlier claim, "Cheer's in my family genes." Just as zombies uninhibited by z-bands display incredible strength, agility, and speed, Bucky's and Addison's athletic abilities surpass their peers'. Moreover, unique hair color is an exclusive zombie trait. While zombie hair is green and Addison's is white, neither zombies nor Addison can simply dye their hair. Addison explains, "I can't dye it, nothing sticks. I've tried everything" (Hoen 2018). Only Zed manages to alter his hair color, albeit without dye. When he passes as normal by tampering with his z-band, his hair goes black. This raises the question about what would happen if Addison put on a z-band and adjusted it to make her normal.

Perhaps Addison does not carry zombie genetics. Yet, for her family, the possibility alone warrants repression. Unearthing the truth of the family genetic difference risks destabilizing social order. Such a revelation would lay bare the contradiction that Seabrook's crowning achievement, the cheer team, may entirely depend on the zombie genetics of Addison's family. Because belief equates with fact in the context of myth and identity, the act of repression instantiates her genetic deviance. It doesn't prove that Addison is mixed, but it proves that her parents and Bucky either believe that she is or fear that the citizens of Seabrook will perceive her as such. When she reveals her true hair color at the homecoming game, her appalled peers reject her. Like the romantic hero, the errand of the American is to reject society and go into the wilderness but also to master that wilderness for society. The assent of the national consciousness determines the efficacy of the ritual performance. Addison's errand remains incomplete until she exercises sufficient Nietzschean will to power to regain the approval of the Seabrook community.

SARTORIAL SIGNIFICATION

The spectacle of Addison's white hair appears artificial until the film parades an armamentarium of increasingly racialized signifiers for inscribing the genetic distinction between normals and zombies. Rita McGhee oversaw costume design and sacrificed nuance for immediate readability for the adolescent viewers of *Zombies*. As Peter Corrigan observes, "it is typical of utopias that the social function of individuals or groups is immediately readable from their dress" (2008, 15). Although McGhee's sartorial exaggerations may appear foppish, the social distinctions dress offers are integral to ensure comprehensibility of the visually coded social hierarchy.

The normals' wardrobe adheres to a classic aesthetic, albeit one comprised exclusively of pastels. Garments for women include 1950s era classic length dresses and skirts frequently limited to a single pastel tone. The attire of the school-aged Addison and her peers often incorporates an additional solid tone that reflects the Seabrook High School colors, pink and green, but with slightly higher hemlines. Otherwise, teens' clothing mirrors the minimalist 1950s outfits of the adult women. Men don pastel classic suits, and school-aged boys are similarly outfitted, though in more casual variants, occasionally substituting shorts for pants. If the possibility for diversity in the clothing of normals seems limited, the wardrobe for zombie adults and children of all genders appears even more homogenized and suggestive of prison uniforms. In his half of the opening monologue, Zed explains: "Zombies have to wear government-issued coveralls" (Hoen 2018). The z-bands that surveil and control their behavior evoke comparison to parolee ankle monitors. While some variation exists among the coveralls, most ensembles consist of baggy pants, t-shirts, and a vest, jacket, or hoodie made from heavier cotton designed for workwear. In contrast to the pastels of normals, zombies wear all earth tones. To parallel the Seabrook pink and green, zombie clothes feature muddy red and toxic green. These colors are even reflected in the architecture of the buildings on their side of the wall. Overall, the zombie aesthetic showcases a hip-hop, grunge syncretism. The hip-hop influence is brandished with loose fitting clothing, especially oversized hoodies and jackets, where the distressed clothing, frayed edges, and patchwork signal a grunge affect. In his opening monologue, Zed continues, "But we make 'em look pretty cool" (Hoen 2018). He gestures to the patches sewn onto the clothing. Other zombie textiles are embroidered with writing, presumably in zombie language, but the line style and character design are conspicuously Asian.[5] The strong codes of clothing are "immediately readable" and make distinguishing a normal from a zombie easy, even from a quick glance at a distance.

The racial signification of zombies extends beyond prisonlike coveralls.[6] Like their unified hair color, zombies' ash-colored skin is an uncomfortable blackface analogue.[7] Moreover, the zombie language, Zombie, almost exclusively used by Zed's other close friend, the novelty sidekick Gonzo, warrants attention. Because Gonzo speaks no English, Zed must translate for him. Gonzo's lines in the opening song are "Zig-zag quig quad / Ziggy gag za ziggity za yo" (Hoen 2018).[8] While the words mean nothing to the audience, the silliness and oversimplicity of Zombie underscores an absence of civilized culture. In addition to an appearance that approximates hip-hop culture, zombies prefer rap in their musical numbers.[9] Similarly, zombie dancing is distinctly hip-hop with its breaking, popping, and locking while normals' dancing revolves around cheer. As their relationship develops, Zed sneaks Addison into Zombietown after curfew for a Zombie Mash, a party held in a dilapidated industrial facility. Addison joins the zombies in a performance of "BAMM," a Disney-glossed hip-hop song. Costuming for the musical number exaggerates the urban edge of zombie chic with baggy, low-slung pants, and gold overcoats with giant hoodies. Zed's friend Eliza wears a red jacket and matching pants reminiscent of Michael Jackson's memorable red leather couture in "Thriller" (1983). The idiosyncratic bling of these outfits deviates from the earth tones of their government-issued uniforms, presumably because this clothing would not normally be permitted.

NEGOTIATED ASSIMILATION

Seabrook's government, comprised of the city council and the Zombie Patrol, along with the school principal and cheerleading team administer and mediate power. Addison's parents are merely figureheads, so their involvement in decision-making or even daily operations is nominal. Addison's mother is the mayor but not in any visible way. At the opening of the film, Missy says, "Addison, you know that Seabrook's won every cheer championship since . . ." Addison interjects, "Forever." Missy continues, "Forever. But now that city council's having our zombies in our schools, we need cheer more than ever. As mayor, I beseech you. You make that team and win that cheer championship!" (Hoen 2018). Missy admits that the city council decided to integrate and that she holds little power. Her admission reveals the real authority of Seabrook lies in the city council, located off-screen and out of reach for the students of Seabrook as well as zombies in general. Addison's father, Dale, leads the Zombie Patrol, yet never overtly directs their actions or gives orders. Despite a similar visual absence, the Zombie Patrol spontaneously emerges during moments of crisis, such as when it restrains Gonzo at the pep rally, shuts down the after-curfew Zombie Mash, and detains those with hacked z-bands after the homecoming game. Such surveillance invokes comparison to Michel Foucault's analysis of the panopticon. Foucault asserts "the inmate must never know whether he is being looked at at any one moment; but he must be sure that he may always be so" (1995, 201). As such, the Zombie Patrol maintains a constant, if invisible, presence.

Frustrated by the unequal treatment of zombies, Addison and her zombie friends repeatedly confront these authorities to fight social injustice. To enact change, Addison and Zed direct their attention to the school administration and the cheerleading team. Like the mayor, Principal Lee also denies her own authority. When she welcomes the zombies to their basement classroom and introduces them to their janitor . . . ahem . . . teacher, Lee says, "I'm Principal Lee. We are thrilled to be forced to have . . . you here" (Hoen 2018). Unlike Missy, however, Lee does display the authority and willingness to negotiate social order. She has power over what happens in the school even if she doesn't get to decide who enters and exits. After Zed demonstrates his athletic prowess by rescuing Addison from near disaster, Lee permits him to join the football team and agrees to accelerate the integration of zombies in the schools on the condition that he lead the team to victory. Bucky also exerts limited authority over the interactions with zombies, but his approach stands in stark contrast to Lee's. He rigorously enforces segregation and discourages all student contact with zombies. Bucky and Lee, two visible figures of authority within reach, present competing models of negotiating power. As such, the demonstrated efficacy of their examples, or lack thereof, function as a guide for maintaining social order. Bucky's inability or unwillingness to accommodate results in disaster for the Seabrook cheerleading team. His rigidity reflects an internalization of the Seabrook jeremiad and drives him to expel any member who expresses sympathy toward zombies. Without sufficient numbers, the remaining skeleton crew cannot complete their performance at the Cheer Championships and loses for the first time in forever. Whereas Bucky fails because of his attempts to preserve totalizing distinctions between zombies and normals at the expense of genetic anomalies like Addison, Lee negotiates with zombies and allows them to enter normals' society but only on her terms. With frightening honesty to racial stereotypes, Lee bases the conditional desegregation on athletic performance. Acceptance of zombies depends on Zed's contribution to win football games. Her approach counterbalances the jeremiad with the errand into the wilderness; she ensures the stability of Seabrook by colonizing the zombie frontier.

ZED AND THE Z-BAND

The government and school may administer power, but the z-band enforces it. Zed states, "We've come a long way since the outbreak, thanks to the z-band. This puppy delivers a dose of soothing electromagnetic pulses that keep us from eating brains. Now zombies can live happy lives and have handsome, yet humble, kids" (Hoen 2018). The apotheosis of colonialism, the z-band visually signifies control and the galvanic machinery of forced assimilation. As already mentioned, the device elicits comparison to the ankle monitor used by our criminal justice system. It offers the Zombie Patrol the ability to always regulate zombies, even in their private homes in Zombietown. As such, the z-band is Jeremy Bentham's panopticon technologically manifest as a wearable wristband. Foucault's description of the panopticon's purpose could be easily mistaken for the z-band:

> Hence the major effect of the Panopticon: to induce in the inmate a state of conscious and permanent visibility that assures the automatic functioning of power. So to arrange things that the surveillance is permanent in its effects [. . .] that this architectural apparatus should be a machine for creating and sustaining a power relation independent of the person who exercises it; in short, that the inmates should be caught up in a power situation of which they are themselves the bearers. (1995, 201)

Thus, zombies do not live merely as prisoners on their side of the wall. The z-band ensures the permanent visibility and active management of their behavior. Wearing one signifies submission and simultaneously makes the zombie responsible for their own imprisonment.

When uninhibited by the z-band, zombies exhibit superhuman strength and athleticism. Zed's illicit hacking of this further reveals that zombie savagery and strength can be and is regulated like a faucet. Early in the film, during a pep rally, Zed's band temporarily malfunctions, allowing him to burst through a formation of Seabrook football players to catch Addison from a possibly fatal fall. The near catastrophe leads him to the epiphany that he can modify the z-band to unlock his suppressed strength and gain an advantage on the football field. His misuse of the device discloses the particularized and continuous control that Seabrook exercises over the bodies of all zombies. In *Discipline and Punish*, Foucault also outlines the fulfillment of "subject and practised bodies, 'docile' bodies" (1995, 138). He writes, "the object of the control [. . .] was not or was no longer the signifying elements of behaviour or the language of the body, but the economy, the efficiency of movements, their internal organization; constraint bears upon the forces rather than upon the signs" (Foucault 1995, 137). Although signification gives way to discipline in Foucault's hierarchy of biopolitics, the z-band coextends through both forms of power.

Zed regularly adjusts the device to discretely inhabit four persistent functional states of zombification. The first, full zombie, occurs if the z-band is completely deactivated. Zed and other zombies tap into their savage nature, exhibiting superhuman strength and apoplectic rage. Zed's muscles and veins swell, his mascara gets really dark around his eyes, and his skin becomes blotchy and red. He chases after normals in an attempt to eat their brains until he is subdued by a taser. To win football games, Zed calibrates the z-band to minimally suppress his zombie nature. In the second state, he has access to increased strength and speed but does not manifest the uncontrollable rage. He can nimbly avoid opponents and effortlessly toss aside anyone with the unfortunate audacity to try to tackle him. His muscles and veins still swell, and the heavy mascara returns, but less noticeably. To avoid arousing suspicion, Zed can only utilize this state when his football attire conceals the visible changes of his body. It's uncertain whether or not the audience is expected to believe that Lee, the football coach, or the community of Seabrook don't notice Zed's temporary transformations during games. Clearly, Zed's racial otherness, situationally condoned on the football field where it benefits the school, is excluded elsewhere. The third state, the Seabrook zombie, is induced by a properly operating z-band, so we can assume the community prefers to maintain zombies this way. Both savagery and athletic attributes are fully repressed. In fact, zombies resemble normals except for two aspects of their visual appearance—the green hair and ashy skin. In this state, zombies are functional isomorphs of normals. When Zed decides to pass as normal, he adjusts the z-band to its fourth state, making himself an urbane brunette with a healthy pallor and visually indistinguishable from a normal. These incremental adjustments highlight the discomforting racial signification of the zombie's otherness and Seabrook's discrete regulation of its visual and corporeal instantiation.

Prior to the homecoming game, Addison's parents insist on meeting Zed, unaware that he is a zombie. It's unclear where he gets the clothes, but by donning a pastel pink suit and adjusting his skin color with his z-band, he passes as normal and ingratiates himself with them. Emboldened by this success, Zed takes Addison on a date to a Seabrook ice cream parlor. While excited by the novelty, Addison expresses discomfort that Zed could get caught and that he suppresses his identity. More likely, Addison's reaction is symptomatic of her identification with Zed's sartorial duplicity. His transgression too closely mirrors her own deception: wearing a wig. For Zed, recalibrating the z-band is not an act of defiance but wish fulfillment. Given the opportunity, he would presumably continue to pass as normal. The range and precision of Zed's adjustments to his hacked band illustrate the totalizing control Seabrook maintains over the zombies. Because the sophistication of the z-band permits discrete regulation, it becomes clear that Zombie Patrol and the Seabrook government choose to suspend zombies in a state of functional but not visual isomorphism. Seabrook excludes use of the first two states of full zombie as they would risk giving zombies too much power. However, the only possible explanation for choosing the third over the fourth state is to conspicuously mark zombies as different. Like the government issue overalls, the z-band reifies the zombies' otherness, which proves integral to maintaining social hierarchy. Read in such a way, the z-band is realization of totalizing biopolitics that simultaneously exerts power over signification and discipline of the body.

BUCKY'S FAILURE

Excitement grows around Zed's success on the football team, and even normals are enthusiastic about his contributions. Some students who previously conformed to the unofficial Seabrook dress code begin to wear t-shirts with a logo of Zed's face on them or fabric wristbands that resemble z-bands. Like the semipermeable boundary between Zombietown and Seabrook, normals' cultural appropriation of zombie chic reveals that they have the privilege to penetrate the boundary at will, while zombies remain restricted. That said, zombie chic offends Bucky because it pushes against the horizon of the permissible. Having internalized Seabrook's jeremiad as cheer captain, Bucky assumes responsibility for preserving the distinction between normals and zombies.

After Seabrook's homecoming victory, the cheer team focuses on preparing for their regional competition. As Bucky's frustration increases, he expels any member of the team who sympathizes with zombies. Where Addison's encounter with Zed in the saferoom causes her to doubt society, Bucky's abjection prompts him to see evidence of defilement everywhere. This cathexis of the pre-object results in narcissism. Kristeva clarifies that this narcissism is not idyllic self-absorption or "the wrinkleless image of the Greek youth in a quiet fountain." Instead, "The conflicts of drives muddle its bed, cloud its water, and bring forth everything that, by not becoming integrated with a given system of signs, is abjection for it" (1982, 14). Bucky increasingly panics, and even his most devout teammates question his decision-making. His pathological narcissism muddies the identity of the cheer team. When the day of the competition arrives, expectations for the Seabrook team are high. However, during their performance, they are unrecognizable to the judges. The routine is disorganized, and they cease to function as a body. When the audience breaks into laughter, Bucky leaves the stage, disgraced. In his attempt to purify the self by negating the zombie, he fragments the team. His own desire for prohibition enslaves him. Addison and her zombie friends take the stage, joining with current and former members of the cheer team to perform a new routine, enacting the hero's return. Unlike their response to the white hair reveal, the audience revels in the performance, and even Bucky concedes to participate in the spectacle. The audience approval reclaims Addison and recasts the homogenous identity of the community. The performance not only galvanizes the cheer team but also builds trust between normals and the zombies.

CONCLUSION

The closing scene occurs after the regional cheer championships. Addison narrates, "We didn't win the cheer championship. But we did something even better. We brought everyone together and we threw an awesome block party. Even my parents came" (Hoen 2018). The celebration signifies growing acceptance of zombies. Normals and zombies reprise "BAMM" and "Our Year." Unlike previous versions of these songs, zombies and normals are integrated. No longer juxtaposed, they form heterogenous dance groups. Because so little time has passed, it's impossible to identify the extent of the acculturation. More normals ornament themselves in token zombie chic yet are careful not to risk being misrecognized as zombies. The line may be fuzzy, but it is never obscured. Normals conform to their traditional solid color pastel attire and only wear zombie accessories. Addison pushes the boundary the furthest by donning a floral print dress. The clothing is still pastel, but the gesture is novel. She also continues to flaunt her white hair, signifying her difference and letting her freak-flag fly. Notably, the zombies still wear government issued clothing including z-bands, and the block party takes place in Zombietown. The implication that zombies remain confined to Zombietown except for school-related activities affirms the superficiality of this celebrated cultural revolution. They still bear the chains of slavery with the z-band, now recalibrated to prevent hacking. In the final celebration scene, Zed reminds the audience that Seabrook retains explicit control over the savagery of every zombie via the bands. He proclaims, "But now all zombies are getting software updates. No more 'tweaking' them. Sweet. Eliza, they have Wi-Fi now" (Hoen 2018). None can go native without Seabrook's permission, nor can they pass as normal. The social stratification remains intact. Seabrook simply has a new hybrid category for Addison, signification of the cultural tendency toward homogenization. Through the ritual of constructing national identity, society internalizes Addison's abjection. The community can celebrate the accommodation of disruption, sutured into the material culture of her pastel floral print dress.

If, as Herbert Marcuse famously uttered on Sigmund Freud's behalf, "the history of man is the history of repression" (1966, 11), then the synchronic and diachronic study of myth reveals the work of civilization, enacting and concealing that repression. According to its own logic, American identity justifies its existence by maintaining distance from the decadent civilization of Europe and the savagery of uncivilized indigenous peoples. From this self-determination of the national subject emerges the ritual of American identity, the daily mythopoetic production of the present as the destiny of the past. Each individual functions as representative of the nation by performing the ritual anew, an entelechy continually affirming what it means to be American. As such, the hero transgresses boundaries of the self, a synecdoche of the state, and encounters the other on the frontier. Consensus politics of Nietzschean will to power validates the efficacy of the ritual. In the film, the community disavows Addison when she initially reveals her white hair but later sanctions her transgression when she and her zombie friends bring recognition to Seabrook at the regional cheer competition. Addison's acculturation to the frontier, vis-à-vis her transgression, is ratified by Seabrook's willingness to accept her back into their circle. Transposing this ritual onto the topography of the frontier reduces the temporality of history to "homogenous, empty time" measured instead by geographic sublation (Benjamin 2007, 261). The three narratives of the Disney film *Zombies* reenact this ritual of American identity. Zed's narrative of assimilation legitimizes the cultural violence of colonialism via his enthusiastic participation in his own imprisonment. Addison, the romantic hero, encounters an internal frontier and resolves abjection by mastering it for Seabrook. Bucky and Principal Lee reveal how authority must adapt to appropriate the work of Addison. Bucky's adherence to tradition signifies a cautious reminder of the dangers of intractable decadence, whereas Lee's diplomacy negotiates the transformation of zombies into docile bodies made ready for assimilation into an increasingly homogenous society, albeit a little less white. As such, the film provides a framework for racial integration and utilizes the community's reaction to the characters' decisions in each narrative to indicate the efficacy of their choices.

NOTES

1. In the context of American history, this is not a particularly surprising move. Thomas Jefferson pioneered such a conflation when he personally revised the proposed constitutional amendment to admit Louisiana into the Union by limiting citizenship to "white inhabitants" (Ellis 2007, 231–232).

2. *Zombies* repeatedly uses the term "normals' to indicate non-zombies. The school even designates entrances for "Normals" and "Zombies" (Hoen 2018).

3. The phrase "errand into the wilderness" comes from Samuel Danforth's 1670 election sermon titled *A Brief Recognition of New England's Errand into the Wilderness* (2006). Perry Miller subsequently titled his 1956 essay collection *Errand into the Wilderness* (1993).

4. During the voyage on the Arabella to the Massachusetts Bay Colony, Winthrop states on April 8, 1630, "for wee must Consider that wee shall be as a Citty upon a Hill, the eies of all people are uppon us; soe that if wee shall deale falsely with our god in this worke wee have undertaken and soe cause him to withdrawe his present help from us, wee shall be made a story and a by-word through the world" (1965, 93).

5. Asian script seems out of place until understood in terms of the narrative's allusion to the civil rights movement. In her book *Liberated Threads* (2015), Tanisha Ford traces the history of "soul style" during the civil rights era and explores efforts to reclaim precolonial African heritage. Unlike African-Americans, however, the zombies of Seabrook have no cultural legacy. Prior to the power plant catastrophe, they were normals. The adoption of street style by zombies is a mimetic gesture of soul style that substitutes anything exotic, such as Black styles and Asian script, for the absence of a cultural inheritance.

6. It should be noted that the cast of normals is primarily but not exclusively white. Addison and her immediate family are white but some of her classmates, including her close friend Bree, are racial minorities.

7. At one point, Zed's zombie friend Eliza complains of feeling sick and asks "Do I look green? Greener than usual?" suggesting that zombie skin color is akin to looking ill (Hoen 2018).

8. Gonzo's untranslated language results in a fascinating interaction between Eliza and Zed. Eliza interjects, saying, "He just dropped that in Zombie" in order to introduce the audience to the fact that zombies have unique and valuable cultural constructs of their own. Zed quickly undermines her by translating, "Yeah, all he said is he's hungry" (Hoen 2018). This conversation shows Zed prefers submitting to authority and sustaining current structures of authority. He desires to assimilate.

9. Interestingly, Zed raps when with his zombie peers. When alone with Addison, he sings, indicative of his conscious desire for assimilation.

REFERENCES

Anderson, Benedict. 2006. *Imagined Communities: Reflections on the Origin and Spread of Nationalism*. New York: Verso.

Balibar, Étienne. 1991. "The Nation Form: History and Ideology." In *Race, Nation, Class: Ambiguous Identities*, translated by Chris Turner, 86–106. New York: Verso.

Barthes, Roland. 1972. "Myth Today." In *Mythologies*, 109–59. New York: Farrar, Straus and Giroux.

Benjamin, Walter. 2007. "Theses on the Philosophy of History." In *Illuminations*, 253–64. New York: Schocken Books.

Bercovitch, Sacvan. 2012. *The American Jeremiad*. Madison: University of Wisconsin Press.

Corrigan, Peter. 2008. *The Dressed Society: Clothing, the Body and Some Meanings of the World*. Los Angeles: SAGE Publications.

Danforth, Samuel. 2006. *A Brief Recognition of New-Englands Errand into the Wilderness: An Online Electronic Text Edition*. Lincoln, NE: University of Nebraska-Lincoln. https://digitalcommons.unl.edu/libraryscience/35.

Ellis, Joseph. 2007. *American Creation: Triumphs and Tragedies at the Founding of the Republic*. New York: Alfred A. Knopf.

Ford, Tanisha. 2015. *Liberated Threads: Black Women, Style, and the Global Politics of Soul*. Chapel Hill: University of North Carolina Press.

Foucault, Michel. 1995. *Discipline and Punish: The Birth of the Prison*. Translated by Alan Sheridan. New York: Vintage Books.
Fruzinska, Justyna. 2014. *Emerson Goes to the Movies: Individualism in Walt Disney Company's Post-1989 Animated Films*. Newcastle upon Tyne: Cambridge Scholars.
Hobsbawm, Eric. 2013. *Nations and Nationalism Since 1780: Programme, Myth, Reality*. New York: Cambridge University Press.
Hoen, Paul, dir. *Zombies*. 2018; Burbank, CA: Disney Channel. DVD.
Jehlen, Myra. 1986. *American Incarnation: The Individual, the Nation, and the Continent*. Cambridge, MA: Harvard University Press.
Kristeva, Julia. 1982. *Powers of Horror*. New York: Columbia University Press.
Marcuse, Herbert. 1966. *Eros and Civilization: A Philosophical Inquiry into Freud*. Boston: Beacon Press.
Miller, Perry. 1993. *Errand into the Wilderness*. Cambridge: Harvard University Press.
Pratt, Mary Louise. 1991. "Arts of the Contact Zone." *PMLA* 91, no. 34: 33–40.
Said, Edward. 1994. *Culture and Imperialism*. New York: Vintage Books.
Trouillot, Michel-Rolph. 1995. *Silencing the Past: Power and the Production of History*. Boston: Beacon Press.
Turner, Frederick Jackson. 1938. "Problems in American History." In *The Early Writings of Frederick Jackson Turner*, 71–83. Madison: University of Wisconsin Press.
Winthrop, John. 1965. "A Model of Christian Charity." In *Puritan Political Ideas 1558–1794*, 75–93. New York: Bobbs Merrill Company.

II

REGULATED WORLDS OF (RESISTING) CHILDREN

4

DO YOU WANT TO BUILD A CHILDHOOD TRAUMA?

Parental Agency and Authority in Disney's *Frozen*
Denise A. Ayo

"Why did they lock Elsa up?" my three-year-old daughter asked on our drive home almost every day for a month. We had recently watched *Frozen*, and thus its songs provided our afternoon soundtrack. As I endeavored to answer this question on a daily basis, as well as wrestle with its ambiguity ("they" who?), I grew increasingly disconcerted. I realized who "they," the film's true adversaries, are. It is not Elsa herself—a character loosely based on Hans Christian Andersen's Snow Queen. Nor is it Prince Hans or the Duke of Weselton, who fear Elsa's powers and covet her wealth and position. "They" are Arendelle's original King and Queen, Elsa and her sister Anna's parents.

We tend to forget the King and Queen. They do not have names, at least in the first film, and die in a little over ten minutes. However, *Frozen*'s remaining hour and a half repeats what happens in these first few moments in which the parents hold all the authority and make all the decisions. When warned that society could perceive Elsa and her powers as dangerous and frightening, they elect to treat their daughter as dangerous and frightening. They teach her to be ashamed and afraid of herself, instruct her that her only options are to conform to or leave society, and deny her of true love and acceptance. Elsa and Anna must overcome these parental lessons to reach the film's conclusion, and thus

I would argue that *Frozen* offers audiences a cautionary tale on how not to care for children.

Like everyday viewers, many popular and academic critics also forget about the King and Queen. They instead focus on the bond between the sisters, ignoring the parents completely or citing their role in separating Elsa and Anna as a plot point not worth exploring.[1] A few bloggers offer reproachful, albeit brief, evaluations. For example, Aurelia (2016) describes the King and Queen as invalidating and unsupportive, and Luttrell (2014) recounts, "Elsa's parents isolate her, teach her that she's dangerous, and demand that she emotionally castrate herself." Resene (2017), an academic scholar who reads Elsa's powers as representing physical, mental, and intellectual disabilities, examines the King and Queen's "mishandling of Elsa's condition" and suggests that they, along with the trolls, erect a "psychological barrier" that drives Elsa to isolate herself even after her parents die. For Resene, the King and Queen merely satisfy society's requirement that difference conform or be locked away.[2] I agree that *Frozen* raises important questions about social norms and values. But I also believe that caregivers have agency in communicating these messages to their children. The King and Queen's beliefs and actions warrant further analysis, especially since this film targets children and their caregivers.

Frozen begins with five-year-old Anna, awoken by aurora borealis, jostling her eight-year-old sister Elsa awake. The two sneak down to the castle ballroom where Anna urges Elsa to "Do the magic! Do the magic!" Elsa, in response, swirls her hands and stomps her foot to create a winter wonderland, using her powers of ice and snow. Their play soon gets out of hand. Anna begins to leap into the air ("Catch me!") with Elsa creating progressively taller snowbanks on which her sister lands ("Gotcha!"). Elsa struggles to keep up with Anna ("Wait! Slow down!") and, in her panic, slips on the icy ballroom floor (Lee and Buck 2013). Anna fails to notice and leaps into the air with nothing to catch her. From the ground, Elsa thrusts her hand out in desperation. Ice shoots from her hand, striking Anna in the head. The King and Queen rush in, pull the ice-cold Anna from Elsa's grasp, and whisk their daughters off to see the trolls in the Valley of the Living Rock.

Once there, the troll leader Grand Pabbie recommends removing all magic from Anna, "Even memories of magic," as the safest way to heal her. After the troll finishes this process, he turns to Elsa to warn her about the danger that her burgeoning powers hold. "Your powers will only grow," he says while creating an image of a blue female figure making ice flurries with her hands and surrounded by other blue figures. "There is beauty in it," he explains, as the group watches the woman create a large snowflake. "But also great danger": the snowflake explodes into a giant red mass. "You must learn to control it. Fear will be your enemy," Grand Pabbie cautions as the crowd turns from blue to red, their expressions changing from awe to anger. They collapse in on the blue woman, eradicating her and the image. Elsa gasps and turns to her father's side as the King cries out with alarm in his voice, "No!" He then proclaims, "We'll protect her. She can learn to control it, I'm sure. Until then, we'll lock the gates. We'll reduce the staff. We will limit her contact with people and keep her powers hidden from everyone, including Anna" (Lee and Buck 2013).

Grand Pabbie seems to warn the family about society's fear, which could spread quickly among the townspeople and cause them to turn on Elsa if her magic backfires or suggests a threat in any way. In the troll's imagery, panic does not cause the snowflake to explode. It explodes because great power is intrinsically dangerous. The explosion creates the sense of peril, represented by the red color. However, the woman remains blue, thus seemingly unimpacted until the mob attacks her. Yet when this scene plays out after Elsa's coronation thirteen years later, the woman is already red with terror. Elsa's fear causes the outburst that, in turn, incites the crowd.

We learn from the film's onset that when circumstances cause Elsa to feel distress, her magic expresses her emotion in unintentional and unguided bursts. The ballroom floor, walls, and door ice over as Elsa holds her unconscious sister, as does the forest path when she and her family rush to the Valley of the Living Rock. Between the troll's warning and its fulfillment, however, Elsa develops an intrapersonal fear that exists without external cause. Her powers do not frighten her immediately after the accident; they react to her concerns about her injured sister. She learns in the intervening years to perceive her abilities as dangerous and to believe that she will hurt someone or invoke society's wrath. Her persistent dread leads to an increasing inability to control her magic, which further exacerbates her terror. This vicious cycle becomes Elsa's constant emotional state. Her internal fear threatens to reveal her powers at her coronation and indirectly does when Anna, fed up with her sister's hiding, pushes the already terrified Elsa too far. Anna demands, "Why do you shut me out? Why do you shut the world out? What are you so afraid of?" In response, Elsa shouts, "I said, enough!," and accidently releases a wall of barbed ice (Lee and Buck 2013).

Fear is certainly Elsa's enemy. But how do we get from society's fear of Elsa to Elsa's fear of herself? A stark contrast exists between the eight-year-old girl who can create a wonderland on a whim and the twenty-one-year-old woman who cannot hold a candlestick without freezing it solid. It is natural that Elsa would respond to the townspeople's trepidation with her own, so perhaps Grand Pabbie's warning about society's impending panic sets off an emotional spiral within the young Elsa. Yet the extent to which terror consumes the adult Elsa calls for a closer look at her coming of age. Before Hans, Weselton, and the townspeople appear in the film, the King and Queen spend their ten minutes on screen as the troll's red crowd. Grand Pabbie sets the tone. He erases Anna's memories and gives an alarming prophecy. However, "the trolls don't tell Elsa's parents to lock her up," as one blogger clarifies, "It is Elsa's parents who have such an extreme and unnecessary response" ("Disney's *Frozen* and Autism" 2013). The King and Queen blame Elsa. They worry what society might do to her, and they worry what she might do to Anna. They lock Elsa away and teach her to suppress her powers. The accident and the troll's words frighten Elsa and her parents. The King and Queen maintain and grow this emotion until Elsa fears herself as much as, or more than, she fears society or society fears her.

When audiences meet the King and Queen, these characters are scared and accusatory.[3] As they rush into the frozen ballroom, the King demands, "Elsa, what have you done? This is getting out of hand" (Lee and Buck 2013). Their panic is understandable: one of their daughters lies unconscious on the floor. Their attribution is logical: the ballroom is frozen, and Elsa is older and conscious, and possesses magical powers. But there is never any mitigation of their reaction despite the film portraying the event as a blameless or co-created accident. Instead, Elsa accepts all culpability: "It was an accident. I'm sorry, Anna" (Lee and Buck 2013). The King and Queen offer no forgiveness or understanding either. They decide to isolate Elsa until she can learn to control herself, which sounds more like punishment than protection. They then leave others to execute this order. Servants lock the gates and shutter the castle, and Elsa closes her new bedroom door, accepting the arrangement without question or protest, and shamefully averts her eyes when she catches Anna's gaze. Elsa assumes the blame for not only the accident but also the subsequent isolation and seems to hang onto the guilt indefinitely.[4] Anna, who cannot offer forgiveness due to her ignorance of the accident and her parents' decision, identifies Elsa as the reason for their separation.

After Elsa dutifully shuts her bedroom door, the song "Do You Want to Build a Snowman?" begins and covers the sisters' maturation from ages five and eight to nine and twelve, and then to fifteen and eighteen. In this song, Anna returns again and again to implore her sister to end their estrangement and, in doing so, establishes a closed door as a symbol for Elsa's active role in her own isolation. Beginning with the aforementioned shot, the song portrays Anna begging her sister through a keyhole to build snowmen, ride bikes, or explain her absence, and it ends with Elsa still refusing to open the door in the wake of their parents' deaths. At the song's conclusion, the equally distraught and lonely sisters sit on either side of Elsa's door: Anna, surrounded by warm tones that seem to convey her desire to connect, and Elsa, surrounded by ice that appears to represent both her fear and her intractability.[5] The connection between Elsa and a closed door appears throughout the film. Anna sings the duet "Love is an Open Door" with Prince Hans, a visiting dignitary to whom she becomes engaged on the same day that they meet, and Elsa tries to retreat through a closed door after refusing to bless the hasty engagement. Later, Anna comments, "That's a first," when Elsa's ice palace doors open, but then Elsa's giant snowman guard Marshmallow throws Anna and Kristoff (the ice harvester who agrees to help Anna find her sister) out these same palace doors (Lee and Buck 2013). Each time a closed door appears in the film, it evokes the image of Elsa shutting her little sister out.

While Anna fixates on Elsa as the source of and only solution to her loneliness, the King and Queen teach Elsa to be scared. Rather than celebrate Elsa's talent as a gift worth wielding, as a few critics point out, the King and Queen construe it as an aberration to be secreted away

("Disney's *Frozen* and Autism" 2013; Aurelia 2016; Resene 2017). At the opening of "Do You Want to Build a Snowman?," the newly isolated Elsa accidentally freezes her bedroom windowsill when she notices something outside that makes her smile. We see Elsa lose control of her powers without provocation for the first time, and thus we must assume that her magic responds to a fear within herself. In the next shot, the King inserts his eight-year-old daughter's hands into a pair of gloves, and Elsa then obediently pledges:

KING: Conceal it.

ELSA: Don't feel it.

KING AND ELSA: Don't let it show. (Lee and Buck 2013)

The parents drive this initiative like they do the sisters' separation, and Elsa, once again, unquestioningly accepts it as her own by sharing its articulation. In isolating Elsa and teaching her to hide her difference, the King and Queen cultivate their daughter's fear of society as well as substantiate society's fear of their daughter. In predicating Elsa's release on the capable quashing of her abilities, they place her in an impossible situation. When frightened, Elsa loses control of her magic, and this inability to restrain herself makes her more scared and out of control. And, because she assumes responsibility for her parents' plan, she feels deeply ashamed when it, inevitably, fails. It is no wonder that the lines Elsa shares with her father haunt her throughout the film and reverberate in all of her songs.

As "Do You Want to Build a Snowman?" progresses, Elsa's powers grow, as does—and perhaps more importantly—her terror. At twelve, Elsa cowers in a corner covered with ice:

ELSA: I'm scared. It's getting stronger!

KING: Getting upset only makes it worse. Calm down.

ELSA: No! Don't touch me! Please, I don't want to hurt you. (Lee and Buck 2013)

Whereas a younger Elsa allows her father to glove her hands, this Elsa beseeches her parents not to touch or come near her. She believes she is

Figure 4.1. Elsa recoils from her father's attempt to embrace and console her (Lee and Buck 2013).

dangerous and perceives isolation as her only option. The King's admonishment to calm down appears hypocritical when we reflect on his and the Queen's behavior until this point. Yet, in this scene, they look at Elsa with sadness and concern on their faces and attempt to pacify her as if she were a terrified animal that might harm itself or others in its panic. Elsa appears irrational when compared to her uneasy yet collected parents, and the King and Queen treat her as such even though she simply embodies their lessons. By the end of the song, their manner towards eighteen-year-old Elsa verges on condescension. Elsa says goodbye to her parents before they depart on the sea voyage that costs them their lives by curtsying at arm's length and pleading, "Do you have to go?" This constrained farewell differs significantly from the family embrace the King and Queen share with Anna. With a smile and pitying look, the King offers the assurance, "You'll be fine, Elsa" (Lee and Buck 2013). The parents no longer seem to share their daughter's fear, despite fostering it with their extreme initial reactions and detrimental teachings. The King and Queen, having sufficiently frightened Elsa, have either successfully suppressed the emotion themselves or completely passed its burden on to their daughter. Either way, they assume a position of calm authority and distance from the consequences of their behavior while Elsa preserves her parents' fear as her own just as she undertakes their mandate to conceal and not feel.

Although transpiring three years after the King and Queen's fatal journey, the song "For the First Time in Forever" picks up exactly where "Do You Want to Build a Snowman?" leaves off in screen time and subject matter. It reestablishes Anna's loneliness and Elsa's growing fear and inability to control her powers. It also depicts how the sisters understand these insecurities in the context of society's reintroduction into their lives. Anna, still running around the castle halls, sings about finding "the one" and returns to the castle gallery to interact with courtship paintings instead of befriending a portrait of Joan of Arc as she does in the previous song (Lee and Buck 2013). However, her envisioned mate, like the fifteenth-century French youth, only serves as a superficial substitute for Elsa. The film demonstrates this a few scenes later when Anna abandons Prince Hans, moments after their betrothal, to follow her sister up North Mountain.[6]

Elsa, in "For the First Time in Forever," desperately tries to keep her pledge as her coronation ceremony approaches. Paralleling her first scene in "Do You Want to Build a Snowman?," Elsa gazes out her window at the advancing townspeople and sings, "Don't let them in / Don't let them see." She then turns to a large painting of her father holding the coronation orb and scepter, singing, "Be the good girl / You always have to be." Even with society encroaching on her, Elsa makes it clear that concealment is primarily not about fearing what the townspeople might do to her but rather about parental expectations. She repeats the pact that she made with her father as she gazes at his portrait and takes off her gloves: "Conceal / Don't feel." She alters the last bit, "Put on a show . . . ," as she turns with a jewelry box and candlestick in her hands, imitating her father's stance in the painting (Lee and Buck 2013).

Figure 4.2. Elsa stands nervously beneath her father's portrait (Lee and Buck 2013).

The King's image looms large over Elsa as she tries to put on a show of normalcy. The objects instantly begin to freeze. Elsa looks down at her hands with panic, confusion, and helplessness, stuffing them back into her gloves after throwing down her practice orb and scepter. Her dependency on gloves underscores her parents' influence. Elsa exerts, both intentionally and unintentionally, her powers with her feet throughout the film, freezing ballrooms, solidifying fjords, and constructing ice palaces with a stomp or stride. Gloves are a useless totem of her parents' teachings that she clings to as desperately as the teachings themselves.

Concealing and not feeling, Elsa discovers, is an unattainable goal. She will never satisfy the King and Queen's conditions and, thus, must remain alone forever. When she involuntarily unleashes her magic after her coronation, she casts herself into self-exile just as her parents isolated her after the initial accident. Audiences and critics tend to perceive "Let It Go," which Elsa sings as she escapes Arendelle and constructs her ice palace, as a triumphant anthem of freedom and renewal.[7] Yet I contend she only repeats what she has been taught to do when her powers are involved in an accident. She looks directly into the viewer's eyes before closing her palace doors, shutting out the audience as well as her sister. Yes, she does this with a look of confidence instead of shame. Yes, she slams the door instead of quietly closing it. Feeling some love and acceptance from herself, she seems to renounce her parents' lessons in "Let It Go." After once again revisiting her promise ("Conceal / Don't feel") with a slight alteration ("Don't let them know . . ."), she offers a rebuke: "Well, now they know!" Her confidence, however, is short lived. "The fears that once controlled [her]," still control her despite her claims to the contrary in "Let It Go." We see this when Anna catches up with her at the ice palace and begs Elsa not to abandon her again in "For the First Time in Forever (Reprise)": "Please don't shut me out again / Please don't slam the door." Elsa, flashing back to the first accident, maintains that she is dangerous and tries to protect her sister by retreating: "Just stay away and you'll be safe from me." Anna continues to push, and Elsa grows increasingly frantic: "I can't control the curse . . . There's so much fear." Elsa attempts to escape but ends up hurting Anna again. After she strikes Anna in the heart, we see Elsa telling herself, "Don't feel. Don't feel," as her palace crackles around her (Lee and Buck 2013).

As if circling a point of trauma, *Frozen* reenacts its first ten minutes over and over again. Anna goads Elsa (to create a winter wonderland, to offer her blessing, to unfreeze Arendelle), and Elsa reacts under pressure and out of fear, leading to an accident (trying to catch Anna and hitting her in the head, trying to get away from Anna and shooting ice at everyone, trying to convince Anna to leave and striking her in the heart). Elsa is then locked up (in her bedroom, in her ice palace, in the castle dungeon), and Anna chases after her sister to prod her once more. Unsurprisingly, some critics, including a clinical psychologist, have found Elsa's behaviors following the initial accident (shutting out loved ones, hiding the precipitating event, existing in an agitated emotional state) comparable to those seen in individuals suffering from posttraumatic stress disorder (Feder 2014; Scarlet 2014). Notably, Elsa's parents teach her these behaviors. Moreover, the reexperienced trauma in the film is not limited to the accident. The plot also repeats the traumatic aftermath, and the repetition does not stop until Elsa's magical outbursts are met with a new response. The King and Queen's mishandling of the accident and their daughter's burgeoning powers creates the cycle. Anna breaks it with love and acceptance.

Anna does not fear her sister. She shouts to Elsa during "For the First Time in Forever (Reprise)," "You don't have to protect me! I'm not afraid!" She repeatedly tries to defuse concerns about Elsa. She tells Hans, "Elsa's not dangerous. . . . She's my sister. She would never hurt me." When Kristoff asks her, "So you're not at all afraid of her?," Anna responds, "Why would I be?" Audiences, who retain their memories of the first accident, may understand Anna's fearlessness as naïveté. The film even seems to mock her trust in her sister when it shows the comical and clueless Olaf, also in response to Kristoff's question, calling Elsa the "nicest, gentlest, warmest person ever" as he accidentally impales himself on an Elsa-created icicle. The snowman's confidence in this scene mirrors his confidence, two scenes earlier, in his ability to spend the summer months with his "snow up against the burning sand / Prob'ly getting gorgeously tanned" (Lee and Buck 2013). We laugh at Olaf facilitating his own demise, and we knowingly smile at Anna's misguidedness.

But we cannot forget that Anna's unwavering faith in and relentless pursuit of her sister also stem from how the opening accident is handled. Grand Pabbie cures Anna's frozen head by removing her memories of

Elsa's magic, and the King and Queen interpret this as a prescription to separate the siblings and never tell Anna anything about Elsa or the accident. Reflecting on this parental decision, Colman (2014) pointedly asks, "If, when [Anna] is old enough to understand the implications, her parents or even Elsa were to sit her down and say, 'Look, there's something you should know about your sister, . . .' would the ice in her head grow back?" The ice does not return when Anna learns about Elsa's magic. Elsa inadvertently puts it back when Anna continues to provoke her. In keeping Anna ignorant, the King and Queen leave her to not only underestimate her sister's capabilities but blindly chase after Elsa for explanation and reconciliation. Her dogged quest goes beyond a need for companionship. As Colman also contends, young Anna was probably not isolated like her sister. Servants still had to manage the castle, and the King and Queen still had to govern Arendelle. Anna, shown freely roaming about as a child, would likely have come into contact with castle staff as well as the numerous other individuals that monarchs rely on to run a kingdom. In addition, the film shows Anna having, unlike Elsa, an affectionate relationship with her parents. Anna's lonely desperation throughout the film centers around the unexplained estrangement from her sister and best friend. Anna does not want to connect with just anyone. She wants to connect with Elsa. Even her search for a husband only masks her desire to reconcile with her lost sister.

Anna seeks to mend the rupture that her parents create and, in the process, ends up counteracting the King and Queen's treatment of Elsa. Anna describes her sister's explosive display following the coronation as unintentional and holds herself accountable. In words equally applicable to the first incident, she argues with Hans and Weselton: "It was an accident. She was scared. She didn't mean it. She didn't mean any of this. Tonight was my fault. I pushed her." When Elsa injures Anna again, Anna does not reproach her sister or dwell on the mistake. In fact, she sacrifices her life for Elsa. Anna and Elsa's encounter at the ice palace leaves Anna with a frozen heart, which Grand Pabbie declares only an act of true love can thaw. Understanding this to mean a lover's kiss, Anna rushes off to find Prince Hans, who presses Anna upon their reunion: "You said she would never hurt you." In response, Anna states, "I was wrong," and immediately refocuses on her need for a kiss (Lee and Buck 2013). Without further comment or censure, she admits that she misjudged her sister's capacity to harm her. Hans, however, refuses to kiss Anna because he only proposed in order to become Arendelle's king. He leaves Anna to die and uses her impending death to justify ordering Elsa's execution. Anna then determines that Kristoff loves her and begins looking for him. As Anna espies Kristoff, she hears Hans unsheathe his sword to kill Elsa. Choosing her sister's life over her own, Anna dives in front of Hans's sword as her sister's magic overtakes her body and freezes her to solid ice. Regardless of how we judge Anna's behavior (her fearlessness as naïve, her pursuit as reckless, her responses as overgenerous), her conduct towards Elsa appears striking when compared to what her parents offer their eldest daughter. Anna's gradual discoveries about Elsa's powers and their dangerous potential never deter her.

Anna's determination results in Elsa experiencing true love. Elsa, believing that she cannot harm Anna any further, embraces her frozen sister for the first time since the King and Queen pulled them apart years earlier. Anna's self-sacrifice serves as the act needed to cure her own frozen heart, and she begins to thaw in Elsa's arms. But Elsa does not stop holding her sister. Anna has taught Elsa that love is the secret to wielding her magic. Blame and fear lead to Elsa's isolation and loss of control. Acceptance and love resolve both. Anna's success reveals just how much the King and Queen fail their daughter.[8] Signaling that loving Elsa was always the solution, the white stripe in Anna's hair, which develops after the initial accident and grows worse after Elsa freezes Anna's heart, disappears.

Rather than read Grand Pabbie's directive to control their daughter's powers as an impetus to isolate her until she can suppress them, what if the King and Queen read it as a need to embrace and empower Elsa? The troll's words can be understood as instructions to respect, train, and harness Elsa's magic as easily as they can be to fear, conceal, and not feel it.[9] Instead of teaching Elsa to conform to social expectations, the King and Queen could have encouraged her to fight against them. Discrimination—which Grand Pabbie both warns against and, frankly, participates in when he asks, "Born with the powers or cursed?"—neither starts nor ends with caregivers (Lee and Buck 2013). But, while society originates and sometimes first communicates the message, it is the role of caregivers to interpret or reject it for their children. We all have a choice as to whether we will maintain or challenge society's dictates. The King and Queen fail Elsa, and they set her up for failure. Grand Pabbie may or may not have stoked Elsa's fear with his ominous warning, and at least Colman (2014) believes the parents' actions pale in comparison to the damage done by his words.[10] However, I would point out that the King and Queen had ten years to love their daughter and mitigate their brief exchange with the troll.

The glimpse that viewers get of the King and Queen shows them as having much in common with many other animated Disney parents. A (nearly) silent yet nurturing mother and a strict yet caring father are not unusual in Disney films (Holcomb, Latham, and Fernandez-Baca 2015). It is also quite common for biological parents to die or be otherwise removed. However, unlike other Disney films, *Frozen* does not explicitly point to the role that the King and Queen's thoughts, feelings, and behaviors play in their children's lives or portray their deaths as significant to the plot. Instead of actively rebelling against extreme beliefs and harsh restrictions like Ariel in *The Little Mermaid* (1989) and Miguel in *Coco* (2017), Elsa accepts them as her own. Instead of parental death leading to an evil stepparent who threatens the protagonist as in *Snow White and the Seven Dwarfs* (1937) and *Cinderella* (1950), Elsa becomes the problematic caregiver Anna must overcome. The King's and Queen's deaths mean Elsa must eventually take over as Arendelle's ruler. But their sudden absence does not force the sisters to grow up by introducing them to the cold cruel world like in *Dumbo* (1941), *Bambi* (1942), and *The Lion King* (1994).[11] Elsa is eighteen when her parents die and has already experienced discrimination at their hands. Likewise, the King's and Queen's deaths only aggravate the loneliness that they create in Anna when they separate her from her sister. *Frozen* breaks the mold here, too. Children are frequently mistreated in Disney animated films, and emotional maltreatment is the most common form; however, unlike in *Frozen,* the perpetrators are rarely biological parents, and the films almost never explore the negative ramifications (Hubka, Hovdestad, and Tonmy, 2009).

In her analysis of Elsa's mistreatment, Resene (2017) suggests that *Frozen* shifts the blame from society to Prince Hans. She contends that when Hans reveals his villainous plot to assume Arendelle's throne, the film invites audiences to focus on him and ignore the larger forces contributing to Elsa's ostracization. She explains that this move helps to assuage our guilt as viewers of the film and members of a culture that discriminates. I am intrigued by Resene's conceptualization of Hans as a scapegoat. He, after all, repeats the King and Queen's actions. His imprisonment of Elsa in the castle dungeon reenacts her parents' confinement of their eight-year-old child. He shackles Elsa's hands for the same reason that the King gloves them thirteen years earlier. Perhaps we can even see similarities between Hans's mercenary marriage proposal (which he explains he directed towards Anna because "no one was getting anywhere with [Elsa]") and the King and Queen's conditional acceptance of their daughter based on her ability to abide by social norms (Lee and Buck 2013). Hans's dungeon and shackles seem cruel in comparison to a castle bedroom and satin gloves; however, the assessment changes when your parents reject and imprison you. Is Hans's appearance as a villain and scapegoat in the film's final fifteen minutes a continuation of the shifting responsibility that we see in the first ten? Although the King and Queen instigate and cultivate much of the fear, onus, guilt, and shame tied to their daughter's abilities, Elsa assumes the entire burden by the time they die. She shuts the door that Anna wants open, and this struggle drives the remainder of the film.

At its core, *Frozen*'s story is one of familial love, withheld by Elsa's parents and then given freely and uncompromisingly by her sister. But we only see Elsa and Anna or, more accurately, Elsa versus Anna. The King and Queen get lost. They get lost in how the sisters' separation takes place. They get lost in our instinct to empathize with Anna locked out of her sister's life—after all, we get a door shut in our face too. They get lost as Elsa absorbs all the fear and accepts all the blame. They get lost with their untimely deaths and removal from the narrative. The story becomes Anna overcoming Elsa's panic and detachment, and the film seems to allow, perhaps encourage, us to forget about the parents who start it all.

Frozen offers audiences a meditation on how much caregivers should allow society to dictate how they raise their children. Will we allow societal fears to become our children's in our efforts to protect them? Or will we challenge these fears and empower our children to combat prejudice with our unconditional love and acceptance? It is unfortunate that these questions get obscured. Perhaps this move is necessary for the same reason that Hans must take the blame: guardian-filled audiences may only be able to handle so much self-reflection before projecting their guilt elsewhere. Personally, I am uncomfortable abandoning my agency and authority as a parent, even if I am permitted to do so. As I ended up telling my daughter on our afternoon drives home, "Elsa's parents locked her up because they were scared. That was bad. Parents need to cherish their children and celebrate their talents."

NOTES

1. For example, Heatwole (2016, 7), writes, "*Frozen*'s princess Elsa must mend her relationship with her sister, Anna, after years spent hiding a dangerous secret.... In the end, *true love* in *Frozen* is recorded as sisterly love, and in the great rescue scene the sisters save each other." Other popular and academic examples include Feder (2014), Law (2014), Elnahla (2015), and Kowalski and Bhalla (2018).

2. Other scholars who pay extended attention to how Elsa's parents treat her tend to be more concerned, like Resene, with how these parental actions connect to social constructs. Streiff and Dundes (2017), for example, read the King's demand that Elsa conceal her powers as the patriarchal desire to control female sexuality.

3. I assume that the Queen agrees with what the King says and does in the film since she has very little dialogue and always appears at her husband's side.

4. The accident haunts Elsa as a flashback late in the film but is never discussed again. Despite reconnecting with Anna and rejoining society at *Frozen*'s conclusion, Elsa spends the two featurettes that come out after the main film either trying to make amends or blaming herself for the years the sisters were apart. In *Frozen Fever*, Elsa painstakingly arranges a perfect birthday celebration for Anna to make up for all the birthdays Anna "spent outside [her] locked door" (Lee and Buck 2015). As the sisters try to figure out how to celebrate their first Christmas together in *Olaf's Frozen Adventure*, Elsa explains to Anna, "After the gates were closed, we were never together.... It's my fault we don't have a family tradition" (Deters and Wermers 2017).

5. Elnahla (2015, 124) writes, for example, "In *Frozen*, 'cold' is not just a temperature, it is an isolation from other people, and it takes sisterly loyalty, devotion, solidarity and selfless love ... to thaw Elsa's icy heart."

6. Law (2014, 19) identifies how Hans's appeal for Anna is rooted in her longing for Elsa: "a charming and understanding prince from a neighboring kingdom who offers Anna the love and companionship that she never received from her sister." Anna seeks in Hans a substitute for Elsa. She characterizes

him and their budding romance as an open door in direct contrast, yet inextricably linked, to her sister's perpetually closed one. Notably, the opening notes of Hans and Anna's duet "Love is an Open Door" start playing while they swap stories about sibling neglect.

7. Resene (2017) describes "Let It Go" as "an anthem of independence," and Law (2014, 22) calls it "an anthem about forgetting the past and moving towards a freer life." Likewise, Feder (2014) writes, "In this song, Elsa releases herself from these pressures and allows herself the freedom to make mistakes and live how she chooses."

8. In *Frozen II*, Elsa and Anna learn that their parents died trying to discover the source of Elsa's powers. Elsa immediately blames herself for their deaths. Anna consoles her sister: "You are not responsible for their choices," and asserts that Elsa and her magic are gifts from the spirits, a reward for their mother saving their father who was her enemy at the time (Lee and Buck 2019). *Frozen II* portrays King Agnarr and Queen Iduna as heroic individuals who overcome with love the hatred between the people of Arendelle and the Northuldra tribe. But I would argue that the film also raises the question of whether Elsa and Anna's parents would have died if they had been less concerned with finding answers (which they probably did in an effort to help Elsa conceal her powers) and more concerned with loving their daughter and accepting her, powers and all, as a blessing. In addition, Anna's words in *Frozen II* remind us that the King and Queen have agency in *Frozen*. Her point that their choice to travel to Ahtohallan is not Elsa's responsibility could be extended to their choice to blame and isolate Elsa.

9. The King and Queen's interpretation arguably makes less sense than the one I suggest, as the YouTube series "How It Should Have Ended" demonstrates. The series's *Frozen* spoof shows Grand Pabbie voicing his outrage and concern ("What? That's not what I said. That's a terrible idea! . . . Are you even listening? I just said fear is her enemy. . . . Oh, wow. You guys are bad parents") as the King and Queen react to his comments about Elsa's growing powers ("So you're saying we should lock her up alone in a castle until she's safe to be around? . . . So you're saying we should teach her to be scared of herself?") ("How It Should Have Ended" 2014).

10. Colman (2014) argues, "regardless of how badly Elsa and Anna's parents interpret the Troll King's warning, the damage is already done. The Troll King steals Elsa's agency too, by needlessly scaring the living shit out of both her and her parents. They are frightened, they are vulnerable and they are desperate, and so the Troll King decides to tell them about Elsa's growing powers in the most frightening and ominous way he possibly could, indelibly equating Elsa's ability with the very fear she needs to avoid."

11. In a *Glamour* interview, Don Hahn explains this common plot point in Disney films: "Disney films are about growing up. They're about that day in your life when you have to accept responsibility. Simba ran away from home but had to come back. In shorthand, it's much quicker to have characters grow up when you bump off their parents. Bambi's mother gets killed, so he has to grow up" (Radloff 2014).

REFERENCES

Aurelia, Autumn. 2016. "9 Reasons Elsa's Storyline in Frozen Is the Perfect Metaphor for Mental Illness." *The Mighty* (blog). December 6, 2016. https://themighty.com/2016/12/elsa-frozen-just-like-people-with-mental-illness/.

Colman, Dani. 2014. "The Problem with False Feminism (or Why *Frozen* Left Me Cold)." *Medium* (blog). February 1, 2014. https://medium.com/@directordanic/the-problem-with-false-feminism-7c0bbc7252ef.

Deters, Kevin and Stevie Wermers, dir. *Olaf's Frozen Adventure*. 2017; Burbank, CA: Walt Disney Studies Home Entertainment, 2018. DVD.

"Disney's *Frozen* and Autism." *The Third Glance* (blog). December 21, 2013. https://thethirdglance.wordpress.com/2013/12/21/disneys-frozen-and-autism/.

Elnahla, Nada Ramadan. 2015. "Aging with Disney and the Gendering of Evil." *Journal of Literature and Art Studies* 5, no. 2 (February): 114–27. https://doi.org/10.17265/2159-5836/2015.02.004.

Feder, Shira. 2014. "Slamming the Door: An Analysis of Elsa." *The Feminist Wire*, October 16, 2014. https://thefeministwire.com/2014/10/slamming-door-analysis-elsa-frozen/.

Heatwole, Alexandra. 2016. "Disney Girlhood: Princess Generations and Once Upon a Time." *Studies in the Humanities* 43, no. 1–2 (February): 1–19. ProQuest.

Holcomb, Jeanne, Kenzie Latham, and Daniel Fernandez-Baca. 2015. "Who Cares for the Kids?: Caregiving and Parenting in Disney Films." *Journal of Family Issues* 36, no. 14 (December): 1957–1981. SAGE Online.

"How It Should Have Ended." 2014. "How *Frozen* Should Have Ended—Reissued." June 4, 2014. Video, 3:00. https://youtu.be/Dach1nPbsY8.

Hubka, David, Wendy Hovdestad, and Lil Tonmyr. 2009. "Child Maltreatment in Disney Animated Feature Films: 1937–2006." *The Social Science Journal* 43, no. 3 (September): 427–41. ScienceDirect.

Kowalski, Christopher, and Ruchi Bhalla. 2018. "Viewing the Disney Movie *Frozen* through a Psychodynamic Lens." *Journal of Medical Humanities* 39, no. 2 (October): 145–50. SpringerLink.

Law, Michelle. 2014. "Sisters Doin' It for Themselves: *Frozen* and the Evolution of the Disney Heroine." *Screen Education* 74 (June): 16–25. ProQuest.

Lee, Jennifer, and Chris Buck, dir. *Frozen*. 2013; Burbank, CA: Walt Disney Studies Home Entertainment, 2014. DVD.

———. *Frozen Fever*. 2015; Burbank, CA: Walt Disney Studies Home Entertainment, 2015. DVD.

———. *Frozen II*. 2019; Burbank, CA: Walt Disney Studies Home Entertainment, 2020. DVD.

Luttrell, Gina. 2014. "How Disney Nearly Ruined *Frozen*." *Thoughts on Liberty* (blog), January 15, 2014. http://thoughtsonliberty.com/how-disney-nearly-ruined-frozen.

Radloff, Jessica. 2014. "Why Most Disney Heroines Don't Have Mothers and So Many More Secrets from the Disney Archives." *Glamour*, September 10, 2014. https://www.glamour.com/story/disney-secrets-beauty-and-the-beast.

Resene, Michelle. 2017. "From Evil Queen to Disabled Teen: *Frozen* Introduces Disney's First Disabled Princess." *Disability Studies Quarterly* 37, no. 2 (June). http://dx.doi.org/10.18061/dsq.v37i2.5310.

Scarlet, Janina. 2014. "Psychology of *Frozen*: What Makes This Disney Movie Unlike Any Other." *Superhero Therapy* (blog). July 12, 2014. http://www.superhero-therapy.com/psychology-of-frozen-what-makes-this-disney-movie-unlike-any-other/.

Streiff, Madeline and Lauren Dundes. 2017. "Frozen in Time: How Disney Gender-Stereotypes Its Most Powerful Princess." *Social Science* 6, no. 2 (March). https://doi.org/10.3390/socsci6020038.

5

"BECAUSE MY WORLD WOULD BE A WONDERLAND"

Fantasy Circumscription and Adult Constructions of Girlhood in *Alice in Wonderland* (1951) and *Peter Pan* (1953)

Joseph V. Giunta

Alice in Wonderland, Disney's 1951 animated adaptation of Lewis Carroll's *Alice* book series, begins with an inattentive Alice sewing a crown of flowers for her kitten, insouciant to her older sister's history lesson about the Norman conquest of England. Openly voicing her preference for a world in which all books are filled with pictures instead of words, Alice declares, "If I had a world of my own, everything would be nonsense. Nothing would be what it is because everything would be what it isn't" (Geronimi, Luske, and Jackson 1951). As audiences experience the film's first musical number, "In a World of My Own," they gain access to Alice's ideal world of fantasy: cats and rabbits wearing trousers, flowers that can converse with her for hours, and a personal allotment of bluebirds, among other fanciful imaginings. However, as the film's narrative progresses, it becomes clear that Alice is unprepared for the literal rabbit hole her own imagination is about to lead her down. Rather, she feels frightened by her unchecked fantasy, quickly realizing that her comparatively disciplined reality, where order reigns over nonsense, is a much preferable and safer space. Alice and her Wonderland, representative of Disney's tidy structuring of cinematic worlds, provides its protagonist with regulated spaces where young audiences can avoid distressing aberrations from conventional decorum. *Alice in Wonderland*

(1951), as well as *Peter Pan* (1953), especially represents a particular adult framing of childhood in which children are cultivated as caretakers of the status quo while also learning about normative behaviors regarding gender, family values, sexuality, race, and class.[1] Though they are adopted from different source texts (children's novel, stage play) and on the surface do not relate in their respective stories (unhinged fantasy, coming-of-age), they not only recurrently become the definitive version of these tales but also assist in constituting children's understandings of the social world and their placement within it (Rothschild 2009; Somers and Gibson 1993). Both narratives, despite their penchant for magical adventures, consistently reinforce societal morals and ideals by concluding their young protagonists' journeys with returns to the safety of hearth and home. These two films, and others released during the 1950s, must be interrogated so we can comprehend their influence on both historical and contemporary constructions of children and childhood (Pomerantz 2009, 147–48).

Although academic research for nearly a century has expressed children's ability to comprehend the content of moving pictures, defining the genre of children's film, as well as its intended youth demographic, remains a contested classification (Holaday and Stoddard 1933; Wojcik-Andrews 2000). Diverse cultural contexts, didactic strategies, and conceptualizations of childhood make universalizing the genre an increasingly difficult undertaking (James 2004; Wojcik-Andrews 2000). However, as Cornell (2015) professes, "a children's film is assumed to have value for society; it is valued if it can serve a readily apparent cultural-pedagogical function . . . to turn children into citizens" (10). Faulkner (2011), introducing her monograph on the history of children's entanglement with innocence, expresses her firm belief that, "Worrying about children is a national vocation" (1). From advertising tactics and religious formation to educational practice and family law, children are constantly the subject of adult anxiety, regularly caught between institutional attempts to correct the failures of the past and socially prepare for what the future may bring (Aird 2004; Hearst 2004; Lindner 2004; Mayall 2001). Manichaean depictions of heroes and villains, closed narratives concluding with "happily ever after," and strict adherences to the contemporary period's traditional family values encompass key components of the genre.

The adult-centric structuring process of modern mediatic depictions of childhood incessantly harkens back to an imagined "Golden Age" of freedom and unrestricted play (Buckingham 2000; Taylor 2011). However, what perspectives did films released during this conceptual Golden Age advocate for in actuality? Deconstructing these timeless classics reveals not only adults' nostalgia for images of young lives but also how children and childhood are often employed as symbols for developing ideologies of nation. Historically and culturally contextualizing the world of Hollywood filmmaking, and the nation at-large, helps situate Disney's animated feature output in the early 1950s. Kammen (1993) succinctly describes this era for artists and writers seeking success in the postwar period: "Patriotism was basically 'in' and cynicism was 'out' for more than fifteen years following the end of the war" (546). After the Second World War, Hollywood acquired a taste for dated value systems that affirmed American exceptionalism. The social and moral lessons offered in Disney films reinforce gendered understandings of the American Dream by preparing young audiences for society's expectations of them as upstanding figures of domesticity, ready to accept their "proper" role as presumptive mothers-to-be.[2] The power in these stories, Wasko (2001) maintains, imitates contemporary society's power dynamics, with control firmly and unquestionably sitting with men.

This chapter, by examining *Alice in Wonderland* and *Peter Pan*, endeavors to break down these sociocultural imaginings of femininity and childhood and, in doing so, concludes by pointing toward alternative and transgressive readings that empower, rather than subjectify, young audiences. Both films map their young female protagonists' escapes from reality into fantasy lands that devolve into perceived physical danger and culminate with their return to the secure and predictable spaces of home (Kavey 2008). Alice's constraint of fantasy's power and decision to "grow up" is mirrored by Wendy in *Peter Pan*. Both promote ideal gender behaviors and societal expectations at two different stages of development, providing didactic lessons in response to the evolving pressures of each girl's coming-of-age. The intersection of cinema and media studies, girlhood studies, and childhood studies helps provide analytical and theoretical frameworks. An interdisciplinary spirit opens up these films to nuanced interrogations that articulate Disney's reaffirmation of adult framings of childhood and American ideals of nation.

POSTWAR DISNEY: EMBRACING AMERICANA IN THE MAGIC KINGDOM

William H. Short, the executive director of the Motion Picture Research Council, commissioned a study in the late 1920s and early 1930s that examined the influence of cinema on children. This research, known as the Payne Fund Studies (PFS), was conducted by psychologists, sociologists, and educators and concludes that, "Moving pictures make a profound appeal to children of all ages" (Charters 1933, v).[3] Though Charters (1933) himself regarded the commercial movie industry as "an unsavory mess," he realized the medium's educational potential and firmly believed films could serve as "beautiful, fascinating, and kindly servant[s] of childhood" (55; 63). The PFS also aligned with critical and social scientific theories of the 1930s and 1940s that claimed mass media profoundly impacted rates of juvenile delinquency and that the splintering of families during the war left young people even more vulnerable to the negative effects of cinema (Spigel 1998). Discussing the 1950 White House Conference on Childhood and Youth, Wojcik (2016) points out that the postwar period shifted public concerns from "impoverished, orphaned children in the 1910s, 1920s, and 1930s" to the developing personalities of "primarily white middle-class children" (102). This mélange of postwar sentiment, scientific research, popular literature, and institutional symposiums did not go unnoticed by the film industry, who proficiently adapted to these anxieties and achieved incredible commercial success by reinforcing traditional family values (Wojcik-Andrews 2000). Disney was in a particularly privileged position and soon capitalized on and cemented their presence in Hollywood as the choice film studio for children's consumption.

Kammen's (1993) discourse around public memory, a gradually shifting combination of ideology, tradition, and pseudo-memory, assists in understanding Disney's reemergence in the 1950s. Parsing through scholarly conversations on this subject, he recognizes how traditional value systems shift over time and how the ideological importance of public memory is defined by its ability to "shape a nation's ethos and sense of identity" (13). Disney's history of oversimplifying social constructions of class and beauty pervade their animated texts: inherent goodness is conflated with appealing physical attributes and higher-class status. This amalgam of morality, comeliness, and wealth serves as a model for young audiences, depicting the reputed fruits of ideal behavioral patterns rather than astute societal realities. Through depictions of gracious princesses and wretched queens, the class systems within these tales often align with their moral spectrums. Disney's young female protagonists' successes, relative to their respective character arcs, are directly tied to their upstanding righteousness, purity, and inherent goodness. These storylines' placement outside of documented history, their ability to mask moral, social, and cultural didacticism under the veil of fantasy and family entertainment, and a broad appeal to mainstream American values positions Disney as producers of a specific ideological value system that systematically conforms to white, middle-class America (Giroux 1995). With *Alice in Wonderland* and *Peter Pan*, Disney promulgates cultural myths regarding motherhood, young girls' positionalities, and gendered stereotypes of 1950s America (Haas 1995).

Evolving from earlier twentieth-century advertising techniques in which advisory voices are woven into solicitations for commodities intended to address maternal concerns, women of the 1950s, as Coontz (2016) attests, "were products of even more direct repression" compared to previous decades (35; Kline 1998). Similar to a modern harkening back to a dehistoricized American "Golden Age," authors in the 1950s waxed nostalgic about traditional family values from the Victorian era, confining women to domestic spaces where they should remain morally beholden as caretakers of their children and separated from working men (Coontz 2016; Spigel 1998). Popular women's magazines of the era reproduced ideologies of domesticated middle-class womanhood that contradicted prevalent understandings of American identity. While American value systems celebrated individual achievement, active independence, and an indefatigable spirit, sociocultural conceptualizations of women emphasized docility, dependency, and child rearing (Deys 2009). In her critique, Deys (2009) details how magazines advanced following gendered norms as "an honorable duty" and ostracized those who failed to meet these standards of morality as "outside of womanhood" (84, 79).[4] Alanen (2009), summarizing Connell (1987), defines these supervisory power dynamics as "the social processes that affect the regulating, organizing, and positioning of people into different social locations within the gender structure or gender order" (168).

Within the Magic Kingdom, however, this process of gendering metamorphosizes into a more pointed form of the regulation of children, in order to prepare young women to fulfill society's expected role for them as mothers-to-be.

A PEEK INTO DISNEY'S NARRATIVE SAUSAGE FACTORY

Walt Disney's personal nationalist and anticommunist activities, demonstrated through his support of McCarthyism and testimony at the House Un-American Activities Committee (HUAC) in the late 1940s, is mirrored by the Disney Company's alliance with the American government throughout the Second World War to create propaganda films and military insignia designs (Wojcik-Andrews 2000). Disney's animated films in the early 1950s were decidedly not constructed for the American government; however, the Disneyfication process of "oversimplification, sanitization, repression and ideological mystification" was, and to some extent remains to be, influenced considerably by Walt's personal ideological values, combining his dogmatic principles with tradition and historicized memory (Buckingham 1997, 290; Kammen 1993).[5]

Disney's reproduction of clichéd feminine identities sustains sexist and heteropatriarchal logics that emulate Walt's ideological perspective by merging moral maxims from the original literary tales with resurfacing historical inclinations toward traditional family values and conservative gender roles, providing covert education that can be made overt when examined as a body of conceptual work (Rifà-Valls 2011; Rothschild 2009). *Alice in Wonderland* and *Peter Pan*, by presenting girls who gracefully choose to fulfill their preordained gender roles, specifically cater to young women coming-of-age and choreograph society's expectations of them with the intention of assuaging adult anxieties surrounding gender in postwar America. Disney's films are marketed as family-friendly because they depict examples of expected behavioral patterns for young viewers. Alice is seven years old, while Wendy is thirteen. These representations of young female protagonists offer models that children can comprehend as they mature into womanhood. Girls' identity formation processes, a confluence of factors that define them as gendered beings through available discursive assemblages, are influenced by children's films' existence as agents of socialization (Jones 1993). As a result of Alice and Wendy's active decisions to retreat to the ostensible safety of home, childhood is reduced to a developmental steppingstone on the way toward a particularly gendered social acculturation.

Disney's oeuvre of animated tales follows a nearly identical narrative structure: the young protagonists, due to a conflict stemming from their coming-of-age, are transported from their typical livelihoods to another space in which, through a serious of adventures, magical activities, and/or harrowing exploits, resolve their inner strife through journeys of self-discovery,[6] and return home with a newfound acceptance for what society anticipates of them (Wojcik-Andrews 2000). Deceased or entirely unaccounted for parents, storylines with overtly expressed values, and reaffirmations of conventional ideological systems are also common, most notably around depictions of gender and sexuality (Haas 1995; Ohmer 2008; Wasko 2001). The children in these films are bestowed false agency; they habitually reach "natural" moral, ethical, and social conclusions on their own that reinforce adult virtues under the guise of self-realization. Alice's adventures in Wonderland, and more specifically how and why they must end, properly introduce us to the rabbit hole that is Disney's pedagogic practices and make for a firm foundation with which to begin this chapter's analysis.

PROSCRIBING *ALICE*'S PREPOSTEROUS IMAGINATIVE POWERS

While children's films customarily instruct young people on how to satisfy adult expectations of them, they also demonstrate what behaviors and desires to categorically avoid—how *not* to be a child (Cornell 2015). Disney's features first establish an opposition to a set of social practices coded as grotesque, improper, and unbecoming, followed by a preferred set of sociocultural expectations their young viewers should adopt (Frankel 2012). *Alice in Wonderland*'s unrestrained fantasy, produced by Alice's own creative capacities, falls into this oppositional classification. Once she follows the White Rabbit down his rabbit hole, a series of increasingly nonsensical trials and episodic adventures ensues: swimming through keyholes, nearly being set on fire, entertaining a duo's endless tall tales, celebrating multiple un-birthdays, and appearing at a corrupt trial encompass only part of Alice's serpentine experiences through her own mind. Alice's imagination runs amok, branching off into explorations of the innermost machinations of thought, rather than fulfilling the Disney princess narrative's requisite dreaming of romantic futurities (Rothschild 2009).[7] When young female Disney protagonists do not fantasize about romance, they must self-correct their imaginatory powers. Especially in storylines where adult figures are predominantly or entirely absent and children's worlds are spatiotemporally displaced from those of adults, characters must adopt adult ideological positions to "naturally" ascertain their proper place in society (Faulkner 2011). Thus, Alice's alternate world where history books contain only pictures and nonsense reigns supreme cannot exist—in reality or in Disney's animated universe. Through her daydreaming's test of endurance, Alice's resistance against normative modes of order and education proves fruitless, as the world of nonsense she has created rebels against her own imagination. Her disobedience does not prevail, resulting in her wish to return home where logic holds sway.

Toward the end of Alice's adventures in Wonderland, she expresses a desire to escape her mind's fanciful abstractions. Losing her sense of direction after a creature sweeps away the only path remaining, she sits down and begins to reflect on her powerlessness to heed her own counsel. Her attraction to peculiarities repeatedly overpowers her better judgment, and she unabashedly admits, "Be[ing] patient is very good advice, but the waiting makes me curious, and I love the change should something strange begin" (Geronimi, Luske, and Jackson 1951). Alice also thoroughly understands that at some point she will be punished for these actions ("I should've known there would be a price to pay someday.") Bursting into tears with the acknowledgment that nobody will likely rescue her from her current dilemma, she asks, "Will I ever learn to do the things I should?" (Geronimi, Luske, and Jackson 1951). Alice does not simply express her desire to mature and comprehend society's value systems; she specifies acquiring a base of knowledge about the things she *should* learn, ascribing intentionality and responsibility to this set of social principles.

Figure 5.1. After losing her sense of direction as the walking paths are swept away, Alice (voiced by Kathryn Beaumont, pictured in center) reflects on her inability to listen to good advice, crying as fantasy creatures emerge from the surrounding darkness and listen to her woeful self-examination (Geronimi, Luske, and Jackson 1951).

After coming to terms with her frustrating tendency to get into trouble, Alice is punished by her own imagination. Cornell (2015) purports, "Rebellion is fine, appropriate even, as long as it remains within limits of fantasy and has some desirable result" (23). Alice, threatened with beheading by the Queen of Hearts after being caught painting the Queen's roses red, is further tortured by the Cheshire Cat's antics during the ensuing courtroom trial, which forces her to run away from her imagination before it kills her. Awaking from her fantasy-turned-nightmare, Alice learns a valuable, adult-prescribed lesson: don't let your imagination get the best of you. As Alice's adventures in Wonderland increasingly seem to put her in harm's way, Kavey (2008) observes they "are remarkably physical and often center around her own body, which allows for an easy comparison with the growing emotional and physical pains of adolescence" (3–4). Oscillating between gigantic, miniature, and standard versions of herself, Alice's physical transformations only empower her for short periods of time and habitually lead to immediate risks to her health. Unable to control this reverie, she must flee the perils of her own mind's creation. This raises questions about Alice's period of self-reflection on her journey: why are some value systems and behavioral patterns preferable over others? Why must she pay for clamoring for imaginative alternate worlds? Why does she first react to getting lost by staying put so that someone can find her?[8] Finally, and perhaps most importantly, what about young viewers who may *not* align with the adult-approved morality and pedagogic lessons of these animated fairy tales? In order to conform to *Alice in Wonderland*'s didactic purpose, Alice must literally fight her fantasy, framed as undisciplined and hysterical, in the most explicit self-policing of deviant behavior among Disney's films from the era. *Peter Pan*, released only a couple of years later, centers the experience of another young female protagonist whose fantastic journey concludes with a warm embrace of her ensuing motherhood, providing a gendered twist to *Alice*'s circumscription of fantasy.

"PROPER" PUBERTY AND NEVERLAND'S PRISON IN PETER PAN

After the box office failure of *Fantasia* (1940), Disney contracted the services of George Gallup's acclaimed Audience Research Institute (ARI) regarding casting, promotional campaigns, and even the titles of projects far along in the development process (Ohmer 1991). Considering Disney's transitional period in the late 1940s, in which market adjustments were actively made to recover from the war and position themselves as an industry leader in the decades to come, Disney utilized Gallup's research to remain cost efficient (Ohmer 1991; Wasko 2001). A specific poll commissioned by Disney before *Peter Pan*'s production returned peculiar results: though the public exhibited little interest in an adaptation of this story, audiences were still fascinated with Disney's brand of filmmaking (Ohmer 2008). Throughout the mid-to-late 1940s, Walt was concerned not only with *Peter Pan*'s possible spectator response but also the future of feature-length animated film as a popular cinematic format entirely. The results of this ARI poll found Disney films were still a desirable commodity, and Walt would continue to turn out his animated adaptations of classic literary tales.

From the original J.M. Barrie tales to the stage plays they inspired, Disney's animated reproduction of *Peter Pan* emerges from an already highly mediated text. The film follows Wendy Darling as she escapes to Neverland with Peter Pan, a figure whose presence is inextricably tied to the childhood imagination of the Darling matriarchs.[9] After her father threatens her with eviction from the nursery—a space she shares with her younger brothers Michael and John—due to her budding adolescence, Wendy's adventures with Peter serve as episodic lessons on growing up and embracing societal expectations of young women. A magical fantasyland where aging is stunted and children reign supreme, Neverland presents Wendy with a place to elude her father's fury and the gendered responsibilities society ascribes to her as a result of her own maturation. After progressing through a series of daring adventures and close calls with the Lost Boys (children who have decided to remain in Neverland and not return home), jealous mermaids, and plotting pirates, Wendy recognizes her inherent calling to motherhood and returns home prepared to enter the next stage of her feminine existence.

Before Wendy even arrives in Neverland, Peter ascribes her the status of mother so that she can tell him and his friends stories. When presented with the Lost Boys' craving for warmth and nurturing, Wendy does not simply become a protective babysitter, she wholeheartedly accepts the role of mother. Due in part to the Darling children's neglectful parents who are too distracted by an upcoming social occasion to properly care for their children's needs, Neverland serves a dual purpose for Wendy, allowing her to suspend her exodus from the confines of asexual childhood while appraising her prescribed future as a maternal figure. Away from the pressure of her parents, Wendy can safely perform a "dress up" of sorts and try on the role society has assigned to her as a young woman. Wendy's lessons, like Alice's, teach young female audiences to take responsibility for adapting to society's expectations of them, which again naturalizes this pedagogic process into one of self-realization.

Surprisingly, the film's forbidden subtext is never directly spoken of: puberty. Perhaps standing in for parents' reluctance to openly discuss children's nascent sexuality, or the unwillingness to directly address gender's covert role in this fairy tale, Disney's purposeful omission of this vital aspect of *Peter Pan*'s narrative allows it to exist on the periphery of the story, circumvented by fantasy and Wendy's enthusiastic welcome of traditional femininity. From Mr. Darling's initial reasoning for Wendy's departure from the nursery, in which he exclaims, "The child's growing up—it's high time she had a room of her own" (Luske, Geronimi, and Jackson 1953), to unfavorable framings of sexuality that impart lessons about aspects of adolescence to avoid, the film is littered with indirect references to Wendy's coming-of-age.[10] She initially travels to Neverland to escape puberty and her banishment from the nursery but instead learns about and is thrust into maternity (Giunta 2018). At multiple points throughout the film, spectators witness Wendy's continual frustration at the Lost Boys' unruliness and perpetual playtime, tying this lack of discipline to a lack of adult authority—in this case, absent mothers. Her lullaby, "Your Mother and Mine," simultaneously soothes the Lost Boys' insubordination while glorifying motherhood, inadvertently fostering Wendy's budding affection for motherhood. Upon her return from Neverland, Wendy confidently voices her reformed willingness to leave the nursery by stating, "I am ready to grow up" (Luske, Geronimi, and Jackson 1953). Wendy's newly cultivated nurturing traits are attained of her own accord rather than through the influence of her parents, attributing a false sense of agency to this decision that conceals the adult proscription of Neverland's endless adventure in favor of a reunion of the nuclear family.

Disney's production of *Peter Pan* emphasizes characters with entertainment value (Ohmer 2008).[11] This pleasurable façade, however, obfuscates the film's promulgation of normative gender roles as Wendy's emotional journey progresses from jealousy to motherliness. Although crowning Peter as the main protagonist of this film seems predestined, he does not conform to Disney's standard narrativization of culturally didactic childhood. His existence serves as a foil to Wendy's "mature" decision to openly embrace popular constructions of femininity, while his noticeable dearth of pedagogic circumstances (lacking responsibility, maturation, lessons to learn) confine him to Neverland's eternal boyhood. Wendy embodies the period of time immediately following traditional delineations of childhood, in which adolescent bodies are "rendered problematic and at the same time are able to remember

Figure 5.2. After John (pictured left) and Michael Darling (pictured center, held by Wendy) return from their adventuring with Peter Pan and the Lost Boys, Wendy Darling (voiced by Kathryn Beaumont, pictured center right) sings them a lullaby that celebrates contemporary gendered stereotypes associated with mothers and motherhood (Luske, Geronimi, and Jackson 1953).

a childhood past when the relationship between gender and identity could be flexible and open" (Prout 2000, 10). In order to avoid this precarious period of uncertain self-identity, *Peter Pan* juxtaposes the "timeless prison of Neverland" with Wendy's actualization of her expected position in society, realizing her father's previously abhorred directive to exit the nursery was simply to prepare her for her future role as maternal nurturer (Faulkner 2011, 83). Neverland, albeit portrayed as an entertaining fantasyland of never-ending adventure, is not a viable or ideal location for children to become acculturated members of society.

The ironic element of Wendy's lessons about motherhood and conventional gender roles in Neverland is striking: though devoid of adults, their pervasive influence still seeps into this fantasy space (Taylor 2011). While Alice's journeys through Wonderland are circumscribed because of their excessively imaginative and unbridled qualities, deemed unrealistic and irresponsible, Wendy's adventures in Neverland are delimited and focalized to help her recognize and appreciate her predetermined duty as an affectionate woman, appeasing a more gender-specific adult anxiety. Both narratives feature protagonists who initially resist society's expectations of them, with Alice's challenge of conservatively organized worlds and Wendy's refusal to grow up and embrace clichéd femininity. However, they ultimately shun these notions, framed as childish, ludicrous, and even dangerous, within their respective cinematic storylines, and, instead, reach their experiential truths by accepting proscribed roles and behavioral patterns.

CONCLUSION

Disney's characterizations of Alice and Wendy embody distinct moments in the enculturation process (ages seven and thirteen) and begin to establish a narrative progression for youth audiences consuming these imaginative tales as they shape their own individuation processes. Rothschild (2009), drawing on work at the crossroads of developmental psychology and gender studies, highlights these two specific intervals in children's lives—between ages six and seven and early adolescence—as periods of "gender intensification" in which they are uniquely "preoccup[ied] with gender-stereotypical behavior and interests" (15). Alice and Wendy impart curated sociocultural, behavioral, and gendered frameworks for young girls to prepare them for the road ahead, acting as parent-approved role models of generationing, which Castro (2019) establishes as the management of generational power differentials between girls and boys, necessitating an interrogation of "hegemonic, patriarchal societies to truly understand the girlhoods and boyhoods of childhood" (265–66). As reflections of their time period's conservative gender divisions, these constructions of girlhood conform to the neatly ordered realms of heteropatriarchal logic, a pattern replicated across the various eras of Disney's film library. These texts about and intended for children are based on adult understandings of childhood, which are fundamentally limited and delimiting (Charters 1933; Giunta 2019). Without apprehensible moral and cultural pedagogy,[12] adults express anxieties over the possibility of overwhelming fantasy within these mediated worlds and require didactic lessons with which young people can be conditioned to societal expectations of them.

The frequent circumscription of genuine childhood for representations of youth heavily affected by adult wish fulfillment and normative ideology is poignantly ironic. The antagonists' presences provide an essential built-in "Other" for children to comprehend as inappropriate and deplorable (Butler 2004) instead of inclusive of young people's positional plurality. This meticulous narrative construction permits pleasurable instances of adventure to exist, but, as Wasko (2001) notes, "Fantasy is carefully controlled, and little is left to the imagination" (118). *Alice in Wonderland* and *Peter Pan*, embedded within 1950s postwar American society, regulate fantasy within a particular preexisting value system (Cornell 2015). Alice's realization that clamoring for nonsensical worlds is immature and unrealistic and Wendy's recognition of her intrinsic nurturing capabilities and embrace of motherhood both work to proscribe Disney's depiction of magical moments and lands of fantasy and escapism within what adults deem as proper societal values. The destinies of the young female protagonists in *Alice in Wonderland* and *Peter Pan* are then harmoniously linked to cozy returns to hearth and home.

According to the Disney hierarchical structuring of the universe, children need to discover what figures of authority, namely their parents and other adults, want them to learn, rather than pursue education for its own sake. Disney's moral binaries of good/evil, hero(ine)/villain, and right/wrong construct similar oppositions to those explored in childhood studies: being/becoming, powerful/powerless, and independent/vulnerable. Pomerantz (2009) expresses her belief that these dichotomies, in effect, "freeze the 'child,' as either/or, limiting not just how adults/researchers conceptualize children, but also the subject positions made available to young people in the social world" (154). The myriad permutations and positionalities girls can occupy, however, cannot and should not be delineated into specific categorizations; as Pomerantz (2009) asserts, "one size will never fit all" (155). The behavioral patterns that Alice and Wendy *should* learn do not encompass the full potential of agentic qualities that girls can embody, instead prioritizing specific sets of contemporary values and gendered conduct adults believe best for child audiences. However, expecting young viewers to precisely absorb these lessons would be imprudent: their reception to them maps across a complex and diverse spectrum of understanding and application in their own lives and peer groups.

Alice in Wonderland and *Peter Pan*, to varying degrees, both rebel against the traditional hierarchies set within their fantasy worlds, only to be regulated by conclusions that favor normative sociocultural structures. These films reinforce Alanen's (2009) notion of generational ordering, in which modern societies classify children as "a social category, and circumscribes for them particular social locations from which they act and thereby participate in ongoing social life" (161). Despite the ubiquity of this adult-enforced system, childhood studies has come to recognize children's involvement, in spite of their unequal positions of power, as agential beings in the (re)production of adult cultures in their own lives, peer groups, and conceptual constructions (Alanen 2009; James 2004). The value systems, although presented as unitary visions of childhood, are not digested precisely as intended. Instead, children interpret them in a more complex web of social, cultural, and moral entanglements. As children's films continue to manufacture particular representations of children and childhood, Cornell (2015) considers "the possibility that children will read the films differently, finding pleasure in the wrong places, and behavioral models in the denigrated, outlaw roles, or ignore the moral outcome in part or entirely . . ." (20). We must consider young audiences' multiple viewings and multimediatic relationships with these stories (Bell 1995; Buckingham 2000). Newcomb (2016) firmly maintains that these ideations of girlhood, "generated between author and reader," are inherently unstable; there is invariably room for multiple interpretations that adapt and rebuff the didactic framings of childhood fantasy (145). Despite Walt's best efforts, there remains an experiential flexibility present within these timeless classics.

Rather than compare Disney's films to onscreen texts that diametrically oppose the strict social, cultural, political, and gendered representations espoused in the Magic Kingdom, it is paramount to instead recognize and embrace the messiness of the relationship between adult anxieties, their resultant ideological structures, and children's interpretations and reproductions of them (Oswell 2016). In the hope of spurring interdisciplinary research on alternative and even subversive readings of narratives about young people within their historical and cultural contexts, this chapter examines a specific moment in America. I hope to contribute to an intricate history of children's filmic and televisual representations that reveals a complex and nuanced relationship between young people and adults that unfolds onscreen. The only way to adequately analyze depictions of youth is to understand the children's film genre's lineage by tracing the legacy of adult appeasement, conventional models of behavior, restrictive gender divides, and moral principles. Like Alice's Wonderland, there is a world of nonsense to explore—it is the mission of scholars and cultural workers to irritate the Queen of Hearts's tyrannical reign over cinematic constructions of childhood.

NOTES

1. For the purposes of this chapter, *Cinderella* (1951), though released during this historical period and containing similar themes, does not fit quite as neatly with *Alice in Wonderland* and *Peter Pan*. The film's imbuing of a classic literary tale with popular contemporary social and cultural values, its narrative concentration on young women's passivity and victimization, patriarchal conceptions of intrinsic maternal qualities, and the protagonists' inherent moral goodness provide useful comparisons to the other two films from this era. Its divergent qualities include its constitution as a Disney princess tale and a notable absence of a journey into a fantasy realm. However, the film does provide supplementary context when it dovetails with this chapter's analysis.

2. Mothers faced pressure to be nurturing, but not overbearing, and even hold the "front line of defense against treason," i.e., communism (Coontz 2016, 35–6). This manipulation led to the hiding of subsequent afflictions, including alcoholism, mental health issues, and suicide. For more on how this active/passive dichotomy resulted in unspoken tragedies that became shrouded by the veil of idealized 1950s American nuclear family life, see Coontz (2016), Deys (2009), Eisler (1986), and Hall (1999).

3. Concerns about cinema examined in the PFS included how often young people attended moving pictures and effects on their ideals and attitudes, sleep patterns and health, behavior and conduct, delinquency/crime, moral influences, and memory and understanding experiments. The PFS even attempted to investigate how films affected the onset of puberty (Charters 1933).

4. For a detailed examination of one specific publication's (*Mademoiselle*) messaging toward women during this period, see Deys (2009, 89–90).

5. For more discussion on Walt Disney and his political activities, see Watts (1997).

6. Whereas Disney's Renaissance princesses (Ariel, Belle, Jasmine, Mulan) learn the constructedness of femininity, Alice and Wendy come to understand gender as a natural category by which young women graciously and willingly enter their predetermined position in society (Higgs 2016; Sells 1995).

7. See Rothschild (2009) for more in-depth analysis.

8. This passivity is mirrored in *Cinderella*, where Grand Duke rewards Cinderella's lack of agentic qualities by coming to her home and whisking her away to the prince, whom she immediately marries and will live with happily ever after. For more on Cinderella's passivity and characterization as a "patient sufferer" and "object of pity," and specifically how these attributes conform to 1950s conservative gender roles, see Lieberman (1972).

9. Mary Darling, Wendy's mother, believes that Peter Pan represents the "spirit of youth," and her actions in the film's opening and closing scenes suggest a unique awareness of him. In the live-action sequel *Hook* (1991), Peter marries Moira, granddaughter of the now elderly Wendy, who had originally convinced him to leave Neverland. In *Peter Pan*'s animated sequel, *Return to Never Land* (2002), Wendy's daughter Jane saves Peter in Neverland, despite her initial misgivings about magic.

10. Wendy's jealousy of Tinker Bell, Tiger Lily, and the mermaids; Hook's belief that "A jealous female can be tricked into anything;" and the problematic "What Makes the Red Man Red?" musical number in which American Indians' skin tone is attributed to their embarrassment over sexuality (repeated in *Cinderella* after Cinderella kisses the king) contribute to the film's unsympathetic portrayal of puberty's presumed effects on Wendy (Luske, Jackson, and Geronimi 1953). Ohmer (2008) discusses how the writing team injected Wendy's bitterness toward the other female figures in *Peter Pan* into the narrative for the sake of entertainment, conflating her coming-of-age with romantic rivalry.

11. Ohmer's (2008) in-depth analysis of Disney's internal conferences between 1948 and 1952 demonstrates how *Peter Pan*'s production adapted to fluctuating societal attitudes while maintaining Disney's unique style. Ohmer (2008) notes the specific stylistic changes from the source text, including transforming Captain Hook into a more central and "gusty" character, making Tinker Bell more explicitly sexual, and creating a love triangle between Wendy, Tinker Bell, and Peter (162).

12. Steinberg and Kincheloe (1997) define cultural pedagogy as "the idea that education takes place in a variety of social sites including but not limited to schooling" (4).

REFERENCES

Aird, Enola G. 2004. "Advertising and Marketing to Children in the United States." In *The Body, Childhood and Society*, edited by Alan Prout, 141–53. New York, NY: St. Martin's Press.

Alanen, Leena. 2009. "Generational Order." In *The Palgrave Handbook of Childhood Studies*, edited by Jens Qvortrup, William A. Corsaro, and Michael-Sebastian Honig, 159–74. London: Palgrave Macmillan.

Bell, Elizabeth. 1995. "Somatexts at the Disney Shop: Constructing the Pentimentos of Women's Animated Bodies." In *From Mouse to Mermaid: The Politics of Film, Gender, and Culture*, edited by Elizabeth Bell, Lynda Haas, and Laura Sells, 107–24. Bloomington, IN: Indiana University Press.

Buckingham, David. 1997. "Dissin' Disney: Critical Perspectives on Children's Media Culture." *Media, Culture & Society* 19: 285–93.

———. 2000. *After the Death of Childhood: Growing Up in the Age of Electronic Media*. Cambridge: Polity Press.

Butler, Judith. 2004. *Undoing Gender*. New York, NY: Routledge.

Castro, Ingrid E. 2019. "The Spirit and the Witch: Hayao Miyazaki's Agentic Girls and Their (Intra)Independent Generational Childhoods." In *Representing Agency in Popular Culture: Children and Youth on Page, Screen, and In Between*, edited by Ingrid E. Castro and Jessica Clark, 255–82. Lanham, MD: Lexington Books.

Charters, W.W. 1933. *Motion Pictures and Youth: A Summary*. New York, NY: The Macmillan Company.

Connell, Raewyn W. 1987. *Gender and Power: Society, the Person, and Sexual Politics*. Palo Alto, CA: Stanford University Press.

Coontz, Stephanie. 2016. *The Way We Never Were: American Families and the Nostalgia Trap* (rev. and updated ed.). New York, NY: Basic Books.

Cornell, Julian. 2015. "No Place like Home: Circumscribing Fantasy in Children's Film." In *Children's Film in the Digital Age: Essays on Audience, Adaptation and Consumer Culture*, edited by Karin Beeler and Stan Beeler, 9–27. Jefferson, NC: McFarland.

Deys, Kellie Leigh. 2009. "Consumperialism: American Consumer Imperialism, the Rhetoric of Freedom, and Female Embodiment." Ph.D. diss., Binghamton University. ProQuest Dissertations Publishing: 3355892.

Eisler, Benita. 1986. *Private Lives: Men and Women of the Fifties*. New York, NY: Franklin Watts.

Faulkner, Joanne. 2011. *The Importance of Being Innocent: Why We Worry About Children*. New York, NY: Cambridge University Press.

Frankel, Sam. 2012. *Children, Morality and Society.* New York, NY: Palgrave Macmillan.

Geronimi, Clyde, Hamilton Luske, and Wilfred Jackson, dir. *Alice in Wonderland.* 1951; United States: RKO Radio Pictures.

Giroux, Henry A. 1995. "Memory and Pedagogy in the 'Wonderful World of Disney': Beyond the Politics of Innocence." In *From Mouse to Mermaid: The Politics of Film, Gender, and Culture,* edited by Elizabeth Bell, Lynda Haas, and Laura Sells, 43–60. Bloomington, IN: Indiana University Press.

Giunta, Joseph V. 2018. "'Did They Send Me Daughters When I Asked for Sons?': Fortifications and Confrontations of Gendered & Social Hierarchies from Disney to Miyazaki." *Red Feather Journal* 9, no. 2: 19–33.

———. 2019. "'Why Are You Keeping This Curiosity Door Locked?': Childhood Subjectivities and Play as Conflict Resolution in the Postmodern Web Series *Stranger Things.*" In *Child and Youth Agency in Science Fiction: Travel, Technology, Time,* edited by Ingrid E. Castro and Jessica Clark, 25–53. Lanham, MD: Lexington Books.

Haas, Linda. 1995. "'Eighty-Six the Mother': Murder, Matricide, and Good Mothers." In *From Mouse to Mermaid: The Politics of Film, Gender, and Culture,* edited by Elizabeth Bell, Lynda Haas, and Laura Sells, 193–211. Bloomington, IN: Indiana University Press.

Hall, Nancy Lee. 1999. *A True Story of a Drunken Mother.* Boston, MA: South End Press.

Hearst, Alice. 2004. "Recognizing the Roots: Children's Identity Rights." In *Rethinking Childhood,* edited by Peter B. Pufall and Richard P. Unsworth, 244–61. New Brunswick, NJ: Rutgers University Press.

Higgs, Sam. 2016. "Damsels in Development: Representation, Transition, and the Disney Princess." *Screen Education* 83: 62–69.

Holaday, Perry W. and George D. Stoddard. 1933. *Getting Ideas from the Movies.* New York, NY: The Macmillan Company.

Jackson, Wilfred, Hamilton Luske, and Clyde Geronimi, dir. *Cinderella.* 1950; United States: RKO Radio Pictures.

James, Allison. 2004. "Understanding Childhood from an Interdisciplinary Perspective: Problems and Potentials." In *Rethinking Childhood,* edited by Peter B. Pufall and Richard P. Unsworth, 25–37. New Brunswick, NJ: Rutgers University Press.

Jones, Alison. 1993. "'Becoming a 'Girl': Post-Structuralist Suggestions for Educational Research." *Gender and Education* 5, no. 2: 157–66.

Kammen, Michael. 1993. *Mystic Chords of Memory: The Transformation of Tradition in American Culture.* New York, NY: Vintage Books.

Kavey, Allison B. 2008. "Introduction: From Peanut Butter Jars to the Silver Screen." In *Second Star to the Right: Peter Pan in the Popular Imagination*, edited by Allison Kavey and Lester D. Friedman, 1–12. New Brunswick, NJ: Rutgers University Press.

Kline, Stephen. 1998. "The Making of Children's Culture." In *The Children's Culture Reader*, edited by Henry Jenkins, 95–109. New York, NY: New York University Press.

Lieberman, Marcia R. 1972. "'Some Day My Prince Will Come': Female Acculturation through the Fairy Tale." *College English* 34, no. 3: 383–95.

Lindner, Eileen W. 2004. "Children as Theologians." In *Rethinking Childhood*, edited by Peter B. Pufall and Richard P. Unsworth, 54–68. New Brunswick, NJ: Rutgers University Press.

Luske, Hamilton, Clyde Geronimi, and Wilfred Jackson, dir. *Peter Pan*. 1953; United States: RKO Radio Pictures.

Mayall, Berry. 2001. "Understanding Childhood: A London Study." In *Conceptualizing Child-Adult Relations*, edited by Leena Alanen and Berry Mayall, 114–28. Oxon: RoutledgeFalmer.

Ohmer, Susan. 1991. "Measuring Desire: George Gallup and Audience Research in Hollywood." *Journal of Film and Video* 43, no. 2: 3–28.

———. 2008. "Disney's *Peter Pan*: Gender, Fantasy, and Industrial Production." In *Second Star to the Right: Peter Pan in the Popular Imagination*, edited by Allison Kavey and Lester D. Friedman, 151–87. New Brunswick, NJ: Rutgers University Press.

Oswell, David. 2016. "Re-aligning Children's Agency and Re-Socialising Children in Childhood Studies." In *Reconceptualising Agency and Childhood: New Perspectives in Childhood Studies*, edited by Florian Esser et al., 19–33. New York, NY: Routledge.

Pomerantz, Shauna. 2009. "Between a Rock and a Hard Place: Un/Defining the 'Girl.'" *Jeunesse: Young People, Texts, Cultures* 1, no. 2: 147–58.

Prout, Alan. 2000. "Childhood Bodies: Construction, Agency and Hybridity." In *The Body, Childhood and Society*, edited by Alan Prout, 1–18. New York, NY: St. Martin's Press.

Rifà-Valls, Montserrat. 2011. "Postwar Princesses, Young Apprentices, and a Little Fish-Girl: Reading Subjectivities in Hayao Miyazaki's Tales of Fantasy." *Visual Arts Research* 37, no. 2: 88–100.

Rothschild, Sarah. 2009. "Modeling the Feminine: The Princess Story in Twentieth-Century American Fiction and Film." Ph.D. diss., City University of New York. ProQuest Dissertations Publishing: 3378967.

Sells, Laura. 1995. "'Where Do the Mermaids Stand?': Voice and Body in *The Little Mermaid*." In *From Mouse to Mermaid: The Politics of Film, Gender, and Culture*, edited by Elizabeth Bell, Lynda Haas, and Laura Sells, 175–92. Bloomington, IN: Indiana University Press.

Somers, Margaret R., and Gloria D. Gibson. 1993. "Reclaiming the Epistemological 'Other': Narrative and the Social Construction of Identity." CSST Working Paper 94, The University of Michigan-Ann Arbor, Ann Arbor, MI.

Spigel, Lynn. 1998. "Seducing the Innocent: Childhood and Television in Postwar America." In *The Children's Culture Reader*, edited by Henry Jenkins, 110–35. New York, NY: New York University Press.

Steinberg, Shirley R., and Joe L. Kincheloe. 1997. "No More Secrets: Kinderculture, Information Saturation, and the Postmodern Childhood." In *Kinderculture: The Corporate Construction of Childhood*, edited by Shirley R. Steinberg and Joe L. Kincheloe, 1–30. Boulder, CO: Westview Press.

Taylor, Affrica. 2011. "Reconceptualizing the 'Nature' of Childhood." *Childhood* 18, no. 4: 420–33.

Wasko, Janet. 2001. *Understanding Disney: The Manufacture of Fantasy*. Malden, MA: Polity.

Watts, Steven. 1997. *The Magic Kingdom: Walt Disney and the American Way of Life*. New York, NY: Houghton Mifflin.

Wojcik, Pamela R. 2016. *Fantasies of Neglect: Imagining the Urban Child in American Film and Fiction*. New Brunswick, NJ: Rutgers University Press.

Wojcik-Andrews, Ian. 2000. *Children's Films: History, Ideology, Pedagogy, Theory*. New York, NY: Garland Publishing.

6

IT ISN'T JUST HIS NOSE THAT GROWS

Disney's *Pinocchio* and the Erotic Afterlives of Errant Boys

Vincent A. Lankewish

DISNEY AND DERRIDA ON THE DEUCE

It's early August 1971. Imagine, if you will, a forty-one-year-old Jacques Derrida en route to Montreal to deliver a lecture, "Signature Event Context," the published version of which will question authorial intention and the fixity of a text's meaning and, in turn, spark arguments among literary theorists for decades thereafter. Mssr. Derrida decides to spend a few days sightseeing in the Big Apple, a nickname for New York City that dates back to the early twentieth century, but that was re-popularized in the early 1970s during the city's financial crisis. As Derrida wends his way through Manhattan, he finds himself in Times Square—an area infamous for sex shops and porn theaters, not unlike Place Pigalle, the red-light district that developed in Paris during and after World War II. And so, he wanders down 42nd Street, known to its denizens as "The Deuce," the center of the city's booming sex industry from the late 1950s through the late 1980s. As the lyrics of the title song of Lloyd Bacon's and Busby Berkeley's 1933 movie musical *42nd Street* inform us, it's where "the underworld/ can meet the elite." We discover the appeal of the Deuce as the song continues: "[n]aughty, bawdy/gawdy, sporty" (Keeler and Powell 1932). As Derrida meanders through this seediest of neighborhoods, where drug-dealing and crime run rampant, he is unaware, of course, that just two decades later the area will become the site of an urban Disney World, the result of Mayor Rudy Giuliani's efforts to rid the neighborhood of its vices, made possible in part by the Walt Disney Company's purchase and refurbishing of the New Amsterdam Theatre in the early 1990s. Nor does Derrida know that this raunchy, raucous, rundown region will constitute the landscape of the 2017–2019 HBO series *The Deuce* that chronicles the rise of pornography and prostitution as big businesses.

Suddenly, the marquee of a nearby movie theater catches Derrida's eye: *The Erotic Adventures of Pinocchio: A Bedtime Story for Adults*, starring Alex Roman, Dyanne Thorne, and Karen Smith. Pinocchio? The wooden marionette popularized by Carlo Collodi, the nineteenth-century Italian author of a beloved book about a wayward puppet who wants to be a real boy? Pinocchio, the mischievous, but endearing, protagonist of the 1940 animated feature produced by Walt Disney studios? He stares in disbelief. But a hand-painted poster promoting the film leaves no room for doubt. The illustrated advertisement for director Corey Allen's retelling of a well-known tale—based on a screenplay co-written with Chris Warfield—features a grown-up, bare-chested version of the protagonist with a wry grin on his face and a nose visibly longer than that of any other male porn stars of the period. Yet, as the poster tells us with a knowing wink, "It's *not* his nose that grows" (emphasis mine)! This Pinocchio's playful smirk is assuredly due to the seven women in various states of undress who surround him—perhaps a witty play on the seven dwarfs at Snow White's command in Disney's first animated feature which premiered in 1937. In Warfield's comedy/fantasy, as the film is billed on the International Movie Database, Pinocchio is created by a lonely woman who is a woodcarver. The film's plot is simple: upon coming to life, the unquestionably heterosexual Pinocchio is temporarily forced into prostitution where he has sex with multiple women, but ultimately lands in a monogamous relationship with his one true love, his creator, Gepetta, aptly named after her male counterpart in Collodi's story, Geppetto. Despite Derrida's initial incredulity, he buys a ticket, enters the darkened theater, takes his place among a group of avid cinephiles, and sits back as the show begins. The rigid social norms promoted by Disney's classic and meant to be internalized by its target audience of children are about to be challenged . . . in a *big* way.

Challenging those norms, however, is by no means limited to this single instance of "Pinocchio Porn" but can also be seen in the Disney film itself; in my own childhood experience of it and other Disney productions; and, most recently, in the illustrated script of a musical by Keith Mayerson, entitled *Pinocchio the Big Fag*.

THE POWERS OF DECONSTRUCTION: SETTING PINOCCHIO FREE

In this essay, I will examine several responses to *Pinocchio* that call into question the reception that Walt Disney likely anticipated when it debuted at the Centre Theatre in midtown Manhattan on February 7, 1940, just a little over five months after Hitler's invasion of Poland and the start of World War II.[1] That reception, of course, would comprise parental approval of the lessons that Geppetto's marionette learns as a result of not only his disobedience to his sculptor father and his "guardian angel," the Blue Fairy, but also of his chronic dishonesty. Little boys—or, in this case, a wooden puppet who wants to become a real boy—who fail to heed their parents' instructions and who repeatedly lie to them risk losing their parents' love and trust and, worse, being tricked into running away from home by profit-hungry kidnappers who transform these boys into pack mules and then sell them. Nonetheless, *Pinocchio*, one must admit, fails miserably in its mission to inculcate in children, and boys in particular, a solemn respect for and compliance with Jacques Lacan's account of the Law of the Father, elaborated in *The Psychoses* ([1955–1956] 1993), the third volume of Lacan's *Seminar*. In this segment of his lecture series, Lacan demonstrates the imperative that a son subordinate his incestuous desire for his mother until he has a wife and children of his own or risk the development of psychotic behavior. *Pinocchio*'s failure to teach this vital lesson is illustrated in three specific moments in the film's history: first, in the *frisson* I experienced as a child watching *Pinocchio* and its band of boys—very *bad* boys, I should note—planning to live together forever on Pleasure Island; second, in Corey Warfield's transformation and, hence, perversion of Disney's film in the form of an X-rated sex flick; and, finally, in the irreverent script of Mayerson's *Pinocchio the Big Fag*.

Derrida's "Signature Event Context" proves itself an indispensable tool in examining the unexpectedly queer erotic afterlives of Disney's titular protagonist. The last third of Derrida's essay is the most relevant to my argument as it offers a withering critique of J. L. Austin's 1962 book *How to Do Things with Words*. In this section, Derrida pays particular attention to Austin's well-known discussion of two types of speech acts: the "constative" (e.g., assertions that are true or false) and the "performative" (e.g., the utterance of specific words that itself serves as the completion of an action). In the first two-thirds of the essay, Derrida identifies his objective with respect to the circumscription of oral communication by its specific context as follows: "I would like to demonstrate why a context is never absolutely determinable, or rather in what ways its determination is never certain or saturated" (1982, 310). Moreover, *writing*, according to Derrida, "*extends* very far, if not infinitely, the field of oral or gestural communication" and "manages to loosen the limits, to open the *same field* to a much greater range" (1982, 311).[2] "To write," Derrida continues, "is to produce a mark that will constitute a kind of machine that is in turn productive, that my future disappearance on principle will not prevent from functioning and from yielding, and yielding itself to, *reading and rewriting*" (1982, 316, emphasis mine). Highlighting the inherent instability of speech and writing and the ever-existing possibility that authors cannot control the meanings of their utterances once they circulate in public, he remarks: "This structural possibility of being severed from its referent or signified (and therefore from communication and its context) seems to me to make of every mark, even if oral, a grapheme in general, that is, as we have seen, the nonpresent *remaining* of a differential mark cut off from its alleged 'production' of origin" (Derrida 1982, 318).

Authorial intention, in particular, gets under Derrida's skin, as he takes issue with the teleological implications of Austin's emphasis on "the conscious presence" of speakers for whom "no *remainder* escapes the present totalization" (Derrida 1982, 322). Thus, Derrida disputes Austin's premise that "no 'dissemination' [escapes] the horizon of the unity of meaning" (Derrida 1982, 322). This will not do, and Derrida therefore takes Austin to task for his acknowledgment of the possible failures of and fractures in performative utterances and, in turn, his refusal to concede that these utterances' successes are predicated upon the ever-present possibility of their undoing. After affirming the potential for "infelicities" to undermine his theory, Austin follows up, as Derrida describes it, "with an almost *immediately simultaneous* gesture made in the name of a kind of ideal regulation, an exclusion of this risk as an accidental, exterior one that teaches us nothing about the language phenomenon under consideration" (Derrida 1982, 323).

The flaw in Austin's theory—a vexing flaw that indeed might have been to him a source of perpetual consternation—is that performative utterances or, more broadly, *all* utterances can be "cited." Just before Derrida registers his deep disagreement with Austin, he notes that "[e]very sign, linguistic or nonlinguistic, spoken or written (in the usual sense of this opposition), as a small or large unity, can be *cited*, put between quotation marks; thereby it can break with every given context, and engender infinitely new contexts in an absolutely nonsaturable fashion" (1982, 320). Citationality may invite "the abnormal" or "the parasitical," which, Derrida asserts, is for Austin "an agony of language that must firmly be kept at a distance, or from which one must resolutely turn away" (1982, 324). The discourse of contagion that informs Austin's discussion of failed performatives is palpable in his contention that, "as *utterances* our performatives are *also* heir to certain kinds of ill which infect *all* utterances" (Derrida 1982, 322, emphasis Austin's). When Austin refers to language that is deployed "in ways *parasitic* upon its normal use—ways which fall under the doctrine of the *etiolations* of language," he suggests that such language feeds upon the so-called "normal" (Derrida 1982, 325, emphasis Austin's). As Derrida sums up, for Austin "[a] successful performative is necessarily an 'impure' performative, to use the word that Austin will employ when he recognizes that there is no 'pure' performative" (Derrida 1982, 325). Derrida states that "the category of intention will not disappear; it will have its place, but from this place it will no longer be able to govern the entire scene and the entire system of utterances" (1982, 326). The hegemony that inheres in Austin's statutes about the purity of performative utterances is, in Derrida's words, "grafted onto a 'new' concept of writing which also corresponds to whatever always has *resisted* the former organization of forces, which always has constituted the remainder irreducible to the dominant force which organized the—to say it quickly—logocentric hierarchy" (1982, 329–30). In this light, the near-Biblical commitment to telling the truth, a hallmark of Disney's *Pinocchio*, and Disney films in general, constitutes a pristine, untainted performative utterance whose existence nonetheless is predicated on blasphemous refusals of truth and accepted "truths." These impieties include: *Pinocchio*'s not-so-subtle eroticizing of bad boys and disobedience; *The Erotic Adventures of Pinocchio*'s projection of heterosexual longing onto its protagonist and the fulfillment of that longing; and *Pinocchio the Big Fag*'s explicitation of male-male sexual desire that, I suggest, lies barely beneath the surface of Disney's retelling of Collodi's tale.

This is *not* to say, however—as former *New York Times* chief book critic Michiko Kakutani mistakenly argues in *The Death of Truth*—that a text can be bent into meaning anything to any reader, but rather to demonstrate that texts are available for appropriation, resignification, and parody that lie beyond an author's control. Deconstruction is not, as Kakutani would have it in *The Death of Truth*, the culprit, but instead a means by which we may question the methods through which truth is constituted and, in turn, challenge them when their outcome contradicts reality. In an especially vitriolic passage, Kakutani states:

> Deconstruction posited that all texts are unstable and irreducibly complex and that ever variable meanings are imputed by readers and observers. In focusing on the possible contradictions and ambiguities of a text (and articulating such arguments in deliberately tangled and pretentious prose), it promulgated an extreme relativism that was ultimately nihilistic in its implications: *anything could mean anything*; an author's intent did not matter, could not in fact be discerned; there was no such thing as an obvious or common-sense reading, because everything had an infinitude of meanings. In short, there was no such thing as truth. (2018, 56–57, emphasis mine)

Aside from her false claim that deconstruction promotes the belief that "anything can mean anything," Kakutani seems to dismiss *tout court* literary interpretation and scholarship. Derrida does not endorse ignorance of science or historical record, but he does indicate that a writer's or a speaker's audience may refuse to "buy" supposedly verifiable information presented to it, just as the later twentieth- and early-twenty-first readers to whom I will now turn rejected the seemingly unquestionable lesson of obedience to social norms *Pinocchio* is intended to teach.

PINOCCHIO, A QUEER BOY'S PUPPET

In their encyclopedic study of the world's most well-known marionette, *Pinocchio Goes Postmodern: Perils of a Puppet in the United States*, Richard Wunderlich and Thomas J. Morrissey argue that the genius of Carlo Collodi, the pen name of Carlo Lorenzini, inventor of Pinocchio, has been eclipsed by distorted versions of the story from the late 1930s onward, particularly Disney's animated eighty-nine-minute musical adaptation in 1940 (2002, xiii–xiv). The initial installment of *The Adventures of Pinocchio*, originally titled *The Story of a Puppet*, appeared in a weekly Italian magazine for children, *Giornale per i bambini*, on July 7, 1881 (Wunderlich and Morrissey 2002, 4). Collodi's Pinocchio is far more disobedient than Disney's and in Chapter 15 suffers an ignominious death by hanging for his errors. At the behest of his readers, however, Collodi resurrected his puppet on February 16, 1882, adding nineteen new chapters (Wunderlich and Morrissey 2002, 4–5). Subsequently, the serialized story was published as a novel, retitled *The Adventures of Pinocchio* and illustrated by Enrico Mazzanti in 1883, while Mary Alice Murray's translation of the text into English appeared in 1892. The first U.S. edition was published in 1901 (Wanderlich and Morrissey 2002, 30–31).[3]

Much to the chagrin of Wunderlich and Morrissey, Disney's version of *Pinocchio* is, of course, far better known than Collodi's. The former, with its amicable and adorable figure who repeatedly gets into trouble, but in the end succumbs to the power and authority of his elders, owes a considerable debt to an acclaimed stage version of the novel by Yasha Frank written for the Federal Theatre Project during the Great Depression and first performed in June 1937 (Wunderlich and Morrissey 2002, 87). According to Wunderlich and Morrissey, whose fixation with Collodi's protagonist as a sacrosanct fictional creation echoes J. L. Austin's obsession with the existence of a pure, perfect performative utterance, Frank "must be credited with crafting the first pretender of the puppet's throne. His play radically revise[d] both theme and characters in *Pinocchio*, and it receive[d] widespread audience exposure. Moreover, "it [was] seen *by the general public* and [was] received *enthusiastically by them*" (Wunderlich and Morrissey 2002, 87, authors' emphasis). Disney's film version of Frank's play failed at the box office when it premiered in 1940. But his blissfully family-friendly remake became increasingly popular from the 1960s through the 1980s and is today the *sine qua non* of *Pinocchios* (Wunderlich and Morrissey 2002, 132).

For boys growing up in the 1960s, coming of age in the 1970s, and coming out in the following decade, however, the Disney film well may have served as a locus of emergent homoerotic desire. Indeed, one such instance of an audience's Derridean "refusal" of the elusive "truth" that Kakutani desperately seeks surfaced nearly fifty years ago in a paper delivered to the American Psychiatric Association. In the published version of his talk, Michael Brody argues that Pleasure Island—the destination that the boys in Geppetto's village, including the as-yet nonhuman Pinocchio, are seduced into believing soon will be their new home, where they will be unfettered by any and all rules and regulations—"with its candy, pool tables and cigars, is a 'bad' boy's dream come true" (1976, 354). Brody then catalogues the appeals of this miscreant's fantasy: "You break things and eat and stay awake till you are sick. No school or rules, just enslavement as mules" (1976, 354). This cinematic representation of chaos and anarchy, Brody believes, "touches all of us who were denied staying up late and making cranky asses of ourselves. We had to wait until we become [*sic*] more 'adult' to do this"—an obvious echo of Lacan's theory that a son must pay proper obeisance to his father until he has matured into a man (1976, 354). Opportunities to misbehave and indulge our ids tempt us all. Indeed, Brody advises, "Add to [Pinocchio's saving of Geppetto and himself from the whale i.e., from oral incorporation] the nose growing and the donkey ears as possible impulse signals, much the same as erections, and we see further psychological themes" (1976, 354).[4]

In my case, the Disney-designed Coca-Cola pavilion at the 1964–1965 New York World's Fair, "It's a Small World," eventually became visible as an originary site of same-sex attraction. I was just three-and-a-half years old when my parents brought my brother and me to the Fair when it reopened in the spring of 1965. (The official opening took place in April 1964, but in a further reenactment of deference to Lacanian psychoanalysis, my parents deemed me too young to visit at that point, and I had to wait until its second season began a year later.) Fascinated by the moving, singing dolls whose international identities the ride celebrated, I also evidently couldn't get enough of the ride's signature song that so many fairgoers found hypnotic and impossible to get out of their heads, for I asked my parents to buy me an LP featuring the Disneyland Boys Choir performing "It's a Small World" and an eclectic array of songs from across the globe. Colorful illustrations of boys in their native costumes populated the album cover. Years later, I discovered that I had used a black marker to draw boxes around my "favorites," unknowingly creating my own version of Andy Warhol's homoerotic and highly controversial silkscreen on canvas mural "Thirteen Most Wanted Men."[5] At just three-and-a-half years old and completely unbeknownst to myself, I was verifying Derrida's argument that every sign can "engender infinitely new contexts in an absolutely nonsaturable fashion" through these, *my* "Most Wanted Boys." I don't remember exactly when I first watched *Pinocchio*—most likely on television—but the sight of this puppet, his pal Lampwick, and a wagon jam-packed with boys on their way to an all-male paradise rekindled a desire I first felt sailing in a small boat through Disney's maze of marvelous boy toys. From *Pinocchio*'s fondness for fairies to its unabashed embrace of male buttocks to its tantalizing depiction of a hedonistic homoerotic playground, not unlike the Pines—one of two gay vacation destinations on Fire Island in New York—this Disney film offers ample evidence to support Steven Bruhm's and Natasha Hurley's acknowledgment of children's sexuality. In their edited collection *Curiouser*, Bruhm and Hurley argue that society prefers to ignore children's sexuality as incompatible with childhood innocence, but that it is decidedly understood as heterosexual when given credence at all. "People panic when that sexuality takes on a life outside the sanctioned scripts of child's play," they argue, noting further that "nowhere is this panic more explosive than in the field of the *queer* child, the child whose play confirms neither the comfortable stories of child (a)sexuality nor the supposedly blissful promises of adult heteronormativity" (Bruhm and Hurley 2004, ix). The child who will not be subsumed into Lacan's "symbolic order," therefore, is destined to become the "problem child."

OF FAIRIES, BOTTOMS, AND AN ISLE OF PLEASURE

The opening credits of Disney's feature invite us to enter an enchanted world that ultimately lies inside a storybook whose cover is emblazoned with the title *Pinocchio*. As this image fades, credit is subsequently given to the puppet's progenitor, "From the story by Collodi." Next, we hear the opening lines of the film's most beloved song, "When You Wish Upon a Star," and discover that its crooner is a cricket, Jiminy Cricket, perched above the storybook itself, this time not only bearing the title character's name, but also a silhouette of his hat-covered head. Shifting from his chest voice to quasi-falsetto ("mixing," as the technique is called) to full falsetto, Jiminy serenades us before an angelic-sounding choir interrupts him. "Fate is kind," the choir declares. Moreover, "She brings to those who love the sweet fulfillment of their secret longing" (Luske and Sharpsteen 1940). Unspoken or unspeakable desires may be satisfied after all. In this light, Jiminy, identifiable now as our narrator, enters the world of the book, introducing us to Geppetto, the woodcarver; his pets, the cat Figaro and the goldfish Chloe; and the marionette Pinocchio, whom Geppetto has created. While lying in bed, Geppetto sees in the night sky a "Wishing Star" and prays that Pinocchio will become a real boy. Suddenly, Jiminy sees the star approaching Geppetto's workshop and watches it metamorphosize into a blond-haired, blue-eyed woman, dressed in a shimmering blue gown with wings and wielding a magic wand. "As I live and breathe—a fairy!" Jiminy exclaims. Of course, the cricket refers here to the Blue Fairy who brings Pinocchio to life and promises that he will become human by proving himself "brave, truthful, and unselfish" (Luske and Sharpsteen 1940). Yet the term "fairy" assuredly still resonates with many adult gay male viewers, who might recall its use as a derogatory term designed to mock and hurt them. Some of those viewers, however, have reclaimed the word as a badge of pride and honor, as is the case with members of the New York City Radical Faeries group. The Blue Fairy, on the other hand, reinforces the very rules and regulations that these "other" fairies actively resist. "You must learn to choose between right and wrong," she urges Pinocchio before telling Jiminy, his conscience, to help his ward refuse the many temptations that he will encounter in the world and to guide him along "the straight and narrow path" (Luske and Sharpsteen 1940).

But, as we already know, Pinocchio will not stick to the "straight and narrow path," repeatedly choosing the crooked road instead. Although in the end Pinocchio must reject the queerness of his desire to stray from the course that the Blue Fairy maps out for him, he twice succumbs to the enticements foisted upon him by Honest John, a fox, and his sidekick Gideon, a cat. Matt Roth argues that these two characters are social deviants whose homosexuality is obvious. "The first villain, The Fox," Roth argues,

> is mannered, effeminate, urbane and of the theater. His small, strangely elastic companion, The Cat, constantly slithers around him and through his legs. Clumsily, the two of them often become entwined with each other in a chaos of limbs. They are clearly gay. The Fox entices Pinocchio to the "theater," selling him to the evil Gypsy Stromboli, the most blatant ethnic stereotype in the movie. (1996, 15–20)

Honest John and Gideon do indeed lead Pinocchio first into the dangerous hands of Stromboli, the impresario of a marionette theater from whose clutches Pinocchio escapes only with the help of the Blue Fairy. Thereafter, they introduce him to the Coachman who lures boys into his wagon headed for Pleasure Island to transform them into donkeys destined for a life of hard labor in the salt mines. But Pinocchio doesn't need much nudging from the Fox and the Cat to stray from the straight and narrow by this point. He discovers all on his own that the promise of eternal life with Lampwick, a mischievous, wisecracking pal he meets on the coach and affectionately calls "Lampy," and the bevy of other boys utterly appeals to him.

Identifying Pinocchio and his friends as "fairies" is precisely the kind of interpretive move that Michiko Kakutani would likely see as a sad casualty of deconstruction. Recall for a minute her flustered condemnation of its practitioners as those for whom "anything can mean anything." But it's impossible to escape another exceedingly queer feature of the film: its never-ending displays of the buttocks of boys, men, insects, and animals. Jiminy Cricket travels to the village in which Geppetto lives to warm his bottom, grown cold from wintery winds. Pushing his way under the door with his behind, Jiminy approaches the fireplace where he takes a small glowing piece of coal, stands in front of it, and bends over, prominently pushing his behind up to make the most of the heat the coal generates. Directly addressing his viewers, he begins a sentence—"As I stood there warming my . . . myself"—but quickly cuts himself off before using an anatomic term perhaps inappropriate for children (Luske and Sharpsteen 1940). Yet the remainder of this scene is replete with references to and a host of images of this body part: Geppetto tells the as-yet lifeless Pinocchio that he has crafted him a "little wooden seat in case he falls"; acting as puppeteer, Geppetto has Pinocchio kick Figaro the cat's behind and himself repeatedly rubs Figaro's furry bottom; when all of the clocks in Geppetto's shop begin chiming, one of them features a bad boy's naked backside being spanked by his mother; when Pinocchio listens to Jiminy's little talk on temptation, he bends over and thrusts his behind high in the air; Geppetto even lights a match on Pinocchio's bottom (Luske and Sharpsteen 1940). Later, Gideon the cat pulls the pocket of Pinocchio's shorts back to see if he has any money hidden there. The bear in Stromboli's theater shakes his behind, and when Pinocchio is locked in a bird cage by Stromboli, he and Jiminy bend down "bottoms up" upon the arrival of the Blue Fairy, who rescues them. During Pinocchio's and Lampwick's pool-playing scene, Jiminy scolds Pinocchio, and, as Lampwick leans over the pool table to take a shot, the camera focuses on the seat of his trousers just before a donkey tail pushes itself through the fabric. When the wayward boys all begin turning into donkeys, the Coachman ruthlessly strips them of their britches exposing them as true "jackasses." The spectacle of so many bottoms is inescapably scandalous.

During the 1930s, the latter years of which Disney had begun working on *Pinocchio*, Fire Island's Cherry Grove established itself as a vacation destination for gay men—be they "bottoms" *or* "tops"—lesbians, their friends, and others who enjoyed the broad-mindedness of this barrier island separated about four miles from Long Island by the Great South Bay, according to Esther Newton (2014). Whether apocryphal or not, the story of this coastal sandbar's transformation into an LGBT Mecca has been traced back to gay writers W.H. Auden and Christopher Isherwood who stayed at Duffy's Hotel in Cherry Grove and one night, dressed as Dionysius and Ganymede, were transported about in a gilt "litter" (Newton 2014, 47). (According to the *Oxford English Dictionary*, "litter" is defined as "[a] vehicle in use down to recent times, containing a couch shut in by curtains, and carried on men's shoulders or by beasts of burden.") Whether Disney knew of the increasing popularity of Cherry Grove as a paradise for gay men and lesbians is difficult to know, but *Pinocchio's* Pleasure Island certainly could have been modeled after it or any other emerging sites of queer culture. When

Honest John the Fox and Gideon the Cat attempt to exploit Pinocchio a second time and profit from his ignorance of their deceit, Honest John plays the role of doctor and determines that Pinocchio suffers from an allergy. "There's only one cure," the Fox declares, "A vacation on Pleasure Island," which he describes as "[t]hat happy land of carefree boys where every day's a holiday" (Luske and Sharpsteen 1940)!

Once the Coachman pays Honest John and Gideon for recruiting Pinocchio, we discover Pinocchio sitting next to Lampwick in the front seat of the horse-drawn wagon that takes them and the other boys to a dock where they board a ferry to their final destination. "Be a glutton!" a voice tells the boys as they enter a brightly lit amusement park. As Pinocchio and "Lampy" bond while drinking beer, smoking cigars, and playing pool, Pinocchio remarks, "Being bad's a lot of fun, ain't it?" When Jiminy Cricket finally arrives at Pleasure Island to find and save Pinocchio, he senses something sinister. "Place is like a graveyard!" he exclaims, observing destruction like that visited upon Sodom and Gomorrah. After discovering Pinocchio and Lampwick in the pool hall, Jiminy mocks Lampwick's stupidity. "He's my best friend," Pinocchio replies, propelling Jiminy to admonish his ward with foreboding words: "Make a jackass of yourself" (Luske and Sharpsteen 1940). We then witness Lampwick turning into a donkey and Pinocchio growing a pair of this beast of burden's ears as well as its tail (See Figure 6.1). Prior to taking the boys to the ferry point, the Coachman lets the Fox and the Cat in on his plan: "I'm collecting stupid little boys. You know, the disobedient ones who want to play hooky from school. And I takes 'em to Pleasure Island." Upon arrival, the Coachman also forecasts the boys' fate: "Give a bad boy enough rope, and he'll soon make a jackass of himself." When the boys realize that they are turning into donkeys, he adds, "You boys have had your fun. Now pay for it!" (Luske and Sharpsteen 1940). Of course, Pinocchio is saved in the nick of time and eventually comes to the rescue of Geppetto, who has been swallowed by Monstro the Whale. For his bravery, the Blue Fairy transforms Pinocchio into a real boy, a boy who will henceforward follow the rules and obey his superiors. But, gee, Pleasure Island still seems like it might be a whole lot of fun—at least to me and Derrida.

Figure 6.1. Pinocchio witnesses his friend Lampwick turn into a donkey (Luske and Sharpsteen 1940).

PINOCCHIO PORN ON THE SILVER SCREEN

The Erotic Adventures of Pinocchio is a textbook example of the further "impurities" to which citations—especially consciously irreverent citations—of previous literary works may lead. For Austin, such quotations of authors' original aesthetic productions are no more than the diseased offspring of their progenitors. Walt Disney died five years before this pornographic twist on his classic animated film for children hit movie theaters in the underbellies of big cities in 1971, but we needn't tax our imaginations too hard to picture his head spinning at the sight of his adorable and adored moppet transformed into a male prostitute thanks to his unusual staying power. Pinocchio's seemingly inexhaustible sexual appetite ensures a steady stream of income for his business partners, Jo-Jo the pimp and his girlfriend Mabel.

But, of course, there's an insurmountable snag to Jo-Jo's money-making scheme. The film opens with a welcome from a buxom platinum blond bombshell who immediately announces to the audience, "I'm the Fairy Godmother around here" and then proceeds to strip down to her undergarments before unclasping her bra and exposing her breasts

(Allen 1971). This Fairy Godmother serves both as the narrator of the "once upon a time" tale she begins to tell and as the moral compass of a love story—complete with a happily-ever-after ending—that she is determined to bring to fruition. Thereafter, we meet Gepetta, a lonely woodcarver who wants to be loved and, in turn, decides to whittle herself a "perfect lover," Pinocchio, whom she wishes—"How desperately I wish," she cries out—will become a real man (Allen 1971) (see Figure 6.2). The Fairy Godmother takes pity on Gepetta and brings Pinocchio to life, advising him to behave and resist the temptations he will encounter in the world. Of course, once Pinocchio meets Mr. Jo-Jo, he *can't* resist having sex with as many women as possible, and so the Fairy Godmother punishes him by lengthening his penis each time he engages in fornication. His penis grows so big that eventually he is forced to participate in an orgy that disgusts him and leads to his realization that Gepetta is his one true love. The Fairy Godmother blesses the couple, now destined for a monogamous, married life.

Figure 6.2. Gepetta carves her Pinocchio from wood (Allen 1971).

Notwithstanding the heteronormative conjugal bliss that the film ultimately endorses, *The Erotic Adventures of Pinocchio* nonetheless "undoes" its Disney predecessor and even makes fun of itself in the process as the cast purposefully takes it to camp heaven. Even the "happily-ever-after" conclusion may be construed as a tongue-in-cheek parody not only of fairy tale endings, but of soft-core plot-driven porno films of the industry's early years that avoid any exposure of both male and female genitalia and whose cast members merely simulate sexual intercourse while loudly moaning, groaning, grunting, and screaming.

As *The Erotic Adventures of Pinocchio* proves, Disney's *Pinocchio* is still by no means safe from attempts to undermine the film's propagation of a belief—in the innocence of children and the importance of their obedience to adults—that might be considered insidious deconstructions of its code of ethical conduct. As I will show, Keith Mayerson's *Pinocchio the Big Fag* also actively engages in such a deconstruction, but as I've demonstrated, the queerness of the Disney film itself is on conspicuous display for any observant viewer.[6]

PINOCCHIO THE BIG FAG

The most recent and possibly the most overt deconstruction of Carlo Collodi's novel and Disney's film is the illustrated script of a musical by Keith Mayerson, entitled *Pinocchio the Big Fag*. Mayerson began this project as a graduate student at the University of California-Irvine in the early 1990s, but its daunting scope led him to concentrate exclusively on a series of drawings and watercolors—in some cases accompanied by text—that explicate the queerness of Disney's narrative. In the Preface to his script, Mayerson credits his study of Derrida and Jean-François Lyotard while an undergraduate at Brown University for stimulating his vision of an out gay Pinocchio. Mayerson's drawings debuted in Irvine before the KIKI gallery in San Francisco and the Drawing Center in New York exhibited them. The *New York Times*'s art critic Holland Cotter praised the show and Mayerson's work in particular. Cotter remarked, "The show's high point belongs to Keith Mayerson, who brings innocence and experience together in a hilarious, phantasmagoric series of 46 ink-and-watercolor drawings that recast the tale of the puppet

Pinocchio as a picaresque journey of growing up homosexual in a homophobic society" (1994, C28). The KIKI gallery's press release describes Mayerson's artwork as "a series of children's book plates from 'the book that never happened,' and a collection of animation cell [sic] from 'the movie that never happened'" (1993). Writing in The *San Francisco Examiner*, art critic David Bonetti identifies his favorite image as a watercolor without text of "Pinocchio, still a clumsy boy, having sex with a feral Lampwick [sic], who has turned into a donkey" (1993, E10). "Their just spent semen," he adds, "swirls in the sky like a psychedelic fantasia" (Bonetti 1993, E10). *Art Forum*, among the most prestigious journals of the art world and art historians, also weighed in on the exhibit with critic Lane Relyea giving it a rave. "In the end," Relyea concludes, "'Pinocchio the Big Fag' happily inverts the Pygmalion myth lying underneath Collodi's book. Mayerson's Pinocchio fights for control of the sexuality constructed for him by his Creator, because at stake for the marionette is the chance to surrender control to his own desires" (1994, 92).

Mayerson published the complete illustrated script independently in April 2019, the twenty-fifth anniversary of the exhibition of his paintings at the Drawing Center (Mayerson 2019, 1). Loaded with phallic imagery, the script begins with Gepetto masturbating, ejaculating, and ingesting his semen before sharing his desire to have a son. "And, boy," he says, "would he have a penis" (Mayerson 2019, 7)! After Geppetto's puppet boy is built and brought to life, Pinocchio discovers that his father is a pedophile, and, thus, he flees the workshop, which leads him to several encounters with representatives of law and order. A police officer, for example, tells Pinocchio, "I represent the State, and if you learn anything in this life, it's that your ass is a piece of wood, and the State is the belt sander" (Mayerson 2019, 15). Pinocchio's conscience, wittily named "Hegemony Cricket," warns the puppet, "Woe to those children who disobey their parents and leave home," adding that "[t]he world is full of temptations" (Mayerson 2019, 19, 21). To ensure Pinocchio's obedience, Hegemony inserts himself into the tip of his ward's urethra. When Pinocchio chops off his penis, a new one grows, affirming the power of patriarchal authority.

But Pinocchio refuses to give up on the development of his nascent gay identity, a decision he reaffirms after meeting and having sex with Lamp-Wick (as Mayerson spells his name) and then venturing together to "Fun Island," an obvious homage to Fire Island. Backed by a "Cute Boy Chorus," Lamp-Wick sings a song which tells Pinocchio that they all will find "a wonderful place—to be a boy!" (Mayerson 2019, 101). "Fun Island," we soon see, is the site of a massive all-boy orgy that leads to Pinocchio's transformation into a donkey, a punishment that Hegemony Cricket finds fitting, but that leads Pinocchio to squish him. Earlier in the scene in which he and Hegemony are reunited, the cricket prophesies that Pinocchio will turn into an ass due to his sexual deviance. "It's written in the Decrees of Divine Providence," Hegemony explains, "that little boys who engage in acts of sodomy or otherwise blasphemous, perverted, and illegal behavior will eventually turn into donkeys" (Mayerson 2019, 110).

This knowledge doesn't prevent Pinocchio from seeking out Lamp-Wick. When they reunite, both by now having grown donkey ears, the two boys proclaim their love for each other, but after Pinocchio kisses his pal, Lamp-Wick becomes a full-fledged donkey. Pinocchio rides him to Geppetto's house, where he comes out to his father, who is disgusted at first, but then eventually accepts and embraces his son's queerness. Pinocchio proposes marriage to Lamp-Wick, asking, "Will you be my bride?" (Mayerson 2019, 137). "Anything for you, my little woody," Lamp-Wick replies, leading up to the gay wedding with which the show concludes and ironically enough managing to reinforce the "homonormativity" anathema to critics of same-sex marriage and undermining the text's otherwise queer agenda (Mayerson 2019, 137). But still.

CONCLUSION

We don't have to work terribly hard to envision the reactions of Disney and Derrida to Mayerson's queer parody of Pinocchio's saga, for *Pinocchio the Big Fag* exemplifies the pernicious, parasitic nature of citations of earlier texts that J. L. Austin believes distort and deform their predecessors. Disney would be appalled. Derrida, on the other hand, would delight in the deviations from Carlo Collodi's "pure" performative utterance. Perhaps he might even summon Mayerson's cheeky acts of deconstruction and destruction to prove his point about the seemingly endless iterations that texts may undergo over time. And, in a jubilant celebration of my all too prescient three-and-a-half-year-old self, I may just need to add a drawing of Pinocchio and Lamp-Wick to the cover of my Disneyland Boys Choir that could serve as testimony to Derrida that I, too, am an "heir to certain kinds of ill which infect *all* utterances." Perhaps I should also add a photo of the living, libidinal Pinocchio from the porn film. And maybe a Kodak picture of myself at the World's Fair, too? Pinocchio the Big Fag, *c'est moi*.

NOTES

1. *Pinocchio* opened in cinemas across the country on February 23, 1940. The film was released in France on May 22, 1946.
2. Unless otherwise noted, all italicized words and phrases are Derrida's.
3. In 1901 the first American edition, translated and illustrated by Walter S. Cramp and Charles Copeland, was published.
4. For a psychoanalytic reading of *Pinocchio* that attempts to redress the failure of Italian "Pinnochiologists" to engage with the Freudian concepts of "infantile sexuality, the centrality of the Oedipus and castration complexes, and the unconscious," see Stone (1994, 1). Stone notes: "The resistance to Freud in Italy is such that even an acknowledged 'phallic' nose is subsumed by the innocence of childhood and by the immaculacy of the Virgin Madonna-Fairy-Godmother" (1994, 1).
5. For a detailed and nuanced account of anxieties about Warhol's mural that eventually led to its removal from the exterior of the New York State Pavilion's art museum, see Meyer (2002).
6. Hall examines the erotics encoded in another Disney classic, *Bambi* (1942), in which he sees the rejection of childhood queerness due to the pressures of a toxic masculinity and heterosexuality to which the titular fawn must conform in order to secure his place as Prince and, eventually, King of the forest (1996, 120–25). In a similar vein, Danielle Glassmeyer embraces Nicholas Sammond's contention that during the 1930s, childrearing guidelines emphasized the importance of children's conformity to social norms and of parents' control of their child's wants and desires. "During the trip to Pleasure Island," Glassmeyer notes, "Pinocchio enjoys drink, tobacco, pool-playing and vandalism in the company of Landwick [sic], a Bowery-accented wastrel who needn't work too hard to seduce Pinocchio away from his unmarked accent and clean habits," but whose influence Pinocchio must escape (2013, 106–7).

REFERENCES

Allen, Corey, dir. *The Erotic Adventures of Pinocchio: A Bedtime Story for Adults*. 1971; Portland, Oregon: Cheezy Flicks Entertainment, 2016. DVD.

Bonetti, David. 1993. "A Queer Way to Look at Pinocchio." *San Francisco Examiner*, November 12, 1993.

Brody, Michael. 1976. "The Wonderful World of Disney—Its Psychological Appeal." *American Imago* 33, no. 4 (Winter): 350–60.

Bruhm, Steven, and Natasha Hurley. 2004. "Curiouser: On the Queerness of Children." In *Curiouser: On the Queerness of Children*, edited by Steven Bruhm and Natasha Hurley, ix–xxxviii. Minneapolis: University of Minnesota Press.

Cotter, Holland. 1994. "The Joys of Childhood, Re-Examined." *New York Times*, March 25, 1994.

Derrida, Jacques. 1982. "Signature Event Context." In *Margins of Philosophy*. Translated by Alan Bass, 309–30. Chicago: University of Chicago Press.

Glassmeyer, Danielle. 2013. "Fighting the Cold War with *Pinocchio, Bambi*, and *Dumbo*." In *Diversity in Disney Films: Critical Essays on Race, Ethnicity, Gender, Sexuality and Disability*, edited by Johnson Cheu, 99–114, Jefferson, N.C.: McFarland and Company.

Hall, Donald E. 1996. "Bambi on Top." *Children's Literature Association Quarterly* 21, no. 3 (Fall): 120–25.

Kakutani, Michiko. 2018. *The Death of Truth: Notes on Falsehood in the Age of Trump*. New York: Tim Duggan Books.

Keeler, Ruby and Dick Powell. "42nd Street." By Harry Warren and Al Dubin. Recorded 1932. *42nd Street*. Lloyd Bacon, dir. 1933. United States: Warner Bros.

KIKI Press Release. 1993. San Francisco: KIKI Art Gallery, November 4, 1993.

Lacan, Jacques. 1993. *The Seminar of Jacques Lacan, Book III: The Psychoses (1955–1956)*. Translated by Russell Griggs. New York: W.W. Norton & Co., Inc.

Luske, Hamilton and Ben Sharpsteen, dir. *Pinocchio*. 1940; Burbank, California: Walt Disney Pictures, 2017. DVD.

Mayerson, Keith. 2019. *Pinocchio the Big Fag*. Los Angeles: Independently Printed.

Meyer, Richard. 2002. *Outlaw Representation: Censorship and Homosexuality in Twentieth-Century American Art*. Boston: Beacon Press.

Newton, Esther. 2014. *Cherry Grove, Fire Island: Sixty Years in America's First Gay and Lesbian Town*. Durham: Duke University Press.

Pinocchio. International Movie Data Base. Accessed November 1, 2020. https://www.imdb.com/title/tt0067061/.

Relyea, Lane. 1994. "Keith Mayerson." *Art Forum* 8, no. 2 (April): 92.

Roth, Matt. 1996. "*The Lion King:* A Short History of Disney-Fascism." *Jump Cut: A Review of Contemporary Media* 40 (March): 15–20.

Stone, Jennifer. 1994. "Pinocchio and Pinocchiology." *American Imago* 51, no. 3 (Fall): 329–42.

Wunderlich, Richard, and Thomas J. Morrissey. 2002. *Pinocchio Goes Postmodern: Perils of a Puppet in the United States*. New York: Routledge.

III

CHALLENGING SOCIAL CONSTRUCTS

7

WHO CAN BE SUPER?

Examining the Shifted Ability Spectrum in
The Incredibles
Ethan Faust

For those familiar with Marvel and DC comics, Pixar's *The Incredibles* (Bird 2004) tells a recognizable story: a collection of superheroes protects non-super citizens from an evil villain.[1] But while the film utilizes that familiar superhero story, its themes take a decidedly Pixar-turn. Much like its studio predecessor *Finding Nemo* (Stanton 2003), *The Incredibles* leans on the motifs of family, teamwork, and self-belief to offer a portrait of the human spirit. Though filled with violence, *The Incredibles* takes great care to leave children with clear messages of empowerment and acceptance. When Violet Parr asks her crush Tony "is different okay?" in the final scene, she vocalizes the fundamental question the film seeks to answer affirmatively and stridently (Bird 2004). The primary difference that Violet refers to is inarguably that of ability, the key signifier of the leading superhero family. While no characters have medically defined disabilities, the film highlights disability, nonetheless. "While, for many, disability can be explained in a straightforward way using medical discourses," Katie Ellis (2015) notes, "critical disability theorists recognize that disability is both socially and culturally constructed" (2). By introducing superheroes into a normate world, *The Incredibles* presents a spectrum of ability that offers ample constructions of socially and culturally disabled characters. As the supers move along the spectrum in relation to the largely non-super population, the audience watches the Incredible family in the social and cultural positions of both the nondisabled and the disabled over the course of the film.

Any examination of disability in *The Incredibles* requires an understanding of its complicated history in the two genres that the film lies within, superhero and Disney/Pixar films. Many of the tropes filmmakers utilize from those genres reinforce rather than break down stereotypes of disability, contrasting the film's thesis that "difference is okay" (Bird 2004).

The resulting mess of ideas—a collection of constructive and destructive messages about disability—demands unpacking. A classically super character like Mr. Incredible stands next to his daughter Violet, a worthy hero for those who feel invisible. Syndrome, a supervillain motivated by revenge, somehow offers a powerful message about prosthetics. And though characters with superpowers succeed in the end, the film suggests mutuality will always triumph over the individual. In this chapter, I argue that while it contains some elements of the ableism embedded in the genres it belongs to and does not always champion its characters with differences, *The Incredibles* delivers a varied and compelling portrait of lived experiences of disability within that set of contradictions.

Superhero stories like *The Incredibles* begin to contain frequent representation of disability during the 1960s, the start of the era known as the Silver Age of Marvel comics. Though superheroes of this period retain the uplifting virtue and heroism of their Golden Age predecessors (think Superman), the existential Cold War angst of the 1960s led to the creation of heroes who could give weight to the increasing American anxieties. "Most strikingly," José Alaniz (2014) writes, "disability—rather than remaining largely invisible and marginalized as it had for decades in the genre—[becomes] foregrounded" (20). Disability serves as the primary vehicle through which these stories could communicate vulnerability and anxiety. In a matter of years, Iron Man, The Hulk, Doctor Strange, Thor, and Daredevil all enter the common culture as heroes with a clear form of disability. "In case after case," Alaniz writes, "a superpower 'overcompensates' for a perceived physical defect, difference or outright disability. Almost universally, the superpower will *erase* the disability, banishing it to the realm of the unseen, replacing it with raw power and heroic acts of derring-do in a hyper-masculine frame" (2014, 36). For most characters, the non-super alter ego has the disability, and the superpower allows them to overcome that perceived limitation. Doctor Strange, for example, suffers nerve damage to his hands in a car accident, effectively ending his medical career. Yet by learning to become the superpower-wielding Master of the Mystic Arts, he takes on powers that enable him to effectively annul his disability. Hulk comes from another class of these superheroes for whom the superpower is itself both the imposition of disability and the source of powers. Here too, superheroes must control the disability to perform acts of heroism.

Disability in these Silver Age superhero stories is at once hypervisible and inconsequential. Ever-present, it defines these characters in many ways. Tony Stark, for example, must wear a chest plate to prevent deadly shrapnel from reaching his heart. Iron Man's suit forever carries that visual reminder of Stark's disability. But in rarely inhibiting the superhero or helping them succeed in the end, disability tends to make little impact on either the hero or the story. Tony Stark may need to charge his chest plate every night, but once he becomes Iron Man, the disability matters little as he performs physically demanding stunts. Superheroes have disabilities, but to become or act super, they discard them or minimize their effects. In that ability to effectively leave one body behind for another, they do not experience life as those with disabilities do. Though the increased visibility of characters with disability was itself a positive for kids with disabilities looking for heroes like them, Silver Age portrayals reinforced in the common culture a number of problematic ideas about disability. Only recently, in the decade after *The Incredibles*, have Marvel films and comics given bigger roles to superheroes like Rhodey, also known as War Machine, who fights *with* his disability, not in spite of it across the Avengers films.

We must view *The Incredibles* within one other vast canon of stories, that of Disney/Pixar. In the decade leading up to the release of *The Incredibles* in 2004, two prominent Disney films came under significant attack for their portrayals of disability. In *The Lion King* (Allers and Minkoff 1994), Scar joined *Peter Pan*'s Captain Hook (1953) and *Sleeping Beauty*'s Maleficent (1959) in a long list of villains defined by, motivated by, and even named for a physical deformity. Just as the dark shade of Scar's skin rightly came under fire as a problematically racial indicator of evil, so too did the decision to use disability to mark evil. Two years later, some disability activists argued *The Hunchback of Notre Dame* (Trousdale and Wise 1996) infantilizes and humiliates Quasimodo, the lead character in the retelling of the 1831 Victor Hugo novel, who has what is now categorized as Proteus Syndrome. "Yes, it's a movie, but it's so much more than that," Martin F. Norden (2013) writes (173). "For disabled people, movies such as *The Hunchback of Notre Dame* are harmful and divisive expressions that reinforce negative beliefs that lead to further discrimination" (Norden 2013, 173). Real consequences arose from that depiction of disability, as the use of the word 'hunchback' as a derogatory term increased in schools across Britain (Norden 2013, 173). Helaine Silverman (2002) posits that "as a quintessential form of American public culture, animated movies may be examined as a site where collective social understandings are created and in which the politics of signification are engaged" (299). Children watch and rewatch these films with particularly open minds. Though they cannot yet critically examine them, they still take in the embedded attitudes. As the representation of disability in broader discourse is preciously limited, culturally prominent animated films can unwittingly become the principal purveyors of the understanding of disability. Harmful portrayals in these animated spaces carry an added weight.

In representing disability in a significantly more progressive way, Pixar's *Finding Nemo* (Stanton 2003) did much to right Disney's ship.[2] Nemo, the film's young protagonist clownfish, has a small fin, congenitally differentiated by an attack that harmed his egg. While Nemo's fin appears physically compromising, he calls it his "lucky fin," and in sharing that with his classmates, he learns that many of them boast their own distinctive physical quirks (Stanton 2003). Along his journey to return home, Nemo negotiates the assumptions other fish make about his abilities. For example, his father worries that he is not a strong enough swimmer for the open ocean, and many fish in the dentist's office tank similarly believe he cannot swim up its filter. Nemo comes to realize their instincts to protect him are well-intentioned. However, he finds ways to persist. His disability affects the way he lives, but it does not define and dictate it. "To the mainstream audience, *Finding Nemo* isn't 'about' disability at all," Ann Millett (2004) writes, "because physical difference isn't a glaring spectacle in the film that signals danger or elicits pity." But in presenting disability as "a socially constructed character quality," the film "proves to be an unconventional, transgressive representation of disability" (Millett 2004). Many other characters, such as Gil and Dory, also have differences, like a scar and frequent memory loss, respectively. "All of the more remarkable," Millett adds, "'abnormal,' even freakish characters in *Finding Nemo* swim with and against the undertow, and neither 'overcome' their so-called physical and intellectual 'problems,' nor prevail 'in spite of them,' as conventional narrative and stereotypes would prescribe" (2004). Especially when compared to the Disney films of the 1990s and the superhero genre, *Finding Nemo* offers a startlingly nuanced portrayal of disability.

Unlike *Finding Nemo*, Pixar's subsequent film *The Incredibles* does not present a world full of acceptance. From the opening sequence, its superheroes occupy a privileged position of power over normate bodies. On the shifted spectrum of ability that the film offers, the able-bodied community members, though large in numbers, are socially and culturally disabled in relation to Mr. Incredible and his fellow supers, who are bound by societal code to protect them. The film opens with the supers discussing why they have secret identities. "Who wants the pressure of being super all the time?" Mr. Incredible asks, a sentiment which Elastigirl, his soon-to-be wife, echoes (Bird 2004). "Sometimes I just want [the world] to stay saved," he continues. "I feel like the maid" (Bird 2004). Immediately, his lack of respect for the common people becomes apparent, as Mr. Incredible looks down upon those without his powers whom he tires of saving. He possesses a troubling desire for the lesser-able citizens to disappear, a sentiment he shares with superheroes of the Silver Age. Robert Genter (2007) explains that the focus "upon the lived reality of the superheroes themselves, that is, upon the ways in which the mundane problems of human existence interfered with their crimefighting abilities" differentiates those Silver Age Marvel comics from their predecessors (954). Set in the 1960s, the era of the Silver Age, *The Incredibles* exists in that context, immediately highlighting Mr. Incredible's attitude toward the banal. Notably, at the wedding of Mr. Incredible and Elastigirl, there are no non-supers visible in the audience. The supers may live among the ordinary citizens, but they maintain a community apart from their lesser-able peers. While they have a duty to society, they do not seem to value the people they protect.

Though Mr. Incredible feels superior to those of lesser ability, he maintains a compulsory need to help anyone whom he decides needs saving. Noble though it may seem, Mr. Incredible acts without asking, presuming that everyone wants his aid. The notion that those with lesser ability always want to be saved or cured has long been challenged within the disability community. "All these [surgeries and therapies] are imposed on us with the assumption that we share our parents' or therapists' desire to be 'normal' at all costs," write Richard Rieser and Micheline Mason (1990) of the phenomenon (81). Those with more ability cannot always understand that not everybody living with a disability craves a different bodily experience. "Both mainstream Hollywood and art-house cinema have leaned heavily on the cure narrative," writes Lawrence Carter-Long (2019), "whether it is because most nondisabled people lack the imagination to conceive of anything else or because in terms of storyline disabled people usually don't exist on our own terms" (28). In much the same way that doctors impose "cures" on those with disabilities, Mr. Incredible imposes his view of who requires saving on the citizens. However, *The Incredibles* differentiates itself from other films based on what unfolds next. Two key scenes involve Mr. Incredible seriously injuring people in attempts to rescue them from death without their asking for assistance. The unwanted actions of Mr. Incredible and other supers lead to lawsuits that force them into hiding. Here, in showcasing the experience of those subjected to unwelcome help, the film condemns the ableist mindset of its superheroes.

The narrative then flips when the citizens force the supers into hiding, as the supers now find themselves the objects of discrimination. As markers of physical deviation, their superpowers act here as a form of disability, for their abilities now inhibit their participation in certain societal norms. In this reversal, the normate rejects the different, a problematic trend that has long led to suffering in the disability community. "Freighted with anxieties about loss of control and autonomy that the American ideal repudiates," writes Rosemarie Garland-Thompson (1997), "'the disabled' become a threatening presence, seemingly compromised by the particularities and limitations of their own bodies" (41). Deviation, often a visual indicator of disability, reminds the normate of what it cannot control. The anxiety that a disabled body inspires reflects more on the self than on the other. In rejecting the disabled body, pushing it into separate, unseen spaces, the normate can relieve some of their anxiety. In that rejection, society often conceals those with a marked difference in ability. "We have been hidden," Sami Linton (1998) writes of her experience with disability, "whether in the institutions that have confined us, the attics and basements that sheltered our family's shame, the 'special' schools and classrooms designed to solve the problems we are thought to represent" (3). In their new position along the ability spectrum on the other side of the non-super citizens, the Incredible family comes to live this common experience that people with disabilities often share. Though the supers still dwell among the normate, the government forces them into hiding to shelter society from harm and shame.

Recognizing their power in numbers, the citizens claim the position of power in the social order, pushing the supers to the edges of society. The film heavily emphasizes the irony of the subjugation, as it inverts expectations to see those with such superpowers struggle to conform to dictates of normalcy. Mr. Incredible still maintains his superhero bulk, especially in his upper body, but frequent shots show him, living domestically now as Bob Parr with a family of five, either unable to fit in his allotted space or yelled at by someone much smaller than him. He is even visually or verbally shamed for his added weight four separate times in unnecessary gags that undermine the film's message of acceptance. These moments, in effect, unman Mr. Incredible, who cannot perform his usual displays of hyper-masculine strength. Like Spider-Man and other alter-egos of the Silver Age superheroes before him, Mr. Incredible experiences great anguish when he cannot use his powers. Of this unmanning sensation, Alaniz (2014) writes, "the slightest hint of enfeeblement signals anathema to [the] super-self" (23). Mr. Incredible feels worthless in his new social standing and can only keep himself going by stealing away to secretly continue crime-fighting with Frozone, another superhero in hiding with whom he maintains a friendship. Mr. Incredible attempts to pass as normate, but his suppressed abilities erupt in his anger. He lifts up his car in front of a neighbor in a moment of frustration, and when his boss Lester fires him, he throws Lester through the walls of nearly a dozen cubicles.

These occasions allow Mr. Incredible to experience another feeling known too well by those in the disability community—the stare. "Staring is the social relationship that constitutes disability identity and gives meaning to impairment by marking it as aberrant," Rosemarie Garland-Thompson writes (2001, 347). As Garland-Thompson describes, the stare from the neighborhood boy on the tricycle confirms the strangeness of Mr. Incredible's powers and heightens his persisting anxieties about experiencing difference. "Even if disability is not apparent, the threat of its erupting in some visual form is perpetually present," Garland-Thompson continues. "Disability is always ready to disclose itself, to emerge as some visually recognizable stigmata, however subtle, that will disrupt social order by its presence" (Garland-Thompson 2001, 347). Though there is clearly meant to be humor in these moments, in being stared at and fearing the consequences of unwittingly disclosing his ability, Mr. Incredible, and the viewers of the film, experience some of the common social sensations of living with a disability.

Mr. Incredible and his family do not find living that experience easy. Elastigirl, now stay-at-home-mom Helen, explains their situation best when she says to their son Dash, who himself struggles to behave in school: "Right now the world just wants us to fit in, and to fit in, the world just wants us to be like everyone else" (Bird 2004). When the Incredibles must conform to the normate, they have marital issues, struggle to concentrate on their day-to-day tasks, and outwardly show anger or apathy. Mr. Incredible breaks his car door by shutting it too hard, he cannot focus on the dinner conversation, and he saws through the table when cutting Dash's steak. He can hardly contain his frustration with his new role, even more than a decade into it. He shouts at his wife, "Reliving the glory days is better than acting like they didn't happen," to which she shouts back, "Yes, they happened. But this, our family, is what's happening now, Bob. You're missing this" (Bird 2004). Lamenting the loss of ability causes Mr. Incredible to lose focus on his present reality. The manifestation of the decade of accumulated frustration with his social position culminates in him throwing Lester through the cubicle walls.

While the marital issues underlie the difficulties of becoming less able-bodied for Mr. Incredible and Elastigirl, their kids only know the new experience. Rather than longing for the past as their father does, they long to be a part of the normate for which they try to pass, or in Dash's case with regard to sports, at least get to participate fully in society. Violet, the family's teenage daughter, shouts amid their internal struggles, "We act normal, Mom. I want to *be* normal" (Bird 2004). Though superheroes are typically depicted as confident and comfortable with their powers, Violet struggles with anxiety and doubt. Her superpower of invisibility itself indicates a level of discomfort in her skin. The way she lets her hair fall over her face further suggests that she wants to disappear even without the use of her power. She can control when she hides, and she desires to be unseen in certain situations, but she also experiences invisibility as a social cost of difference, an unwanted consequence for many young women with disabilities (Bauer 2001). It does not always manifest itself as a superpower.

Unlike her parents, Violet has a second power—she can create forcefields. But where her anxiety makes becoming invisible easier, she struggles to use her defensive power. When she and Dash join their mother on a jet, unknowingly bringing themselves out of hiding in the process, she cannot create a forcefield around the plane at a moment's notice, despite her mother yelling at her to do so. The immense pressure causes her to break down, panic etched on her face. Elastigirl manages to save them despite Violet's failure and tells her, "Doubt is a luxury we can't afford anymore, sweetie. You have more power than you realize" (Bird 2004). Though Elastigirl reminds Violet she has tremendous power in order to make her feel better, it is a tragic example of parents expecting able-bodiedness and not giving anxiety its appropriate weight. Violet feels inadequate, and, as she frantically practices, her continued inability to master her power shows that the added expectations hinder her. In a moment of instinct, however, she produces a powerful forcefield to save her brother Dash. After proving her skill, she possesses a new self-confidence. She pulls her hair back behind her ears, no longer hiding her face, no longer wishing to be quite so invisible. For the remainder of the film, she solves nearly every problem the family faces, intelligently figuring out the coordinates for the rocket launch, grabbing the remote control off the street, and saving her brother from the Omnidroid, Syndrome's weapon designed specifically to defeat superheroes.

Violet is a particularly progressive superhero for the disabled community, a creation distinct from her superhero predecessors, for an aspect of the disability that she experiences not only stays with her in her moments of triumph, but itself becomes a source of strength. Where first her invisibility is a manifestation of her anxiety, she learns to channel it into a real superpower. She shows that the class of girls who feel unseen can have tremendous power within them that they alone can bring out. While Violet may appear to *beat* anxiety in an unrealistically quick way, the presentation of self-confidence does not necessarily mean the absence of anxiety. Rather, her continued use of invisibility shows that she always carries some of that anxiety with her, and her power to create forcefields signifies her learned ability to actively keep it at bay, an ongoing process even as she finds success. Violet's arc is unique because it lacks narrative prosthesis, a concept defined by David T. Michell and Sharon L. Snyder. Mitchell and Snyder posit that in storytelling, disability tends to act as a crutch to advance a story, but once it fulfills its function, it disappears altogether (2001). In *The Incredibles*, though everyone in her family feels the ramifications of their new social positions on the ability hierarchy, Violet alone carries that experience forward with her when they come out of hiding. She does not thrust her disability aside. She learns not to define herself by her abilities, and in so doing, she makes an easy transition into the ability-diverse world at the film's end.

While Jack-Jack, the baby, does not play a major role in the story until *Incredibles 2* (Bird 2018), his arc in the original film offers further insight into the expectations that parents have for their children regarding ability. At first, he seems to be the family's lone non-super child. As a needy, lesser-able human, he reminds us that able-bodiedness can be temporary and that it is not a state that people are born into. Elastigirl outright tells Edna Mode, the tailor for the supers, "Jack-Jack doesn't have any powers" (Bird 2004). In caring for her youngest child, Elastigirl does not need superpowers, and she performs the roles of bathing and feeding him without hesitation. However, Mr. Incredible notably engages with his baby in precious few moments. His only on-screen interactions with his non-super son come in the montage after he begins training as a super again, moments when he is at a personal high. The contrast in parenting further highlights the link Mr. Incredible makes between masculinity and ability. Already unmanned by the loss of his own power, he seems eager to avoid the idea that he has fathered a son who does not possess the same level of ability. Accepting that would mean yet another blow to his masculinity.

When the rest of the family joins Mr. Incredible in his fight against the Omnidroid, the villain Syndrome kidnaps Jack-Jack and, in his monologued taunt, criticizes Mr. Incredible's treatment of those with lesser ability. Syndrome uses the baby as a stand-in for his younger self, whose experience as a non-super Mr. Incredible seemed similarly uninterested in. He tells Mr. Incredible, "I'll be a good mentor. Supportive, encouraging—everything you weren't" (Bird 2004). Mr. Incredible knows Syndrome's criticism is partly true, having realized in a prior moment of weakness that he has undervalued his family in a quest to prove his strength. The youngest Incredible reminds parents not to let ability affect the raising of a child. However, Jack-Jack does have powers, and the sudden reveal highlights that unknown abilities can be the strongest of all, for in a moment of dramatic irony, he defeats Syndrome. His and Violet's roles draw attention to the way family members expect ability in their children and put undue pressure on them. But in their eventual success, they show that nobody should be written off based on their outward display of ability.[3]

In his larger arc beyond his interactions with Jack-Jack, Syndrome acts as a foil for the Incredible family. He first appears before the inversion of the ability spectrum, when he shows up to try and help Mr. Incredible fight Bomb Voyage. Syndrome's normate body contrasts with the muscled figure of Mr. Incredible. Because Syndrome does not possess a superpower, he must use prosthetic-like technology to attain the ability of the supers he desires to work with. To do so, young Syndrome develops rocket boots, which give him the power of flight and act as prosthetics in that they push him along the ability spectrum to be on par with the supers. "Not every superhero has powers you know?" he tells Mr. Incredible upon flying in to help. "You can be super without them" (Bird 2004). It is an empowering message. Yet, despite Syndrome achieving and supporting a level of equality, Mr. Incredible rejects Syndrome's pleas to help: "Fly home, Buddy. I work alone" (Bird 2004). Unwilling to see Syndrome's abilities, Mr. Incredible refuses to use Syndrome's chosen name, IncrediBoy. Their squabbles result in Bomb Voyage getting away, which Mr. Incredible pins on young Syndrome as he hands him over to police, effectively pushing him to the shadows. As Michael T. Hayes and Rhonda S. Black (2003) write, "The greatest impediment to a person's taking full part in his society are not his physical flaws, but rather the tissue of myths, fears, and misunderstandings that society attaches to them" (115). Hayes and Black might well have written this sentence about Syndrome himself, as the film plainly shows his relative physical limitations never prevent him from being super.

After the inversion of the ability spectrum and the subsequent time jump, Syndrome creates a superweapon to enact revenge on the supers for dismissing him when he was a boy. Throughout the rest of the film, Syndrome's rage and anger come as a direct result of the super community not accepting him. To supplement his rocket boots, he creates a series of prosthetics to generate the additional superpowers that he supposedly lacks. "Am I good enough now?" he asks when he traps Mr. Incredible with his laser-beam technology. The goading continues when he adds, "Who's super now?" (Bird 2004). Even as he becomes more of a super, he carries the societal rejection he experienced. Once he achieves his desired superiority over Mr. Incredible, he repeatedly uses the word "lame" to put down Mr. Incredible for calling for help (Bird 2004). With his word choice, Syndrome shows his new intent to invert rather than annul their original ability-power relationship. Instead of eliminating the hierarchy of ability with his prosthetics, as he initially sought to do as a child, he wants to reinforce it. By attempting to kill off the supers, Syndrome fulfills the stereotypical villainous role of a person with a disability seeking revenge over able-bodied persecutors.

The origin of Syndrome's new chosen name is never explained, though it carries much significance. While a syndrome, like a scar, only indicates physical or cognitive difference, here, as with the *Lion King*'s Scar, the naming couples malevolence with that difference. Syndrome has no visible physical disability, but his name reinforces that he is of lesser ability and somehow made evil by that distinction. For decades, antagonists across genres have been marked by disability. From Disney's Captain Hook to Marvel's Dr. Doom and DC's Bane, storytellers use physical differences to indicate villainy. Paul Longmore (2003) writes:

> Giving disabilities to villainous characters reflects and reinforces, albeit in exaggerated fashion, three common prejudices against handicapped people: disability is a punishment for evil; disabled people are embittered by their 'fate'; disabled people resent the nondisabled and would, if they could, destroy them. In historic and contemporary social fact, it is,

of course, nondisabled people who have at times endeavored to destroy people with disabilities. As with popular portrayals of other minorities, the unacknowledged hostile fantasies of the stigmatizers are transferred to the stigmatized. (133–34)

Syndrome's name entrenches him in this class of problematic supervillains and brings those prejudices to the fore. The name, perhaps even more so than Syndrome's revenge plot, suggests the filmmakers' ideology aligns with Mr. Incredible's in believing Syndrome's ability lies below the supers' despite his resourceful use of prosthetics.

Syndrome's fundamental desire to put the disabled on an equal level with the able—which in his new plan happens only after the supers have been eliminated and he has lived in power for a number of years—seems fundamentally at odds with his vile actions. "When I'm old, I'll sell my inventions," he says, "so that everyone can be super. And when everyone is super, no one will be" (Bird 2004). Were Syndrome not killing off those on the far end of the ability spectrum and attempting to claim his own spot ahead of everyone else, that idea could be taken as a positive challenge to the hierarchical system that has suppressed people of a lesser ability—the same idea that he approaches Mr. Incredible with as a boy. His creation of prosthetic technology does appear to succeed in eliminating the oppressive ability gap. It puts him on par with the supers, which he loudly touts: "Oh I'm real. Real enough to defeat you. And I did it without your precious gifts. Your oh-so-special powers" (Bird 2004). When he unleashes the Omnidroid on the city, Syndrome plans to intervene only once it wreaks sufficient havoc. He thinks he can fool the crowd into believing his deactivation of the droid is instead a feat of great power. The crowd does recognize his ability initially, shouting, "The supers have returned" when Syndrome flies in. However, his immediate failure to corral the Omnidroid exposes him as a fraudulent super to the public, and his subsequent death further suggests the filmmakers believe his prosthetics never in fact make him an equal in ability to the supers. His classic super-villainy, namely his need to enact revenge over his persecutors, aligns with comic book villains of the past. Ultimately, that clouds and mitigates his welcome intent to dismantle the hierarchy of difference through the use of prosthetics.

Putting aside Syndrome's obvious lack of morality, his demise problematically suggests that the biological always remains superior to the prosthetic. Syndrome's outcome posits that a person with a disability cannot elevate their level of ability to that of the normate, no matter the technology they possess. Mr. Incredible goes so far as to use the word "pretend" to describe Syndrome's status as a super, despite Syndrome no longer having comparative physical limitations (Bird 2004). The critique of the technology-aided hero might also be a statement against transhumanism, the cultural movement that supports the notion that the use and widespread availability of technology can fundamentally improve the human condition. This criticism of technology is not as prevalent in other superhero tales, as Marvel creations like War Machine and Iron Man achieve great success as technology and prosthetic-aided Avengers. As discussed, Tony Stark's command of technology allows him to develop the life-sustaining suit that Iron Man wears into battle. He also creates leg braces that allow War Machine to continue to fight even after paralysis.

Paradoxically, despite the dismissal of prosthetics, the Incredible family's ultimate victory occurs despite their superpowers not being sufficient. As he tries to stop Syndrome's Omnidroid from destroying the city, Mr. Incredible cannot rely on his strength alone. Even when Frozone and his entire family join him in the battle, they cannot topple the rampaging superweapon. To defeat it, they instead learn to operate Syndrome's remote control, an item that anyone of any ability can use, which they track down with each other's help. They succeed in the end not because of their unique physical abilities, but because they work with one another to locate and utilize the available resources. It is similar to Nemo and his father Marlin figuring out that although they cannot free the netted school of fish themselves, they can do so by encouraging them to swim down together. Digging here into its Pixar roots, *The Incredibles* suggests that mutuality and community can triumph over individuality.

As an artifact in the disability discourse within both the superhero genre and the Disney/Pixar world of stories, *The Incredibles* provides a complicated blend of mixed messages. On the one hand, the use of tired stereotyping tropes of villainy feels entirely in line with both the comic book genre and the Disney films of the 1990s. The vilification and demise of the single character who seeks to adjust the hierarchy of ability ultimately reinforces the able body as best. And though technology can allow people to act super, the film problematically underscores that those with prosthetics can never truly *be* super. One must ask whether the film's championing of the supers above the prosthetic not only annuls Syndrome's message about prosthetics but also underscores the hierarchy of differences the film overtly seeks to reject. On the other hand, one can plainly see the critique of the power structures that result in the supers losing their status above the normate citizens. As a result, the film explores not only the physical limitations of disability, but also some of the social and cultural experiences it can bring, just as in *Finding Nemo*. One can see Violet, the empowering, invisible super who once longed to fit in with the normate, affirm that she can thrive in an ability-diverse space when she asks her crush Tony out in the final scene. "Different is great," he responds (Bird 2004). Although the filmmakers do not come close to creating a wholly positive representation of disability, the breadth of disability experiences that they put on screen tips the scale favorably.

In the years since *The Incredibles*, superheroes continue to play an inordinate role in the portrayal of disability, and many of the Silver Age characters have achieved renewed cultural prominence in the twenty-first-century superhero movie boom. Gradually, perhaps buoyed by parts of what *The Incredibles* accomplished, or perhaps because of the influence of Disney, who took over Marvel Entertainment in 2009, Marvel has taken strides to expand its representation of disability. Much like Violet, its superheroes increasingly live and fight with their markers of difference or disability, as opposed to casting them aside. In examining some of the complexities of living with a disability rather than merely putting disability on screen, *The Incredibles* begins showing a path to destigmatizing the myths, fears, and misunderstandings that impact the lives of people with disabilities. The film does not go all the way in championing an ability-diverse space, crucially disavowing the prosthetic experience. But, in highlighting the social and cultural implications of an ability hierarchy, *The Incredibles* advances the portrayal of disability within its genres.

NOTES

1. When *The Incredibles* was released, Disney was in the midst of a ten-year partnership with Pixar Animation Studios, which they would formally acquire in 2006. Pixar had full creative control of *The Incredibles* as a part of the deal. In 2009, Disney would also acquire Marvel Entertainment.
2. Like *The Incredibles,* Pixar's *Finding Nemo* was distributed by Disney.
3. Jack-Jack's powers are the subject of Pixar's *Incredibles 2* (Bird, 2018). Over the course of the film, his parents and siblings each find out about Jack-Jack's abilities on their own, and they express great delight. Notably, the film came under fire from the disability community not for its portrayal of disability, but for its disregard of many of its viewers with disabilities. The scene that involves the villain weaponizing a strobe light effect particularly endangers those in the audience with photosensitive epilepsy and can agitate those prone to migraines, individuals with Autism or ADHD, and those living with seizure disorders. After its opening weekend, theaters began issuing a warning before the film began (Glazier and Ko, 2018).

REFERENCES

Alaniz, José. 2014. *Death, Disability, and the Superhero.* Jackson: University Press of Mississippi.

Allers, Roger and Rob Minkoff, dir. *The Lion King*. 1994; Burbank, CA: Buena Vista Home Entertainment, 2011. DVD.

Bauer, Anne M. 2001. "'Tell Them We're Girls': The Invisibility of Girls with Disabilities." In *Educating Young Adolescent Girls*, edited by Patricia O'Reilly, Elizabeth M. Penn, and Kathleen deMarrais, 29–45. Mahwah: Lawrence Erlbaum.

Bird, Brad, dir. *The Incredibles*. 2004; Burbank, CA: Buena Vista Home Entertainment, 2005. DVD.

———. *Incredibles 2*. 2018; Burbank, CA: Buena Vista Home Entertainment, 2018. Blu-Ray.

Carter-Long, Lawrence. 2019. "Where Have You Gone, Stephen Dwoskin? On Disability Film." *Film Quarterly* 72, no. 3: 26–29. https://doi.org/10.1525/fq.2019.72.3.26.

Ellis, Katie. 2015. *Disability and Popular Culture*. New York: Routledge.

Garland-Thompson, Rosemarie. 1997. *Extraordinary Bodies: Figuring Disability in American Culture and Literature*. New York: New York University Press.

———. 2001. "Seeing the Disabled: Visual Rhetorics of Disability in Popular Photography." In *The New Disability History: American Perspectives*, edited by Paul Longmore and Lauri Umansky, 335–74. New York: New York University Press.

Genter, Robert. 2007. "'With Great Power Comes Great Responsibility': Cold War Culture and the Birth of Marvel Comics." *Journal of Popular Culture* 40, no. 6: 953–78. http://dx.doi.org/10.1111/j.1540-5931.2007.00480.x.

Glazier, Eve, and Elizabeth Ko. 2018. "Ask the Doctors: *Incredibles 2* Strobe Light Scenes Prompt Health Advisories." *The Spokesman-Review*. August 23, 2018.

Hayes, Michael T., and Rhonda S. Black. 2003. "Troubling Signs: Disability, Hollywood Movies and the Construction of a Discourse of Pity." *Disability Studies Quarterly* 23, no. 2: 114–32. http://dx.doi.org/10.18061/dsq.v23i2.

Linton, Sami. 1998. *Claiming Disability: Knowledge and Identity*. New York: New York University Press.

Longmore, Paul. 2003. *Why I Burned My Book and Other Essays on Disability*. Philadelphia: Temple University Press.

Mitchell, David T., and Sharon L. Snyder. 2001. *Narrative Prosthesis*. Ann Arbor: University of Michigan Press.

Millett, Ann. 2004. "'Other' Fish in the Sea: *Finding Nemo* as an Epic Representation of Disability." *Disability Studies Quarterly* 24, no. 1. http://dx.doi.org/10.18061/dsq.v24i1.861.

Norden, Martin F. 2013. "Disability and Otherness in *The Hunchback of Notre Dame*." In *Diversity in Disney Films: Critical Essays on Race, Ethnicity, Gender, Sexuality, and Disability*, edited by Johnson Cheu, 163–78. Jefferson: McFarland.

Rieser, Richard, and Micheline Mason. 1990. *Disability Equality in the Classroom: A Human Rights Issue*. Rev. ed. London: Inner London Education.

Silverman, Helaine. 2002. "Groovin' to Ancient Peru: A Critical Analysis of Disney's The Emperor's New Groove." *Journal of Social Archaeology* 2, no. 3: 298–322. http://dx.doi.org/10.1177/146960530200200302.

Stanton, Andrew, dir. *Finding Nemo*. 2003; Burbank, CA: Buena Vista Home Entertainment, 2003. DVD.

Trousdale, Gary and Kirk Wise, dir. *The Hunchback of Notre Dame*. 1996; Burbank, CA: Buena Vista Home Entertainment, 2002. DVD.

8

RISK AND REFLEXIVITY IN PIXAR'S *THE INCREDIBLES*

Francine Rochford

INTRODUCTION

Pixar's *The Incredibles* (2004) and its sequel *Incredibles 2* (2018) are set in a 1960s alternate universe in which superheroes initially operate openly; however, their activity is declared illegal due to the risk of litigation. Brief, but rich, expository scenes occur early in *The Incredibles* in which Mr. Incredible, the main protagonist, carries out two rescues, one of a suicidal man and the other of train passengers, but in doing so causes injuries. These events lead to litigation against Mr. Incredible and the government, cascading into potential liability for all superhero activity and leading the government to ban it and redeploy superheroes in the "Superhero Relocation Program." The ill-defined government National Supers Agency (NSA), administered by world-weary case worker Rick Dicker, moves the superheroes underground. The film focuses on the Parr family, Bob and Helen Parr, retired superheroes (Mr. Incredible and Elastigirl) who have secret identities, and their children.

The early scenes reference several central themes in law and jurisprudence, particularly ideas of control and responsibility in allocating risk. They pull together some recent controversial developments in the law of civil wrongs, or tort law. In this chapter, I will demonstrate the legal issues explored by *The Incredibles* and draw out the jurisprudential questions arising from them. I will first consider the ways in which the film explores litigation and its consequences. One outcome of civil litigation is opening additional categories of legal action. As new forms of legal claim arise, perceptions of risk change or are actively steered by litigants, the government, and insurers. Among the factors to be managed is the degree of personal responsibility and autonomy of the individual. In discussing this process of change, I will draw upon Beck's "risk society" thesis (Beck 1992) to show that *The Incredibles* centers on the fears of unmanageable risk in America in the movement toward the "second modernity." The relations between citizens and government, law and litigants, the family and roles within it are all taken apart and reassembled in the second modernity. By viewing *The Incredibles* through Beck's sociological lens, we can respond to some of the more common criticisms of the movie as a reflection of conservative values by focusing on its depiction of modern trajectories in law, authority, and power.

LITIGATION AND ITS CONSEQUENCES IN *THE INCREDIBLES*

The establishing scenes of *The Incredibles*, the cynosure of this chapter, occur fifteen years before the main story. Mr. Incredible performs a sequence of interventions and rescues, but due to the interference of ten-year-old Buddy Pine ("Incrediboy," later "Syndrome"), bystanders are injured. A bomb set by villain Bomb Voyage becomes attached to Buddy's cape, and Mr. Incredible's removal of it causes the destruction of a section of train rail and injury of passengers. Later, Mr. Incredible's interference in the suicide attempt of banker Oliver Sansweet results in Sansweet suffering whiplash, as evidenced by a prominent neck brace. The train passengers, many of whom also wear neck braces, and Sansweet are plaintiffs in the legal suit in Superior Court, which, according to the media voiceover, costs the government millions. The use of the neck brace, common in portrayals of American litigation, signals that the plaintiff is engaging in spurious litigation, a perception noted in medicolegal literature: "[m]edia and professional stereotypes often depict the patient with whiplash walking into the courtroom with a cervical collar and grimacing in pain, only to throw off the collar the moment a settlement is reached" (Swartzman et al. 1996, 53). The inference, clearly signaled by the courtroom scene, is that the litigants are "fabricating or exaggerating symptoms for financial gain" (Swartzman et al. 1996, 53).

The details of the legal proceedings in *The Incredibles* are sketchy, literally. The animators depict the courtroom scenes in sketch form, which represents the judicial rule that publication of photographic images is (or historically has been) prohibited to prevent prejudicial publicity (Caffrey 1975). From the newspaper reports it is apparent that Mr. Incredible has been held accountable for the injuries arising from his rescue attempts, although it is uncertain whether the verdict relates to Sansweet's claim or the suit relating to the train rescue. The voiceover, presented as a news report, notes that "Incredible's court losses cost the government millions, and opened the floodgates for dozens of superhero lawsuits the world over" (Bird 2004). The spinning tabloid effect common in animations from the era cleverly underlines the role of spin, or manipulation of the narrative, in the management of public issues. The scenes move quickly from the headline "Mr. Incredible Sued" in the *Municiberg Reporter* to editorial columns in the *Municiberg Tribune*.

The legal actions against Mr. Incredible all involve the law of torts, a type of civil wrong which, if successfully established, results in the payment of compensation. Negligence, the tort most likely represented here, requires that the injured person prove three things: that a superhero owed a duty of care to the person, that the duty was breached when the superhero failed to act as a (notional) reasonable person would in the circumstances, and that, as a result, compensable loss occurred. The tort of negligence is an expanding area of law because of the relatively broad definitions applied to terms such as "reasonable," and the courts' generous attitude to the types of compensable loss. The floodgate effect that the film references is a noted phenomenon in common law jurisdictions based on the precedential force of an authoritative ruling. In a sufficiently superior court, the legal reasoning in a decision will have binding force on courts below it but will only give rise to a floodgate of claims if the precedent changes the previous law. In the law of negligence, this expansion usually occurs when a superior court accepts a new category of duty relationship or compensable damage. The term "floodgate" is typically deployed in conservative arguments (that is, arguments presenting an anti-plaintiff view) to emphasize the policy effects of major changes in case law. It has been used in many jurisdictions, for instance, as an argument for refusing to accept a claim for negligent infliction of purely economic loss (Smith and Burns 1983, 152). The projected effect of expanding the class of litigants or the category of damage on courts' caseloads has acted as a strong reactionary influence on the development of case law for many years.

The question, then, is what is the point of difference between the legal action against Mr. Incredible and previous litigation? What changes in the law resulted in the precedent that ushered in the "floodgate" of cases that followed the decision? The lawsuit against Mr. Incredible has several novel features, all live issues in modern tort law. The most obvious is the rescuer's liability for injuries arising during rescue, known as the "Good Samaritan" problem (Gordon 1965). The second issue is the law's willingness to accept that continuing life is a form of damage, meaning that Mr. Incredible could be liable for thwarting a suicide, and the third relates to the comparative moral culpabilities of the defendant and the actual wrongdoer.

NOVELTY IN THE LEGAL LANDSCAPE OF *THE INCREDIBLES*

In considering the main novel legal themes in *The Incredibles*, I will begin with the Good Samaritan problem, which has two aspects: whether a duty arises in law to come to the aid of another and whether liability can or should be borne by the rescuer when their benevolent actions result in injury. The so-called duty to rescue does not, in common law jurisdictions like the United States, extend to those without an existing duty arising from their position such as doctors or paramedics (Lee and Lindahl 2017, 3.81). The first articulation of the generalized duty of care occurred in the iconic case of *Donoghue v. Stevenson* (1932) in which Lord Atkin proposed the "neighbor principle" as a category of duty but distinguished between the legal and moral duty. The morally correct "Good Samaritan" will assist a bystander, but the legal obligation to help another is enlivened only if an established duty of care exists, such as in a doctor and patient relationship. However, once a rescue is undertaken, a duty arises and in common law jurisdictions, assistance undertaken negligently could result in liability (Lopez and Maccarrone 2017–2018, 105). Therefore, a superhero would be legally safe if they choose *not* to intervene in an emergency. Morally, however, they might feel compromised because they can make a difference but are compelled by the risk of litigation *not* to act. According to this principle, if superheroes are not actually required to aid (for instance, because they are employed by the state, like policemen or firemen), then they could not be liable if they did *not* assist.[1] Most common law jurisdictions recognize that the threat of liability will disincentivize rescue attempts, so legislation typically provides legal immunity to Good Samaritans. In England for instance, the fact of an emergency is salient to the question of breach if Samaritans who "act heroically" are sued to recover damage.[2] In *The Incredibles* universe, we see a manifestation of the Good Samaritan issue in its most problematic form, represented in the United States by the 1964 murder of Catherine "Kitty" Genovese. Thirty-eight witnesses watched the killing of Genovese, none of whom intervened or called emergency services (Yamen, Carr, and Bartholomew 2019). Whilst the case generated copious sociological research on the "bystander effect" in legal policy, the refusal of bystanders to intervene for fear of legal repercussions is a well-known adverse consequence of tort litigation. This reflects a world in which superheroes are inhibited by the risk of liability.

Legal action against Mr. Incredible also presents a novel point in the type of harm caused to Sansweet when he attempts suicide by jumping from a building. Mr. Incredible's rescue means that Sansweet does not die by suicide but instead suffers injury and ongoing pain. The case against Mr. Incredible portrays the so-called "wrongful life" or "wrongful birth" cases, which ask the court to determine the value of a human life. Is it better to live in pain or die, and how can the court calculate the worth of the life? In the press scrum, Sansweet claims that Mr. Incredible did not "save his life," but rather "ruined [his] death" (Bird 2004). The recognition of a new type of harm in Sansweet's legal win could bring a floodgate of litigation, or even a new common law tort of "wrongful living" (Lynch et al. 2008). It is legitimate to ask whether "continued life" should be called "harm," and, in most jurisdictions, courts resist awarding damages merely for "life." Of course, when wrongful life arises from noncompliance with advance medical directives, the discussion revolves around recognition of personal autonomy (Lynch et al. 2008), but legally and medically "not intervening" in a person's death differs from actively contributing to it. In the absence of an advanced directive made in a condition of sound mind, it is legally precarious ground to assert that Mr. Incredible should provide compensation for Sansweet's life or lack of death.

Mr. Incredible's intervention in the L-Train incident also raises unprecedented issues around loss. If he had not intercepted the L-Train, passengers would have suffered certain death or severe harm, instead of the minor damage consistent with a sudden stop. The legal question is whether the harm would have occurred but for Mr. Incredible's act. Of course, stopping the train is a cause of the loss, but other events bring the accident about, and he is not responsible for them. He is far from the most culpable. At the very most, the sequence of events should result in apportionment of liability between wrongdoers in accordance with what the court considers the most just outcome, and given the emergency situation and lack of alternatives, Mr. Incredible may well have no liability at all.

The misalignment between wrongdoing and responsibility is also explored in the potentially novel liability of the government or regulatory agency, the National Supers Agency, for the actions of the Supers. This real-world issue, known as "third party" or "peripheral" liability, occurs when the injured person sues the less-culpable regulator rather than the actual wrongdoer. You could compare it with, say, the Environment Protection Authority being made liable for its failure to prevent polluters from polluting. This "growing feature of modern tort law" (Stapleton 1995, 311) threatens to diminish the link between blameworthiness and liability. As in *The Incredibles*, the "most troublesome form of this phenomenon" (Stapleton 1995, 311) arises when a person or authority is sued for failing to control the actions of another. According to Stapleton, two dangers result from the imposition of liability in this way: it "signal[s] a vast inhibition on freedom," and "deflects attention" from the primary wrongdoer (1995, 311). In the case of the L-Train injuries, primary culpability lies with Bomb Voyage, who robs a bank and smashes through a brick wall before Mr. Incredible intercepts him. However, Buddy Pine ("Incrediboy") distracts Mr. Incredible, compromises the arrest, and flies off, negligently failing to notice a bomb attached to his cape. He is the next most suitable defendant. Mr. Incredible's actions are morally, legally, and logically the least egregious. In the choices made by plaintiffs in litigation, however, the defendant with the most funds (usually the government) or with access to insurance will be preferable to the impecunious defendant or the defendant who cannot be found (as in the case of many crimes). Unless joint and several liability has been replaced by proportionality based on contribution to harm, the extension of liability to superheroes allows access to governmental, or potentially insurance, funds. Liability becomes detached from responsibility.

In *The Incredibles*, the role of the government, as represented by the shadowy National Supers Agency (NSA) and case worker Rick Dicker, is not explicitly framed. The courtroom scene (Figure 8.1) depicts Mr. Incredible in costume. His real identity remains secret, suggesting that he is not being sued in his personal capacity. It seems apparent that superheroes work for the government, which assumes responsibility for their activities. It is unclear whether supers are employees, agents, independent contractors, or unpaid volunteers. Prior to its prohibition, superhero activity is certainly tolerated, and, clearly, there is some expectation of reciprocity. The government, presumably through the NSA, compensates those injured in superhero interventions, covers relocation costs of ex-superheroes, and erases memories as part of the Superhero Relocation Program. According to the newspaper reports, "the Supers would be granted amnesty from responsibility for past actions, in exchange for the promise to never again resume hero work" (Bird 2004). We can infer, therefore, that the government has vicarious liability for the actions of the superheroes, in the same way an employer may be liable for the wrongdoing of an employee.

Figure 8.1. Screenshot of the Courtroom Scene (Bird 2004).

The conflation of the interests of the superhero with the government underlines the narrative of responsibility. Sable (2013) begins to address this point by describing *The Incredibles* as a "call to action, a film that argues that the exceptional powers of a family, and of a nation, should be used and not forgotten" (16). The film delineates the state's initial embrace of superpowers, a retreat from that position after the threat of liability, and a final resumption of superhero activity, with popular acceptance. The trigger for the narrative arc, the litigation against Mr. Incredible, centers on responsibility for the consequences of power. The precedential weight of this litigation, ironically, forces the responsibilization of the individual and the abandonment by the state of the protective role. The report in the (fictional) *Municiberg Tribune* reinforces the idea by noting the absence of superheroes in the response to tropical storm Andrews: "'This is the first storm we've had to bear the full brunt of in some time,' weatherman I. M. Guessing revealed" (Bird 2004). Once a plaintiff successfully argues that the government is legally responsible for injuries caused by superhero actions, the state vacates the protective role. Left without superhero/government protection, plaintiffs try to manage their risks through insurance. The insurer may then seek to minimize payouts (as we see in the scenes involving Parr's employer, Insuricare, considered later) and their future risks by changing the terms and conditions of insurance.

The Incredibles reframes the exploration of the proper repositories of power and responsibility that occurs in other superhero franchises. In *The Avengers* (Whedon 2012) universe, the political fallout from civilian casualties in Lagos prompts the Sokovia Accords, which brings superheroes under the auspices and discipline of a panel of the United Nations. The Keene Act (1977) prohibits vigilantism in *Watchmen* (Snyder et. al. 2009). There are significant parallels in the *X-Men* franchise, where prohibition of mutants drives the primary narrative. The television series *The Boys* (Kripke 2019) features superpowered individuals selected to be part of The Seven who do not work for the government but for a private corporation, Vought International. Damage to citizens arising from the actions of The Seven is managed by media manipulation and settlements brokered by lawyers. Many of those with special powers are portrayed as immoral and vicious.

The moral dissonance in many portrayals of the superhero emerges from the ambivalent attitude toward both state power and that arising from enhanced abilities. Superhero films explore both demand for and resistance to regulation of superheroes. *The Avengers* posits superpower as an analogy to weapons of mass destruction. Notably, *Captain America: Civil War* (Russo and Russo 2016) pits supporters of the Sokovia Accords, including Tony Stark, against perennial good guy Captain America, who has a strong motivation to resist state control after his experiences in World War II. *X-Men: First Class* (Shuler-Donner et. al. 2011), in an "appropriation of the Holocaust as an 'origin story'" (Smith 2017) depicts Magneto's negative attitudes toward government attempts to register and curb superpower as a legacy of the abuse he endured as a Jew in Hitler's Germany. The process by which power is managed differs between these franchises and *The Incredibles*. *The Incredibles* avoids the common tropes of rebellion against state power by exploring instead the manipulation of risk and responsibility and the banal realities of new modernity.

Issues of culpability and responsibility frame the overarching narrative of *The Incredibles*. Attribution of liability to Mr. Incredible alone appears an unjust instance of the plaintiffs managing their own exposure to risk by shifting the loss to the defendant deemed most able to absorb the cost—the government's insurers, via Mr. Incredible. In the reordering of power and authority, using the device of risk as the mechanism of change, the storyline illustrates Beck's risk society thesis. The next section will examine more closely the idea of risk in modernity and the apt placement of *The Incredibles* in the transition between first and second modernity.

ALLOCATION AND MANAGEMENT OF RISK IN A RISK SOCIETY

The themes of autonomy, relative culpability, legal liability, and management of risk in modern society demonstrate the "risk society" thesis, which theorizes that modernization has created new sources of risk, requiring a complex set of techniques to manage, deflect, and transfer it. Beck distinguishes between first modernity, which brought with it the risks of modern, industrial society, and second modernity, which brought "post-industrial, post-risk-calculation" (Ericson and Doyle 2004, 135). First modernity risks are calculable and therefore manageable, but those in second or reflexive modernity are "*un*natural, human-made, manufactured uncertainties" (Beck 2002, 41) since indeterminism and ambiguity are the hallmarks of second modernity. In a second modernity, new sources of uncertainty are not bound by national or social borders or temporal ranges (Ericson and Doyle 2004, 136). In demonstrating second modernity risks, *The Incredibles* captures 1950s anxieties about American and Russian superpowers kept in check only by the promise of mutually assured destruction. In that decade, risks "create social trouble regarding attributions of liability, accountability, responsibility, and response-ability" (Ericson and Doyle 2004, 136). In the denouement of *The Incredibles*, Syndrome's deployment of an Omnidroid against a city demonstrates these unmanageable risks, moving across national borders with incalculable potential damage and ungovernable costs. That the risks *are* unmanageable is emphasized by Syndrome's own inability to control his device.

Risk undermines the legitimacy of authority and results in the responsibilization of the individual to manage their own risks. In *The Incredibles*, this is represented by the government's abandonment of the protective role previously inhabited by superheroes, a vacuum that requires each person to take responsibility for themselves. In fact, the work sequences at Insuricare, Bob Parr's employer, demonstrate that a person is not well-placed to control and allocate risk because policy provisions, information, and resources all disproportionately benefit the insurer and work against the interests of the insured. In this way, insurers reconfigure risks and contribute to the uncertainty in risk assessment in pursuit of their own financial interests. Gilbert Huph, Parr's boss, says, "Don't tell me about their coverage. Tell me how you're keeping Insuricare in the black" (Bird 2004). Huph's instruction represents the pressure of conservative capitalism and a manifestation of neo-liberal governmentality. At a systemic scale, insurers can manage their own risk by using their political, contractual, and market power to rewrite their own exposure and take strategic litigation. By bringing test cases, settling claims to prevent the creation of adverse precedents, and writing one-sided insurance contracts, insurers actively control the litigation landscape. In *The Incredibles*, the government seeks to control its own exposure to litigation by decommissioning superheroes and absolving them of further liability. Similar interventions have occurred in various jurisdictions, where parliaments have legislated government immunity or capped insurer liability, often following a narrative constructed by the insurance industry itself, alongside its other litigation strategies. This situation is expressed by Dicker: "[F]rom now on, you're on your own" (Bird 2004).

CONSERVATIVE VALUES AND THE DISNEYVERSE

Beck's sociological perspective provides a subtle correction to the common analyses of Disney/Pixar films. Typically marketed to either the child or "the child in everyone" (Rojek 1993, 125), Disney has as its audience "that deathless, precious, ageless, absolutely primitive remnant" in everyone (Schickel 1986, 158). Some suggest that early animations present a world of leisure—not subject to rules (even the laws of physics), unconstrained by the necessity to work, lacking in any portrayal of sexuality, an "oleaginous realm where politics supposedly do not matter" (Rojek 1993, 124)—and people exist "beyond good and evil" (Eisenstein and Leyda 1986, 9). Pointedly, Eisenstein (Eisenstein and Leyda 1986, 4) describes animation as a "marvellous lullaby" a sentiment which seems "within a hair's breadth of the notoriously negative 'opiate of the masses'" (Nesbet 1997, 22). Key to its effectiveness is the viewer's obliviousness to the social conditioning occurring throughout Disney's works. But Disney's immense cultural capital renders it an appropriate subject for critical analysis. Recognizing the potency of his brand, particularly in view of the vulnerable target audience, critics scrutinize Disney's conservative values, traditional gender roles, and racism. Cappiccie et al. (2012) note that "Disney has long been viewed as promoting a culture of childhood innocence, protected space, and wholesome family fun" (49) but it is not free of ideology. Rojek (1993, 121) argues that Disney films "support a specific moral order which is heavily moralistic." Portrayals of individual freedom and self-help idealize the "American Way."

A similar critique of conservative stereotypes can be directed at Pixar's *The Incredibles*. At least at first, Mr. Incredible represents a prototype of

American masculinity: his superpower is strength, his body type characteristic of the alpha mesomorphic male, the superhero V-shape of Superman, Captain America, and Batman. The exaggerated muscular physique "portray[s] traits that include power, dominance, strength, sexual virility, and self-esteem" (Baghurst et al. 2006, 87). He is hypercompetitive: as a superhero, he "works alone" (Bird 2004). At home, Bob is the sole breadwinner and suffers from "the emotional isolation of the alpha male" (Gillam and Wooden 2008, 2), required to be reliable and resilient. *The Incredibles* also presents a conservative stereotype of the family unit, recalling Beck's first modernity transitioning into second. They eat dinner together in nightly isolation, typical of the American nuclear family (Sussman 1959). The modernist design of the family home represents the 1950s architectural style, and, in terms of form, incorporates "modern and abstract art and images and furniture, pastel colours [and an] emphasis on home wares. . . . [You] can almost smell the Tupperware" (Hill 2005). This Pixar portrayal aligns with Rojek's view of Disney culture, which reflects "a particular and historical form of white, capitalist society" (1993, 122) and normalizes the social order portrayed.

Other critics, however, note the subversion of stereotypes in Pixar's offerings. In *The Incredibles*, the house design and interior unsettle the apparent critique but in a highly nuanced manner. Rather than the idealized image, the film presents a "sanitized" version of what a "normal" 1950s family and home would look like. The depiction of Eichler's architecture emphasizes hopeful modernity and the normality of the middle-class, planned community (Adamson 2001), but Bob Parr seems constantly at war with his house. He is too large for the space. The plywood of the Charles Eames style chairs and the slim legs and pinched dimensions of the dining room put him at odds with his surroundings. His car is absurdly small. Normality literally cramps him.

Conservative messaging more profound than its depiction of inadept American masculinity arises from the risk analysis in the narrative arc of *The Incredibles*. Some proffer that the criticism of the regulation and marginalization of superheroes is a position of resistance to any form of government restriction of the individual, an "intolerance for anything less than perfect human autonomy" (Nadesan 2013, 27) and "an Ayn Randian or scientologist notion of the special people who must resist social pressures to suppress their superpowers in order to fit in with the drab masses" (Halberstam 2011, 47). The concern for the hurt feelings of the superheroes clearly intends to evoke the sympathy of the audience to "justify sentimentally the competitive hierarchical values of a system that distributes rewards and penalties unequally, without apology and without concern for the inevitable losers. . . . The cries for emancipation of the gifted seem like upscale whining, the piteous complaints of the most favoured and privileged among us" (B. Beck 2005, 22). In *The Incredibles*, the newspaper critiques in the comic universe itself subvert the narrative around the duty to rescue. Fictional journalist Stan Tahl, in a column entitled "Super Menace to Society," argues that "[w]hatever forces granted them unique abilities that set them apart from the rest of normal society, it does [sic] not grant them the right to exercise those same abilities in the name of protecting others" (Bird 2004). Superhero activities, rather than conceptualized as a civic duty, are described as a private right. In framing the tension in this way, critics choose to identify the use of power as selfish and illegal, rather than an act of service. Mr. Incredible and the other banished Supers might demonstrate the anomie and alienation resulting from a conflict of moral worldview. Mr. Incredible considers rescue an obligation. *The Incredibles* has thus been criticized for denoting a negative attitude about government regulation of superheroes with a "right-wing dystopia of a kind generally associated with Ayn Rand's ideas: an oppressive regulatory regime [glorifying] a utopian 'free' capitalist economy in contrast" (Lauer 2013, 35). Meinel (2014) detects American exceptionalist logic in the denial of recognition to superheroes but argues that *The Incredibles* actually "ushers in a neo-liberal paradigm" which subverts and undermines American exceptionalism (193). Mr. Incredible is no longer confined to American soil, and the new order is based on individual competition, illustrated by Syndrome's selection of the most powerful of all superheroes in trial by battle.

Critical analyses aligning *The Incredibles* with Randian support of laissez-faire capitalism are misplaced. Clearly, the government originally supports superheroes through the NSA and pays compensation for damage caused by their activity. "[L]itigation [becomes] a regulatory device as a result of courts more frequently issuing decisions with widespread regulatory effects" (Luff 2011, 74). The neoliberal paradigm that creates the tort law crisis is not depicted positively, despite the suggestions of critics. Risk management does its work through indirect oversight. It is a form of governance at a distance and manipulation of governmental forms by private industry, rather than the leveling influence of progressive government. This manifestation of risk-shifting strategies mediated by contracts (for employment and insurance, as well as for provision of government services) and by government retreat from a range of activities signals the refusal to take responsibility for the acts of superheroes, leaving individuals to look after themselves.

CONCLUSION

This chapter reflects upon the legal context in which superheroes in *The Incredibles* are made liable for the ramifications of their socially motivated actions and then prohibited from exercising their superpowers. The animation presents parallels to tort law and its reform in various western jurisdictions and illustrates the shifting ground between autonomy and responsibility. The narrative suggests that the trend to emphasize autonomy, which mirrors the tendency in the real world, leads to the individualization of risk (resulting in the dominance of insurance companies) and the retreat of the government. Pixar and the Disneyverse have been subjected to critical analysis in proportion to their influence and the vulnerability of their audience. However, contrary to the typical critique that these movies promote ideologically conservative values, Pixar's *The Incredibles* represents a highly sophisticated and grounded analysis of risk allocation in second modernity. Beck's analysis of the responsibilization of the individual for risks provides a useful lens with which to view the anomie of the unwanted superhero. The individual is poorly situated to negotiate risk against the capacities of the government, large corporations, and insurers, who manage cascading effects of litigation. The childish desire to return to pre-modernity values where a "superhero" protects the individual is an unsurprising result of the individualization of risk.

NOTES

1. In some jurisdictions, notably civil systems, there is an obligation to rescue, or even to intervene to assist those in dangerous circumstances (Yamen,

Carr, and Bartholomew 2019). This has been incorporated into jurisdictions with similar legal bases (French civil law) such as in the Province of Quebec, where there is a legal duty to rescue arising from Quebec's *Charter of Human Rights and Freedoms* (1975, Article 2).

2. See the *Social Action, Responsibility and Heroism Act* (2015). See also in New South Wales, Australia the *Civil Liability Act* (2002); in Victoria, Australia the *Wrongs Act* (1958).

REFERENCES

Adamson, Paul. 2001. "California Modernism and the Eichler homes." *The Journal of Architecture* 6, no. 1: 1–25. https://doi.org/10.1080/13602360010024804.

Baghurst, Timothy, Daniel B. Hollander, Beth Nardella, G. Gregory Haff. 2006. "Change in Sociocultural Ideal Male Physique: An Examination of Past and Present Action Figures." *Body Image* 3, no. 1: 87–91. https://doi.org/10.1016/j.bodyim.2005.11.001.

Beck, Bernard. 2005. "It's a Gift: Ray, *The Incredibles* and Lives of Greatness." *Multicultural Perspectives* 7, no. 3: 20–23. https://doi.org/10.1207/s15327892mcp0703_4.

Beck, Ulrich. 1992. *Risk Society—Towards a New Modernity*. London: Sage.

———. 2002. "The Terrorist Threat: World Risk Society Revisited." *Theory Culture and Society* 19, no. 4: 39–55. https://doi.org/10.1177/0263276402019004003.

Bird, Brad, dir. *The Incredibles*. 2004; United States: Buena Vista Pictures.

———. *Incredibles 2*. 2018; United States: Walt Disney Pictures.

Caffrey, Denise. 1975. "United States v. CBS: When Sketch Artists Are Allowed in the Courtroom, Can Photographers Be Far Behind?" *Duke Law Journal* 188–205. https://www.jstor.org/stable/1372101.

Cappiccie, Amy, Janice Chadha, Muh Bi Lin, and Frank Snyder. 2012. "Using Critical Race Theory to Analyze How Disney Constructs Diversity: A Construct for the Baccalaureate Human Behavior in the Social Environment Curriculum." *Journal of Teaching in Social Work* 32, no. 1: 46–61. https://doi.org/10.1080/08841233.2012.640252.

Charter of Human Rights and Freedoms 1975 (Quebec).

Civil Liability Act 2002 (New South Wales).

Donoghue v. Stevenson [1932] A.C. 562.

Eisenstein, Sergei and Jay Leyda. 1986. *Eisenstein on Disney*. Translated by Alan Upchurch. Calcutta: Seagull Books.

Ericson, Richard V. and Aaron Doyle. 2004. "Catastrophe Risk, Insurance and Terrorism." *Economy and Society* 33, no. 2: 135–73. https://doi.org/10.1080/03085140410001677102.

Gillam, Ken and Shannon R. Wooden. 2008. "Post-Princess Models of Gender: The New Man in Disney/Pixar." *Journal of Popular Film and Television* 36, no. 1: 2–8. https://doi.org/10.3200/JPFT.36.1.2-8.

Gordon, Gerald L. 1965. "Moral Challenge to the Legal Doctrine of Rescue." *Cleveland-Marshall Law Review* 14, no. 2: 334–55.

Halberstam Jack. 2011. *The Queer Art of Failure*. Durham: Duke University Press.

Hill, Michael J. 2005. "A Home for Heroes: The Incredibles Domestic Design." *UTS: Design, Architecture and Building, Symposium Papers—Imaginary Worlds* 1–17. http://hdl.handle.net/10453/1405.

Kripke Eric, dir. *The Boys*. Season 1, Aired July 26, 2019, on Prime.

Lauer, Emily. 2013. "Coming of Age in Dystopia." In *Contemporary Dystopian Fiction for Young Adults: Brave New Teenagers*, edited by Balaka Basu, Katherine R. Broad, Carrie Hintz, 47–62. New York: Routledge.

Lee, J. D., and Barry A Lindahl. 2017. *Modern Tort Law: Liability and Litigation*. Thomson Reuters.

Lopez, Victor D., and Eugene T. Maccarrone. 2017–2018. "Should Emergency Good Deeds Go Unpunished: An Analysis of the Good Samaritan Statutes of the United States." *Rutgers Law Record* 45: 105–44.

Luff, Patrick. 2011. "Risk Regulation and Regulatory Litigation." *Rutgers Law Review* 64, no. 1 (Fall): 73–116.

Lynch, Holly Fernandez, Michele Mathes and Nadia N. Sawicki. 2008. "Compliance with Advance Directives." *The Journal of Legal Medicine* 29, no. 2: 133–78. https://doi.org/10.1080/01947640802080298

Meinel, Dietmar. 2014. "'And When Everyone Is Super [. . .] No One Will Be': The Limits of American Exceptionalism in *The Incredibles*." *European Journal of American Culture* 33, no. 1: 181–94. https://doi.org/10.1386ejac.33.3.181_1.

Nadesan, Majia Holmer. 2013. "Autism: Profit, Risk, and Bare Life." In *Worlds of Autism: Across the Spectrum of Neurological Difference*, edited by Joyce Davidson and Michael Orsini, 117–42. Minneapolis: University of Minnesota Press.

Nesbet, Anna. 1997. "Inanimations: Snow White and Ivan the Terrible." *Film Quarterly* 50, no. 4: 20–31.

Rojek, Chris. 1993. "Disney Culture." *Leisure Studies* 12, no. 2: 121–35. https://doi.org/10.1080/02614369300390111.

Russo, Joe, and Anthony Russo, dir. *Captain America: Civil War*. 2016; United States: Walt Disney Studios Motion Pictures.

Sable, Anna. 2013. "Passing on Democracy: A Look at Discourse in Post-911 Animated Film." *Summer Research* 199. http://soundideas.pugetsound.edu/summer_research/199.

Schickel, Richard. 1986. *The Disney Version: The Life, Times, Art and Commerce of Walt Disney*. London: Pavillion Books.

Shuler-Donner, Lauren, Sheldon Turner, Bryan Singer, Ashley Edward Miller, Matthew Vaughn, James McAvoy, Jennifer Lawrence, Kevin Bacon, Michael Fassbender, and Henry Jackman, dir. *X-Men*. 2011; Beverly Hills, CA: 20th Century Fox Home Entertainment.

Smith, J.C. and Peter Burns. 1983. "Donoghue v. Stevenson: The Not So Golden Anniversary." *The Modern Law Review* 42, no. 2: 147–63. https://www.jstor.org/stable/1095489.

Smith, Scott Thompson. 2017. "A Likely Jew: Magneto, the Holocaust, and Comic-Book History." *Studies in American Jewish Literature* 36, no. 1: 1–39.

Snyder, Zack, Lawrence Gordon, Lloyd Levin, Deborah Snyder, David Hayter, Alex Tse, Malin Akerman, et al., dir. *Watchmen*. 2009; United States: Warner Brothers.

Social Action, Responsibility and Heroism Act 2015 (UK).

Stapleton, Jane. 1995. "Duty of Care: Peripheral Parties and Alternative Opportunities for Deterrence." *Law Quarterly Review* 111: 301–45.

Sussman, Marvin B. 1959. "The Isolated Nuclear Family: Fact or Fiction." *Social Problems* 6, no. 4: 333–40.

Swartzman, Leora C., Robert W. Teasell, Allan P. Shapiro, Ann J. McDermid. 1996. "The Effect of Litigation Status on Adjustment to Whiplash Injury." *SPINE* 21, no. 1: 53–58.

Whedon, Joss, dir. *The Avengers*. 2012; United States: Walt Disney Studios Motion Pictures.

Wrongs Act 1958 (Victoria).

Yamen, Sharon., Nanci K. Carr and Aaron Bartholomew. 2019. "Am I My Brother's Keeper: How Technology Necessitates Reform of the Lack of Duty to Rescue or Duty to Report Laws in the United States." *Boston University Public Interest Law Journal* 28, no. 2: 117–46.

9

OUT THERE

Science Fiction and Surveillance in Pixar's
WALL-E and Up

Farisa Khalid

WALL-E (2008) and *Up* (2009), two of Pixar's most innovative films, are prime examples of how contemporary three-dimensional computer animation can create vivid world-building within the realm of fantasy and speculative filmmaking. They are entertaining, bittersweet, coming-of-age adventure films that deal with death, grief, and loneliness in profound ways. David Denby, in his 2009 *New Yorker* review of *Up*, observes that "[t]hese [Pixar] movies are fashioned as much for adults as for kids . . . they are built around an exhilarating drive for achievement." This chapter examines how WALL-E and *Up* demonstrate Pixar's engagement with the science fiction (SF) genre to offer salient commentary on contemporary themes: surveillance, the abuse of corporate power, and environmental destruction at the hands of corporations and unscrupulous individuals. The first part of the chapter focuses on WALL-E, its adherence to SF genre conventions, and its satirical depiction of consumerism and surveillance. The second half analyzes *Up*, particularly how the film functions as an adventure story and a critique of surveillance.

Released nearly fifteen years ago, WALL-E and *Up* are still among the most original of Disney and Pixar's animated films. The two films also mark a shift in Pixar's storytelling. During the early 2000s, Pixar directors moved away from their characteristic style developed by chief creative officer John Lasseter. The Lasseter approach endured unabated for a decade, from *Toy Story* (1995) to *A Bug's Life* (1998) to *Cars* (2006), which are all coming-of-age stories of masculine reawakening. However, in the years after 9/11, filmmakers at the studio realized that they needed a fresher story model for animated feature films that differed from the typical Lasseter narrative (that had succeeded so well in *Cars*, a nostalgic carryover from the late 1990s Pixar films that was becoming repetitive) They began to develop material considered more inclusive of the experiences of young audiences forced to adapt to new geopolitical realities after 9/11.

WALL-E and *Up*, produced and released after the terrorist attacks of September 11, 2001, reflect the anxieties and fears of the post-9/11 age when the United States government increased its surveillance apparatus both domestically and abroad. The prevalence of portable technology, such as cell phones, PDAs, and digital cameras that contained personal images, data, and consumer habits, enabled government agencies to monitor the public with greater ease. Strangers could easily seize, in an instant, another person's photograph. Corporations could almost effortlessly obtain a person's internet history. Identities became increasingly tied to online data patterns. With the establishment of the Department of Homeland Security in November 2002, and in partnership with the National Security Agency (NSA), the United States government intensified surveillance across the country. In January 2006, Mark Klein, a former AT&T engineer and whistleblower, revealed details of AT&T's cooperation with the NSA in installing network hardware to monitor, capture, and process telecommunications. This smoking-gun evidence revealed that the United States government spied on its citizens (Shorrock 2008, 311). In July 2008, the United States Congress voted to override the rights of Americans to petition for a redress of grievances, thereby absolving the NSA and AT&T of any culpability (Lee 2015, 154). In June 2013, the *Guardian* and *The Washington Post* revealed that the U.S. government, through the NSA and various telecommunications companies, notably Verizon, Facebook, and Google, monitored millions of people across the world without their consent. The details came to the forefront of media scrutiny thanks to the efforts of an NSA whistleblower, Edward Snowden, a then twenty-nine-year-old cybersecurity specialist and subcontractor (Annis 2018, 23). Because of Snowden's disclosures, people worldwide could engage in an unprecedented debate about government surveillance.

Pixar, founded by Edwin Catmull, Alvy Ray Smith, and Apple co-founder Steve Jobs in 1986, has a history tied to the development of computer technology, enabling its filmmakers to understand more fully the omnipotence of telecommunications (Paik 2015, 9). The Pixar films made after 2001 reflect the heightened anxieties of their contemporary moment, particularly the abuse of surveillance. Movies such as *Monsters, Inc.* (2001), *Toy Story 3* (2010), *Incredibles 2* (2018), and *Toy Story 4* (2019) demonstrate the abuses of corporate systems and individuals who manipulate surveillance for immoral purposes. The characters exploit surveillance technology do so to curtail individual liberties while creating climates of paranoia and fear: Mr. Waternoose (*Monsters, Inc.*), the Buy-N-Large corporation and Auto (*WALL-E*), Lots-O'-Huggin' Bear (*Toy Story 3*), Evelyn Deavor/"Screenslaver" (*Incredibles 2*), and Gabby Gabby (*Toy Story 4*). Incorporating this trenchant critique of surveillance while still creating palatable stories for young audiences challenged Pixar filmmakers in the post-9/11 era. One solution was to draw upon conventions of science fiction.

SF's ability to combine scientific enquiry with adventure, the real with the surreal, and the probable with the improbable, makes it an ideal vehicle to examine the effects of surveillance within the format of the animated film. During the late nineteenth century, the science fiction romances of Jules Verne and H.G. Wells, serialized in Victorian periodicals such as *The Boy's Own Paper*, inspired boys to equate the genre with the robustness of imperial adventure fiction (Spinrad 1990, xiv). Between the 1920s and the 1960s, these types of adventure stories found their way to science fiction pulp magazines, such as *Wonder Stories* and *Amazing Stories*, reappropriating the tropes of Victorian imperialist masculinity into a suitable vehicle for American boys in a country poised to take Britain's geopolitical place after World War One (Svilpis 1983; Adams 1990). The science fiction adventure story, a type of didactic literature, entertains as well as educates.

Traditionally, SF has provided insight into humans' relationship with technology and their dreams and nightmares of the future. It often presents an alternative view of technological progress from which to judge the effects of society's evolution. SF and its subgenre, the adventure story, provide rich formats where animated films with complex themes about technology and futurism can be marketed to children. It is not surprising that Pixar animators would turn to the SF narrative model for some of their feature films given the studio's dependence on science and technology. Lasseter claimed that there were two major turning points in the history of animation in the United States: the release of Disney's first feature-length animated film in 1937, *Snow White and the Seven Dwarfs*, and then the 1977 premier of George Lucas's SF space opera *Star Wars* (Neupert 2016, 170–71). Lasseter felt the narrative template of Lucas's films would set the foundation for integrating computer technology and animation into mainstream commercial filmmaking. In the early 2000s, after the release of the first of Lucas's *Star Wars* prequels, *The Phantom Menace* (1999), animation studios, reawakened to the commercial viability of SF, produced various films within the genre: *Atlantis: The Lost Empire* (2001) and *Treasure Planet* (2002), both produced by Disney, and *Titan: A.E.* (2000), produced by Fox. *WALL-E* and *Up* were Pixar's entries into the growing body of SF animated films of the early 2000s. While *WALL-E* is a traditional SF film, like *2001: A Space Odyssey* (1968), *Up* falls more within the subcategory of the adventure story, which has counterparts in works like Jules Verne's *Journey to the Center of the Earth* (1864) and Arthur Conan Doyle's *The Lost World* (1912).

Science fiction also provides a mode of enquiry into environmental abuses and ecocritical concerns, themes with which both *WALL-E* and *Up* engage. *WALL-E* depicts a futuristic society set in the year 2805 A.D. where people's slavish reliance on technology disconnects them from the natural world. *Up* is also work of ecological science fiction, where nature, exemplified by beleaguered and oppressed animals, rebels against the abuse of technology. The films have strong environmental messages where each story involves the last of a species—a plant and a bird, respectively—being rescued by reluctant loners pulled out of their routine existences by those needing help. This message is more pronounced in *WALL-E*, which critiques corporate greed, than it is in *Up*, where the threat of natural destruction comes from an individual, not a corporation. The villains in each film use surveillance technology to monitor and control their enclosed environments: the spaceship, the

Axiom, and Paradise Falls in Venezuela. These surveillance-controlled ecosystems, fantastical panopticons, are also dystopian worlds. The main characters' missions are tied to their rebellion against the disciplining mechanisms of their heavily monitored spaces and to protecting the Earth (*WALL-E*) and an endangered animal (*Up*). The films use common SF tropes, such as the generation spaceship, the sentience of artificial intelligence, the mad scientist/explorer, and the mysterious island, to examine the dangers of totalitarianism for the environment, individual, and society. The power of technology is not necessarily the problem, but rather, the technology of power.

WALL-E, a science fiction epic set seven hundred years in the future, consciously draws on a tradition of dystopian narratives written by H. G. Wells and George Orwell. The film, a blistering satire of capitalism and mass consumption, shows how over the course of seven hundred years, people, through their endless need to spend and consume, have polluted the planet so that it is no longer habitable. The air is not fit for breathing, and cities drown in mountains of garbage. In what initially seems like a humanitarian effort, the CEO of Buy-N-Large (BnL) proposes that the large multinational corporation saves the last living humans by whisking them away to space in rescue ships that double as pleasure cruises while Buy-N-Large robots attempt the Sisyphean task of clearing Earth's mountains of waste. The film opens in the twenty-ninth century where a lone robot named WALL-E (referred to by his functional acronym for Waste Allocation Load Lifter, Earth-Class), the last of its kind, remains on Earth clearing and compacting garbage in isolation. The people float in space on the last Buy-N-Large ship, the *Axiom*, unaware that they are condemned to spend their lives trapped in a cycle of eating, spending, and sloth. The film's plot revolves around a solitary photosynthetic plant, which WALL-E nurtures and guards, after discovering it hidden amid the rubble of Earth. Then, a new robot arrives on Earth, the sleek, shiny EVE (Extraterrestrial Vegetation Evaluator), sent to retrieve viable traces of plant life. WALL-E, has human desires and falls in love with EVE. A great deal of the quest involves the struggle of EVE and WALL-E to get the plant into the ship's holo-detector, which will program the engine to return to Earth so those aboard the *Axiom* can live on the rejuvenated planet.

The passengers on the *Axiom* have become habituated to generations of physical and mental degeneration. They embody the nightmare of science fiction's obsession with Darwinian theories of evolution and natural selection, in which *Homo sapiens*, rather than progressing into adaptive physical strength, regress into infantile physical uselessness. For example, Captain B. McCrea (Jeff Garlin) is the latest in a long line of captains who has manned the *Axiom*. Each one has deteriorated as they have grown increasingly more dependent on the ship's technology. Like everyone else aboard the *Axiom* who no longer needs to use their bodies for active survival because Buy-N-Large supplies them with all their needs, McCrea has become an obese, amorphous, blob-like being transported across the ship on a hovercraft.

In its depiction of Buy-N-Large, *WALL-E* cleverly moves from an innocent animated feature film to a scathing critique of corporate greed, presenting a disturbing portrait of the abuse of technology and surveillance through the comedy of commercialism run amok. The Buy-N-Large sponsored pleasure cruise, the *Axiom*, is a mall but also a prison, a Noah's Ark as well as a factory that perpetuates consumerist desire in order to maintain control over its population. The dystopian environment grossly illustrates neoliberal corporate penalization and the privatization of social control. The *Axiom*'s structural model of power hearkens back to the panopticon, the circular utilitarian building conceived by the late eighteenth-century philosopher and social theorist Jeremy Bentham (1784–1832) and cited as an instrument of institutional authority by Michel Foucault in *Discipline and Punish* ([1975] 1995). The holo-screens, administered from the ship's central computer, regulate all activities from the education and indoctrination of children to retail, housing, and hospitality-related needs, while also monitoring passengers at the same time. Bentham's hope was that the prisoners in his panopticon, who never knew exactly when they were being watched, would eventually learn to police themselves. This programmed behavior would, in turn, facilitate state-sanctioned conduct across all sectors of society (Richardson 2015, 143).

The dystopian society aboard the *Axiom* is a satire of the familiar spaces of corporatized leisure, of shopping malls, cruises, megastores, and theme parks, designed to stultify and lull the public into a lazy stupor, so that it is eager for relentless consumption. An army of robot managerial and administrative staff assiduously watch over the humans on the *Axiom* and tend to all of their demands and desires under the strict orders of Buy-N-Large. Michel de Certeau, in *The Practice of Everyday Life* (1984), observes how organizations utilize tactics to manipulate people within certain spaces. This division of space "makes possible a panoptic practice proceeding from a place whence the eye can transform foreign forces into objects that can be observed and measured to 'include' them within its scope of vision" (de Certeau 1984, 36). The simultaneity of vision associated with the panopticon provides the satiric bite of the film's critique of rampant capitalism. Eric Herhuth explains that the type of social control depicted revolves around the fact that "a large part of human nature is about administering the contingencies of life and managing fear . . . [h]ence the *Axiom* is essentially a cruise ship on which all aspects of life are administered" (2014, 65). As a dystopian narrative, *WALL-E* highlights how the rapid development of posthuman technology, according to the requirements of capitalist profit, will have a profoundly disturbing effect on the world. The factory-like conditions of labor and monitoring on the cruise/ark are modeled on the assembly line practices of Frederick Winslow Taylor, which Henry Ford and others adopted to help make the modern industrial state. Much of the comic pantomime that occurs when WALL-E stows away on the *Axiom* and disrupts the Buy-N-Large robots' preordained mechanized routine pays homage to other parodies of Taylorist manufacturing, like Charlie Chaplin's *Modern Times* (1936) and *The Simpsons* (1989– present) (Flaig 2016). The Buy-N-Large model of consumption and monitoring is a comic look at Taylorist retail surveillance at the expense of civil liberties.

The main antagonist in *WALL-E* is the *Axiom*'s ship's steering wheel, named Auto. A classic example of "artificial intelligence gone rogue" in science fiction cinema, Auto is based on HAL 9000 in Stanley Kubrick's *2001: A Space Odyssey*. Like HAL, Auto demonstrates humans' fear of the unpredictable and potentially dangerous sentience of machines, which has been detailed in the SF writings of Karel Čapek and Philip K. Dick: one day the machine created to serve humans will revolt against its masters. Auto is white and black with a solitary red laser "eye," similar to HAL's laser eye. Both also have mellow, monotone male voices and are programmed with commands that cannot be overridden. In Auto's case, secret directive A113, ordered by Buy-N-Large's former CEO, dictates its behavior, even if Captain McCrea tries to supersede it in the best interest of all those aboard the ship. Thus, Auto attempts to destroy the plant that EVE and WALL-E find because he wants to keep the *Axiom* floating in space to sustain Buy-N-Large's control. In doing so, the robot maintains its power on the ship.

In dystopian science fiction narratives, one of the ways in which characters resist totalitarianism is by using surveillance against itself. EVE's introduction of the plant to Captain McCrea, and Auto's subsequent attempt to destroy it, inspire McCrea to veer from his prescribed Buy-N-Large sanctioned routine and research sustainable plant life on Earth. Accessing the ship computer's encyclopedic database and archival videos of waterfalls, forests, and couples line-dancing, McCrea discovers the potential happiness of people living peacefully on land as they nurture their home planet. Among EVE's storage files, McCrea finds the clips EVE recorded during her brief time on Earth, including one from WALL-E's precious video collection: a sample of the musical number "Put On Your Sunday Clothes" from the 1969 film version of *Hello, Dolly!* As McCrea watches the video, he is inspired by the concept of dancing and moving, which he has been unable to do while living on a hovercraft aboard a starliner. As he taps his fat, unused toes, he looks down at them, then at the boot that holds the plant, and finally at the plant itself. WALL-E's media archive causes McCrea to understand the essential symbiotic relationship between humans and nature that can only be sustained on Earth. Like WALL-E at the beginning of the film, McCrea's curiosity and longing, initiated by archival media and surveillance footage, stimulates a desire to leave the safe, stultifying confines of the *Axiom* and to explore Earth as humanity's future home.

When Captain McCrea defies Auto and decides to steer the *Axiom* to Earth, Auto's survivalist instinct, like HAL 9000's, activates and the computer becomes aggressive. The war of wills between McCrea and Auto culminates with McCrea's effort to regain his agency and consciousness against the power of the posthuman machine. Eric Herhuth observes that "Captain B. McCrea is the only human character in an authoritative position over the ship's technologies, and it is he who must physically battle with Auto" (2014, 69). In the case of a controlling computer like Auto, Marcia Landy remarks that "the computer brain may be superior to the human brain in its speed of computation, accuracy, and logical thinking, but [its] coexistence with human beings also [makes it] vulnerable to human error. What is presented is not a simplistic binary vision of the war of man against the machine but a profound interrogation of man's wisdom in dominating the computer brain" (2006, 97).

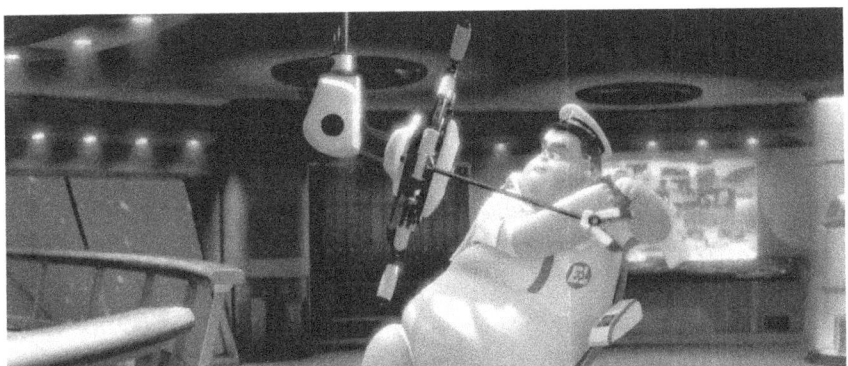

Figure 9.1. *Captain B. McCrea of the* Axiom *attempts to resist the authority of the ship's autopilot, Auto (Stanton 2008).*

Another instance in which surveillance leads to a productive outcome occurs when the robots use the *Axiom*'s cameras against its totalitarian operators. After EVE and WALL-E evade Auto's attempt to destroy them and the plant, they rush back into the ship as their faces are splashed across every holo-screen with the caption, "Warning: Rogue Robots" in the manner of a "wanted" poster. When Captain McCrea sees the flashing images, he starts up the vanity console and projects himself on the holo-screens so that he can instruct EVE and WALL-E about where to take the plant, in defiance of Auto's authority. Here, the heightened surveillance inspires McCrea to assert his authority against the malevolent machine. His manipulation of the computer is an example of the subversion of surveillance in which the human actor, who has been reduced to a small cog within a vast network of technological control, regains his autonomy by impairing the tools used to oppress him. Another part of the heroism of the story involves EVE's rebellion against the capitalist totalitarian order which created her. She develops morality in her desire to save the plant. By the end of the film, the good robots and the captain prevail, and the blob-like *Homo sapiens* aboard the *Axiom* can rebuild life on the parched planet one plant at a time. WALL-E and EVE, the robot equivalents of their biblical forebears, return to the garden to enable it to thrive. Ironically, the robots humanize the humans. This type of heroism also occurs in *Up* as the protagonists struggle to survive and escape the restricting panoptic confines of an isolated tropical setting, which mirrors the claustrophobic seclusion of outer space in *WALL-E*.

While *WALL-E* tells a romantic story set within a technological dystopia, *Up*, released a year later, focuses on friendship amid a tropical, nightmarish landscape. At the center of *Up* is Carl Fredricksen (Ed Asner), a curmudgeonly widower and retired balloon salesman. We first see him in a flashback as a schoolboy (Jeremy Leary) in the 1930s watching a black-and-white newsreel. In it, his hero, the explorer Charles F. Muntz (Christopher Plummer), has recently returned from an uninhabited region of South America called Paradise Falls, having completed a year-long study of the island. Muntz is proud of his discovery, the skeleton of a thirteen-foot-tall tropical bird, whom he calls "The Monster of Paradise Falls." However, scientists claim the specimen is a fake. Muntz is forcibly removed from his position at the National Explorers Society. Vowing that he will be vindicated, Muntz returns to Paradise Falls to obtain a live version of the bird.

The black-and-white film ends, and the narrative shifts to Carl's childhood. He and his tomboyish sweetheart Ellie (Elie Docter) dream of emulating their idol Muntz. Carl and Ellie marry and spend over fifty years together. After her death, Carl stubbornly insists on staying put because their beloved Victorian house symbolizes her presence. When property developers threaten to take the house, Carl accidentally injures a builder, is considered a danger to the public, and is ordered to live in a retirement home. Rebelling against this decision, Carl attaches hundreds of colored balloons to his home and takes off for Paradise Falls. However, Russell (Jordan Ngai), a nine-year-old Wilderness Explorer scout, stows away on Carl's porch. At Paradise Falls, Carl and Russell befriend two animals, a brightly colored female tropical bird, whom Russell calls "Kevin," and a friendly but dim Golden Retriever named Dug (Bob Peterson), who belongs to Charles Muntz. In his nineties, Muntz still searches for the bird, which he believes will restore his reputation. It turns out that the "Monster of Paradise Falls" is none other than Kevin, whom Muntz wants to capture and eventually kill. Realizing that he must save Kevin, Dug, and Russell from Muntz's cruelty, Carl learns to cope with his grief and let go of his bitterness. He discovers the son he never had in Russell and his own youthfulness by fulfilling the adventure that he and Ellie dreamt of in their childhoods.

We first see the role of surveillance in the film in the form of the austere real-estate developer in charge of the neighborhood's urban renewal project, a thin figure in a black suit and sunglasses who constantly watches Carl, trying to intimidate him into selling his house. Under observation by the developer, Carl eventually loses his temper and hits a construction worker. This rash act of violence injures the worker and causes him to bleed. The developer then places a hand on Carl's fence, conveying that the house will soon be his: Big Brother watching from the other side of the window. The court orders Carl to be sent to a retirement home. On its promotional brochure, Shady Oaks Retirement Home appears to be a benevolent place. However, to Carl, it seems like a prison. The Shady Oaks nurses, A.J. and George, wear blue scrubs, uniforms of conformity that signify how the process of care for the elderly is a form of social control. Carl's reluctance to go to Shady Oaks is also part of his inability to accept his integration into larger communities of inclusion. His grief over Ellie compels him to be an egotistical, reclusive loner, like his boyhood hero, Muntz.

Muntz, like Auto, has an obsessive desire to surveil and control the environment around him. In *Up*'s narrative of personal growth and redemption, screenwriters Peter Docter and Bob Peterson craft an adventure story in the mold of those by Verne and Wells. Muntz is a neo-Gothic villain who conforms to the patterns of late Victorian science fiction antiheroes like Captain Nemo and Doctor Moreau, whose desire to master the surrounding physical landscape, in the ocean or jungle, compels them towards murderous actions as they are controlled by their egos. Muntz's persona as an explorer is also based in part on aviators like Charles Lindbergh and Howard Hughes.

The masculine charisma which he demonstrates at the beginning of the film gives way to his dark, murderous desires. Lilian Munk Rösing notes how Muntz's "gestures, his moustache, the enthusiastic crowd" depicted in his 1930s newsreel "give to his amplified voice the connotations of a dictator's" (2015, 151). Like Howard Hughes, Muntz is consumed by obsession. Carl's idolization of his boyhood hero fades as he begins to comprehend Muntz's madness. Muntz reveals to Carl that over the years he has killed several men, whom he suspected of trying to steal his glory. "The 'Surveyor' making a map . . . a 'Botanist' cataloguing plants," Muntz says, menacingly, as he knocks over a series of flight helmets, which fall to the floor like hollow skulls. "An old man taking his house to Paradise Falls. . . That's the best one yet. I can't wait to hear how it ends (Docter 2009). Dietmar Meinel observes that in "uncompromisingly pursuing his dream of scientific glory," Muntz "has lost all the qualities of the adventurer-hero and [becomes] instead . . . a remorseless murderer in the isolation of Paradise Falls" (2014, 75). Muntz's isolation, combined with old age and bitterness, make for a dangerous, destabilizing formula. By forgoing Muntz's adventurous ethos, which Carl and Ellie valued in childhood, Carl lets go of the negative qualities associated with exploration and the traditionally male hegemonic imperialist attitudes that Muntz embodies.

Figure 9.2. *Charles Muntz surveying his map of Paradise Falls, consumed by obsession (Docter 2009).*

While *WALL-E* depicts a dystopia sustained by machines, *Up* presents one maintained by animals: a canine panopticon. Part of the comedy of *Up* involves a subversion and parody of the traditional dog-master relationship habituated by love, devotion, and affection, where dogs inhabit an intellectually inferior position to humans. Muntz has bred a number of dogs, including bulldogs, Labradors, and schnauzers, to obey his commands, each equipped with an electronic collar that functions as a tracking device, radar, walkie-talkie, camera, and translator. Through the use of these surveillance collars attached to his roaming dogs, Muntz can monitor all of Paradise Falls. The collars also enable the dogs to communicate with Muntz through a device that translates their barks into human speech.

The dogs live by a hierarchy in which their names, Alpha, Beta, Gamma, and Epsilon, indicate their social positions. Dug, an enthusiastic, plump Labrador, whose name is as relaxed and as informal as he is, falls at the bottom of the chain of command, where he gets abused and mocked for his lack of aggression. Dietmar Meinel observes that the system of power that Muntz establishes among his crew "indicates the malevolent nature of his enterprise and his character" (2016, 156). His skill at manipulating surveillance technology toward charting and overseeing Paradise Falls in the pursuit of his goal, all the while subjugating the animals he claims to protect, places him into the category of the megalomaniac villain that appears in various Pixar films, from *Monsters, Inc.* to *Toy Story 3*. Michel Foucault explains that through "hierarchized, continuous and functional surveillance . . . disciplinary power becomes an integrated system" ([1975]1995, 176). This type of "surveillance rests on individuals, its functioning is that of a network of relations from top to bottom" (Foucault ([1975]1995, 176). In creating his surveillance network, Muntz brainwashes all of the dogs except Dug, which is ironic because though Dug appears the "weakest," he becomes the first to resist the groupthink mentality that subjugates the other dogs. Like EVE in *WALL-E*, the nonhuman character with the capacity for moral reasoning can resist the dehumanizing conditioning of totalitarian technology.

In *WALL-E*, EVE and Captain McCrea learn to use the tools of surveillance against those in power. Similarly, the protagonists in *Up* escape from Muntz by tampering with the dogs' programmed behavior and psychology. While attempting to rescue Kevin, who is trapped in a cage inside Muntz's airship, Carl sees Dug mindlessly gnawing on the tennis ball on his walker and realizes he can trick Muntz's dogs. Poised on Kevin's cage, Carl teases the dogs, "Who wants the ball" (Docter

2009)? The dogs readily succumb to this deception, proving that their programming can be easily rewired. In another scene, Dug dethrones Alpha by throwing a radar shade on him, convincing the other dogs that Alpha "wears the cone of shame" and that Dug is their new anointed leader (Docter 2009). Similarly, Russell outsmarts the menacing dog pilots flying World War I-era fighter planes (an homage to Hayao Miyazaki's animal pilots and a visual pun that emphasizes the aerial nature of the word "dog fight") by yelling "squirrel!" so they will crash (Docter 2009). Like WALL-E's interactions with the robots and humans aboard the *Axiom*, Carl, Russell, and Dug resist Muntz's authority by using his technology against him in subversive and funny ways.

Carl's decision to save Kevin from Muntz, thereby endangering his and Russell's lives, is pivotal in that it helps Carl realize that the allure of Muntz's explorer/adventurer heroism is a myth that rests on the ruthless exploitation of the environment. In resisting Muntz, Carl and Russell save Kevin and her chicks from extinction, thereby strengthening a fragile ecosystem. *Up*, like *WALL-E,* also ends with a restored environmental landscape. WALL-E and EVE return the last surviving photosynthetic plant to Earth, making the planet habitable for humans, while Carl and Russell allow Kevin's family to prosper peacefully in the jungle without being hunted. The ecological story in each film is framed across a broad ethical register designed to appeal to world audiences. This is particularly resonant in parts of both films in which the storytelling depends largely on nonverbal communication through music and imagery. The environmental messages are connected to critiques of the abuses of surveillance and technology at the expense of individual liberties.

While *WALL-E* is a love story, *Up* focuses on coping with grief and learning to let go of anger. As Carl attempts to save Russell and Kevin from Muntz, he realizes he cannot be consumed by obsession like his former boyhood hero. When Carl and Muntz fight, despite creaking bones and bracing back pain, their battle in the airship's gallery of decaying fossils and dinosaur bones represents a fight between Carl and his *doppelgänger*. The film shows us Carl's instances of anger: he hits a builder with his cane, fantasizes about dropping the stowaway Russell to his death, yells at Russell and Dug, and is even comfortable with abandoning them, briefly, to fulfill his obsession of carrying his house to

Paradise Falls. Muntz represents what Carl might become if he remains consumed by his grief, anger, and selfish desires. Perhaps with the exception of *Coco* (2017) and the short film *Us Again* (2021), *Up* is one of the few Disney/Pixar films that deals honestly with the realities and perils of aging. Carl learns to overcome his grief by accepting the losses associated with growing old. He realizes he can no longer be a recluse like Muntz because the isolation will only exacerbate his paranoia and egotism. By the end of the film, Carl chooses to voluntarily join a community to sustain others when he moves to Shady Oaks and mentors Russell.

WALL-E and *Up* are fascinating films within Pixar's canon in terms of their depictions of interpersonal relationships, as well as dystopias and the horrors of totalitarian control. The science fiction scholar Gary Wolfe notes that one of the genre's core narratives involves how individuals react against absolutism: how static environments become destabilized (2011, 61). Both films function as cautionary tales about the perils of uncontrolled technological power suited to a post-9/11 world. Funded by Disney and Apple, the epitome of corporate entertainment synergy, Pixar tends to make films primarily for young audiences. This leads one to the question of whether a children's film can adequately express corporate and governmental abuses. There is an underlying anxiety about how whatever is shown, no matter how unsettling, could somehow inevitably be reduced to entertainment for mass consumption. *WALL-E* and *Up* ask us to consider whether the framework of conventional corporate-funded media can provide relevant anti-capitalist, anti-totalitarian satire.

However, in their incorporation of science fiction tropes, *WALL-E* and *Up* demonstrate how the science fiction genre highlights the abuse of technology and the value of environmental stewardship to young audiences. Genres change in relation to the times. Our age has been characterized by the tensions that arise between advanced telecommunications, digital technology, surveillance, and the erosion of civil liberties. It is helpful to think about how both dystopian stories fit in and outside of the traditional Disney canon. They reflect a process of struggle against various types of oppression and authoritarianism as they imagine viable possibilities for the realization of utopian settings. In spite of the inherently greed-driven corporate ethos of its parent companies, Disney and Apple, Pixar creates highly original animated films by engaging with important science fiction themes, such as the relationship between humans and nonhumans, age and death, and the dangerous limits of technology. They provide insightful commentary on how the omnipresent camera symbolizes the limits of our struggle for survival and freedom.

REFERENCES

Adams. Michael C. 1990. *Male Desire and the Coming of World War I*. Bloomington and Indianapolis: Indiana University Press.
Annis, Matt. 2018. *Cyber Wars*. New York: Cavendish Publishing.
de Certeau, Michel. 1984. *The Practice of Everyday Life*. Berkeley: University of California Press.
Denby, David. 2009. "The Wanderers." *The New Yorker*. Vol. 85, 8, June 2009.
Docter, Pete, dir. *Up*. 2009; Emeryville, CA: Pixar Animation Studios. Disney Plus.com.
Docter, Pete, and Bob Peterson. 2009. *The Up Screenplay*. Pixar Animation Studios.
Flaig, Paul. 2016. "Slapstick After Fordism: *WALL-E*, Automatism and Pixar's Fun Factory." *Animation* 11, no. 1: 59–74.
Foucault, Michel. (1975) 1995. *Discipline and Punish: The Birth of the Prison*. Reprint. Trans. A. Sheridan. New York: Vintage.
Herhuth, Eric. 2014. "Life, Love, and Programming: The Culture and Politics of *WALL-E* and Pixar Computer Animation." *Cinema Journal* 53, no. 4: 53–75.
Landy, Marcia. 2006. "The Cinematographic Brain in *2001: A Space Odyssey*." *Stanley Kubrick's 2001: A Space Odyssey: New Essays*. Ed. Robert Kolker. Oxford: Oxford University Press, 87–104.
Lee, Newton. 2015. *Counterterrorism and Cybersecurity: Total Information Awareness*. New York and London: Springer.
Meinel, Dietmar. 2014. "Empire Is Out There?!: The Spirit of Imperialism in the Pixar Animated Film *Up*." *European Journal of Media Studies* 3, no. 1: 69–87.
———. 2016. *Pixar's America: The Re-Animation of American Myths and Symbols*. New York and London: Palgrave.
Neupert, Richard. 2016. *John Lasseter*. Champaign, IL: University of Illinois Press.

Paik, Karen. 2015. *To Infinity and Beyond!: The Story of Pixar Animation Studios*. San Francisco: Chronicle Books.

Richardson, Janice. 2015. *Law and the Philosophy of Privacy*. New York and London: Routledge.

Rösing, Lilian Munk. 2015. *Pixar with Lacan: The Hysteric's Guide to Animation*. London: Bloomsbury.

Shorrock, Tim. 2008. *Spies for Hire: The Secret World of Intelligence Outsourcing*. New York: Simon & Schuster.

Spinrad, Norman. 1990. *Science Fiction in the Real World*. Carbondale and Edwardsville, IL: Southern Illinois University Press.

Stanton, Andrew, dir. *WALL-E*. 2008; Emeryville, CA: Pixar Animation Studios. DisneyPlus.com.

Svilpis, Janis. 1983. "Authority, Autonomy, and Adventure in Juvenile Science Fiction." *Children's Literature Association Quarterly* 8, no. 3: 22–26.

Wolfe, Gary. 2011. *Evaporating Genres: Essays on Fantastic Literature*. Middletown, Wesleyan University Press.

10

PIXAR'S COCO

The Power of Celebrity and Its
Impact on the Adolescent Mind
Susan Ray

Disney Pixar's fantastical film *Coco* (2017) received immediate praise for its celebration of Mexican culture, its representation of women as family leaders, and its deliberate subversion of the macho stereotype of Latin romance. Surprisingly, film and academic critics alike have overlooked *Coco*'s insightful messages about the nature of celebrity and its impact on the psyches of young fans. Its protagonist, the music-loving Miguel, plays all the songs from late Ernesto De La Cruz's films, collects his memorabilia, and memorizes his interviews, finding solace in the movie star's body of work and the mythos surrounding him. When the adolescent Miguel discovers a torn photograph of his great-great-grandfather in which only hands holding a guitar remain visible, the boy recognizes the instrument as De La Cruz's and instantly believes the star to be his long-lost relative. Miguel's unwavering belief reflects recent psychological theories regarding celebrity attachment which state such devotion to a famous person is parasocial. That is, one uses the celebrity to fulfill a psychological need unmet by in-person relationships; in this case, Miguel feels detached from his family members who forbid music. As the film unfolds, it thoughtfully presents the ways fandom can positively fulfill a psychological need, particularly for adolescents, while simultaneously demonstrating how an all-consuming attachment to a celebrity can also have deleterious effects. Finally, by revealing the ways De La Cruz carefully crafts his media persona and that he murders Hector for his songbook, *Coco* reminds viewers of the deliberate, and often fictional, construction of the celebrity figure.

THE BENEFITS OF PARASOCIAL RELATIONSHIPS

An aspiring musician in a family that avoids music, twelve-year-old Miguel opens the film by narrating: "Sometimes I think I'm cursed, because of something that happened even before I was born." He explains how his great-grandmother Coco's father, a talented guitar player who abandoned his family for "a dream to play for the world," led Coco's mother, Imelda, to open a shoemaking business in order to support her daughter and to declare music the catalyst that tore her family apart (Unkrich 2017). While Coco is now elderly, infirm, and typically silent, her daughter (Miguel's grandmother, "Abuelita") aggressively enforces the late Imelda's edict that music be outlawed in the Rivera family; a montage shows her snatching a bottle from Miguel when he rhythmically blows across its opening, screaming at a passing car radio, and slamming her shutters against the melodies of passing musicians. As the rest of the family, including his parents, obediently follows Abuelita's lead, Miguel's passion for music causes him to feel isolated and aberrant. He states, "I know I'm not supposed to love music, but it's not my fault! It's his! Ernesto De La Cruz, the greatest musician of all time!" (Unkrich 2017). The film pans to a bronze statue of the late singer, which dominates the plaza where Miguel shines shoes. A tour guide introduces a crowd to the monument, explaining they stand on the spot where De La Cruz "took his first steps toward becoming the most beloved singer in Mexican history," thus demarcating Miguel's hometown as a site of pilgrimage (Unkrich 2017). Living in the rural community of Santa Cecilia, birthplace of the late film star, Miguel reaches into the past and through the silver screen to find a role model and kindred spirit.

We view a montage of a young De La Cruz playing in the plaza, then acting in films while Miguel excitedly narrates, "He started out a total nobody from Santa Cecilia, like me. But when he played music, he made people fall in love with him. He starred in movies! He had the coolest guitar! . . . And he wrote the best songs! But my all-time favorite is 'Remember Me.'" The film then introduces a middle-aged De La Cruz performing the song on stage, surrounded by dozens of female dancers twirling upon layers of illuminated platforms. Miguel explains, "He lived the kind of life you dream about until 1942, when he was crushed by a giant bell." (We witness a fawning stagehand so taken by the performance that he inadvertently leans against a lever to the rope holding the bell above the star, causing the singer's demise.) Miguel adds, "Sometimes I look at De La Cruz, and I feel like we're connected somehow. Like if he could play music, maybe someday I could too" (Unkrich 2017). These details confirm that De La Cruz is not only a celebrity, but a legend and an icon. It is understandable that Miguel, though living in our modern moment, identifies with a movie star from the Golden Age of Mexican Cinema (1930–1954). Sharing the same background, culture, and hometown, the star offers Miguel the musical point of connection his family denies him.

Miguel lacks a musical role model in his immediate social circle, and De La Cruz represents a reflection of the boy's idealized persona. Researchers Derrick, Gabriel, and Tippin remind us that the "difference between [the] ideal self and a person's actual self [is] an actual-ideal self-discrepancy. People who experience this discrepancy to a greater extent than most are more likely to experience dejection-related emotions" (2008, 260). When he's not playing, discussing, or listening to music, we see Miguel as a boy who feels disconnected from family members who expect him to share their passion for shoe making and hatred of music. Their work bores him; thus, the relative Miguel spends the most time with is the only one outside of the workshop: his silent and wheelchair bound great-grandmother, Coco. The lack of interaction Miguel has with his other family members contributes to his sense that he does not belong, and, thus, De La Cruz functions as a surrogate companion and parental figure. The aforementioned researchers explain that identifying with celebrities who fulfill this discrepancy can be a positive coping mechanism. Such parasocial relationships "can provide a safe route for people who have a difficult time with real interpersonal relationships . . . to view themselves more positively with very little risk of rejection" (2008, 263). Miguel's childhood attachment to De La Cruz fosters his musical ambitions and benefits his sense of self.

Sociologist Nick Stevenson considers this phenomenon in his examination of David Bowie fandom in the UK. Examining the parasocial relationships between the British rock star and his fans, Stevenson notes "such relationships may help fans or audiences to construct their own biographies" (2009, 81). As a Latino icon, De La Cruz presents Miguel with a role model from the same background who carved out a path Miguel wishes to follow. Furthermore, Miguel's position as a De La Cruz fan offers him "cultural citizenship" among the singer's throngs of Mexican fans, for "popular culture can be a significant place for the construction of civic identities" (Stevenson 2009, 81). Stevenson repeatedly points to "the power of media to provide the symbolic resources through which ordinary people live their lives" (2009, 82). The tour group standing alongside De La Cruz's statue in the beginning of the movie represents a nation of De La Cruz enthusiasts, a musical community which Miguel belongs to through his fandom.

We are privy to the extent of Miguel's attachment to De La Cruz through not only the music he plays, but the instrument he crafts and the items he collects. After watching Miguel finish the construction of a homemade guitar in the likeness of De La Cruz's famous white one, the audience follows the boy to his hidden alcove above his family's shop. Here, Miguel celebrates and cultivates his imagined connection to De La Cruz. Mirroring his family's ofrenda, where the Riveras place photos and offerings during the Dia De Los Muertos or Day of the Dead celebration, Miguel has created a makeshift shrine to his musical hero. He displays acquired banners, photographs, figurines, albums, newspaper clippings, advertisements, and various memorabilia, all reflecting moments from the star's long career. The items surrounded by lit candles create a religious atmosphere, marking the significance of the space for Miguel. For, as Marshall explains, "The fantasy of celebrity connection . . . provides a pathway out of the prison of the everyday and bestows on the fan a kind of devotional—even religious follower—identity that has both directed purpose and coherence" (2016, 458). Whereas Miguel feels out of place in the shop and among his family members, his shrine to De La Cruz solidifies his identity as a musician and aspiring entertainer. Adjacent to the makeshift shrine, Miguel plays a VHS tape labeled "Best of De La Cruz," and soon begins singing and playing along to its soundtrack, ultimately reciting monologues of De La Cruz's various characters. The singer's line "I have to sing! I have to play! The music is not just in me, it is me! When life is down, I play my guitar" cements Miguel's decision to compete in the annual music competition for the Dia De Los Muertos in the plaza, despite his family's objections (Unkrich 2017).

Figure 10.1. Miguel sits before his makeshift shrine to De La Cruz (Unkrich 2017).

While Miguel's attachment to the celebrity may appear excessive, psychologists tend to mark it as a normal aspect of adolescent growth. Gleason et al. theorize that such "parasocial processes might play a role in helping adolescents address the tasks of this developmental period, such as identity formation and the development of autonomy from parents" (2017, 1). Psychologist Zelda Gillian Knight walks readers through influential 1950s psychologist Erik Erikson's eight stages of psychosocial development. Erikson contends that during each stage, youths confront a specific conflict in which "there is a pair of opposing psychological tendencies, which need to be balanced" (2017, 1049). Miguel is in the throes of the fifth stage, known as Identity versus Role Confusion. Kristin Doran, MS, LPC, explained in a personal interview that this stage is marked by adolescents exploring their independence and developing a sense of self separate from their parents' identities. In his progression toward autonomy, Miguel is leaving behind his family's values in search of his own, and he uses De La Cruz as his compass. Therefore, Miguel's makeshift altar to De La Cruz marks a fundamental part of his psychosocial development as he navigates a psychological pathway from dependent child toward autonomous adult.

After leaving his secret enclave, Miguel's discovery of the torn photo (in which his faceless great-grandfather holds De La Cruz's famous guitar) cements his imagined connection to the star. But having separated themselves from popular culture by avoiding all music, his family is unmoved by the boy's joyful claim that Coco's long-lost father is a celebrated Mexican musician. His father replies, "We've never known anything about this man! But whoever he was, he still abandoned his family. This is no future for my son!" Abuelita adds, "That man's music was a curse! I will not allow it!" as she symbolically smashes her grandson's handmade guitar. A brokenhearted Miguel runs to the plaza, appealing to the statue: "Great-great-grandfather, what am I supposed to do?" Miguel feels answered by the statue's inscription of De La Cruz's famous idiom: "Seize your moment" (Unkrich 2017). Even in death, he offers Miguel comfort, for "parasocial relationship partners can counteract rejection from real [relationships]" as these connections "feel psychologically real and meaningful" (Derrick, Gabriel and Tippin 2008, 262). Furthermore, such an emotional connection with a celebrity for "intense-personal reasons is positively related to neurotic-coping" (Matlby et. al. 2004, 423). Instead of feeling entirely decimated by his family's rejection of his musical ambitions, Miguel's attachment to De La Cruz assuages his anxiety and feelings of isolation. The boy not only finds solace in his perceived link to De La Cruz, but imagines the late star offering him support and guidance. This parasocial relationship creates a faux support system which counteracts Miguel's loneliness, reifies his identity, and benefits his mental well-being.

THE SLIPPERY SLOPE OF CELEBRITY WORSHIP

Miguel's parasocial relationship with De La Cruz first tilts negatively when the boy breaks into his mausoleum. This negative link to a celebrity is often dubbed celebrity worship, a term that connotes a potentially harmful obsession, rather than a beneficial parasocial connection. When none of the musicians in the plaza will lend him an instrument for the competition, Miguel feels entitled to take De La Cruz's famous skull-headed guitar hung above his sarcophagus. Miguel breaks the stained glass to the mausoleum, covering the shattering sound beneath the boom of celebratory fireworks marking the Day of the Dead celebration. As he reaches for the guitar, he speaks to De La Cruz's portrait: "Señor De La Cruz, please don't be mad. I'm your great-great-grandson. I need to borrow this. Our family thinks music is a curse. None of them understand, but I know you would have" (Unkrich 2017). Miguel truly feels he knows De La Cruz, and his adoration has crystalized into an unwavering belief that they are not only connected, but related, and that Miguel can predict De La Cruz's potential thoughts and responses. As Miguel removes the guitar from the wall, he is cursed: the boy transforms into a shadowy phantom of the spirit world, neither living nor dead, which simultaneously marks his transition from positive to negative fandom.

Miguel's dilemma begins when he climbs Maltby's Celebrity Attitude Scale from level one celebrity worship—which is motivated by entertainment and social reasons—to level two, which is marked by a fixation, which is "neurotic, often triggering denial, as well as mental and behavioral disengagement" (Maltby et al. 2004, 423). Celebrity followers with a weak sense of self and who experience unusual levels of boredom are more prone to this level of attachment. Miguel's anxiety about his place in his family and the long afternoons he spends with little to no company make him especially vulnerable. Maltby's fellow researcher, Lynn McCutcheon, coined the term Celebrity Worship Syndrome, which refers to "a condition wherein, at its most severe, the object of our worship becomes the central figure of our life" (qtd. in Stever 2011, 1357). While the white guitar in the torn picture is a significant clue to uncovering the identity of Coco's long-lost father, Miguel's obsession with De La Cruz sparks an unchallenged certainty that the icon is his blood relative and would support him in his quest to become a famous musician. Gaba explains, as "[celebrity] obsession progresses into a true addiction, the individual will begin to believe there is a real relationship with the celebrity. This can lead to detailed fantasies that could potentially escalate into more dangerous behaviors" (2013). Miguel breaks laws by stealing and desecrating a tomb, compromising his future in pursuit of this perceived connection.

As noted previously, Miguel is at a crucial psychological stage of development (identity vs. confusion) and his attachment to De La Cruz no longer serves him positively in this struggle. At this age, youths often feel anxious about themselves and how they fit into their communities, which may lead to unpredictable and impulsive behaviors, but typically parents and family maintain a significant influence as adolescents formulate their own identities and value systems (Kristen Doran, pers. comm., 2020). Yet, Miguel's identification with De La Cruz becomes absolute as his rejection of his family grows. The film presents viewers with the implicit message that not only is healthy adolescent growth achieved through the combination of emerging individuality and family connection, but that all-consuming celebrity worship leads to anxiety, isolation, and even danger. When Miguel transforms into the shadowy figure, his psychological battle begins. He must seek his way back to the Land of the Living—back to reality—beneath his crushing desire to establish a connection with De La Cruz and the obsessive celebrity worship that has led him so astray.

Inside the graveyard, Miguel panics as the living pass through his transparent form and he can suddenly see and communicate with the dead. A local street dog, which he names Dante after De La Cruz's cinematic steed, leads him to his late family members. The extended Rivera family comforts him and leads him to the Land of the Dead, so Mama Imelda may help him break the curse. We see Imelda arguing with an administrator in the "Afterlife Offices," ultimately realizing she cannot pass through to the Land of the Living because she is in the torn picture Miguel removed from the ofrenda. The clerk informs the family that the curse on Miguel occurred because on the night people are to "give to the dead, [Miguel] stole from the dead," and that only a family member's blessing can restore him. Miguel performatively agrees to Imelda's conditional blessing—that he "go home, [to] put my photo back on the ofrenda, and never play music again"—only to immediately steal De La Cruz's guitar once more, and thus reactivate the curse and reappear before his late disappointed family members in the Land of the Dead (Unkrich 2017).

Dante's aid, his extended family's concern, and Imelda's edict ring meaningless against the echoing desire to play his hero's white guitar in the Dia De Los Muertos Competition. Though Miguel is irrevocably fading from body to skeleton, one finger already transformed, he places his attachment to De La Cruz above his own well-being and his reunion with his family in the real world. Sociologist Paul Hollander explains that the dark side of celebrity worship descends when "focus on a celebrity [replaces] the focus that should be on [ourselves]" and those closest to us, and that this is the tipping point that leads to imbalance in one's life (2010, 388). Gratitude, honesty, family, and even self-preservation rank beneath Miguel's desire to symbolically become De La Cruz by playing the celebrity's instrument in the town square that launched his hero's stardom. After this plan is stifled, Miguel hides from his concerned, dead family members in a final act of rejection, gambling with his life by deciding to find De La Cruz and secure the icon's blessing in order to return home.

During Miguel's journey, we meet the celebrity's character foil, Hector. The gangly spirit is not allowed to exit the City of the Dead as a scan reveals no one has placed his photo on an ofrenda in the real world. Hector is desperate, for if he is entirely forgotten in the Land of the Living, he will fade from existence in the afterworld. As Miguel makes his escape from concerned relatives, we witness a desperate Hector try to negotiate his way into the Land of the Living by promising an arresting official an introduction to De La Cruz (after noticing a poster of the star in the office). While Hector is not only Miguel's true great-great-grandfather, but also the composer of De La Cruz's famous songbook, he knows the clerk will not believe in his authorship. Donning tattered clothing, appearing impoverished and desperate, Hector's only option is to try to convince the authority figure that he has access to the icon. In such moments, the film forces the audience to question the value we place upon celebrity. Barry King examines the questionable practice of making "stars and celebrities exemplars . . . and placeholders occupying a preferential place on the societal scale of worthiness of prestige" (2016, 315). As I further discuss in the following section, De La Cruz's star power is founded upon his physical attractiveness, the deliberate media construction that blurs his identity with his film roles, and Hector's songbook. Still, his unknowing fans, both living and dead, value him above fellow citizens, friends, and even family members.

Upon meeting, Hector and Miguel soon strike up a mutually beneficial arrangement: Miguel will take Hector's photo to the Land of Living and Hector will shepherd Miguel to De La Cruz. After Hector sneaks Miguel into the rehearsal space where De La Cruz supposedly prepares for his upcoming concert, Miguel encounters Frida Kahlo. She fastidiously works on her live art performance, which will precede De La Cruz singing at the Sunrise Spectacular Concert at dawn. Despite being perhaps the most celebrated Mexican artist of all time, she immediately engages with the boy as an equal—explaining the purpose of spirit animals, introducing Dante as a guide of wandering spirits, asking Miguel's opinion on her work, and telling the boy, "You have the soul of an artist!" When Miguel asks about finding his idol, Kahlo bitterly remarks, "Ernesto doesn't do rehearsals! He's too busy hosting that fancy party at the top of his tower!" (Unkrich 2017). The first character to refer to the star by his first name, Kahlo humanizes De La Cruz, highlighting his vanity and egotism, but her critique falls upon deaf ears. In complete contrast to De La Cruz (an egomaniac who kills to achieve stardom), Kahlo's character represents artistic collaboration, humility, respect, and creativity, a healthier connection to a celebrity who honors the artist in Miguel, offering him the sense of cultural connection he seeks in De La Cruz. Yet, these lessons are lost upon Miguel as he is locked into his singular purpose of meeting De La Cruz, unable to imagine his idol as a flawed human being.

Miguel and Hector quickly learn that they can gain admittance to the party by winning the music competition in the Plaza De La Cruz. In *Understanding Celebrity*, Graeme Turner explains that "those who invest in celebrity tend to describe it as an innate or 'natural' quality which is possessed only by extraordinary individuals and 'discovered' by talent scouts" (2014, 4). Miguel believes De La Cruz attained stardom because he was a gifted singer and songwriter who could magically connect with his audiences. The competition supports this ideology that celebrity is achieved by the deserving, and a spot among the celebutante at the annual party must be earned. To gain an instrument for the contest, the pair visits Hector's friend Cheech, who agrees to give them his guitar if Hector performs his favorite song. While Miguel is somewhat surprised by Hector's musical talents, he cannot overlook the man's ordinariness: Hector is lanky, clumsy, and poor, and his photograph (which he begs Miguel to display on an ofrenda) shows him as an average looking man with kind eyes, a weak chin, and oversized ears. Hector is the opposite of Miguel's classically handsome, muscular and charismatic idol, and the boy cannot separate talent from the constructed Hollywood image of stardom.

When Cheech fades away before their eyes, as the Land of the Living forgets him, Miguel appreciates Hector's precarious situation. Despite realizing this fate awaits his new friend, Miguel continues to lie, saying De La Cruz is the only one who can send him home. Hector helps Miguel practice for the competition, coaxes him through his stage fright, and ultimately performs "Poco Loco" with him, seemingly securing their victory, but Miguel's appreciation of Hector is short-lived. Upon seeing his late family members enter the plaza, Miguel drags Hector off stage as the host shares "an emergency announcement. Please be on the lookout for a living boy. . . . Earlier tonight he ran away from his family. They just want to send him back to the Land of the Living." Backstage, Hector scolds him for lying to "live out some stupid musical fantasy" and begs for his assistance: "Look at me, I'm being forgotten. I don't even know if I'm going to last the night!" But Miguel remains steadfast, running off to seek his idol. When Dante nips the boy's pant leg, trying to lead him back to his family, he yells, "You're not a spirit guide! You're just a dumb dog! . . . Get out of here!" As Miguel escapes through the bars of a narrow metal gate, Mama Imelda starts to sing, desperate to connect with and ultimately save her great-great-grandson. Despite her pleas, Miguel yells, "Music is the only thing that makes me happy! You'll never understand!" (Unkrich 2017). Instead of trying to reason with her, Miguel again abandons the Riveras in his pursuit of his beloved celebrity. According to Reeves and his fellow researchers, such intense levels of celebrity worship "significantly correlated with lower levels of self-concept clarity and self-esteem" (2012, 675). Locked into his identity vs. conflict stage, Miguel desperately believes that meeting with and connecting with De La Cruz is the only solution to resolving his feelings of anxiety and uncertainty.

After finally sneaking into the party in De La Cruz's mansion, Miguel is overwhelmed by its magnitude and ornateness; designed in homage to the Golden Age of Hollywood, it features lengthy red carpets, art deco pillars, giant marble staircases, and palm trees dressed in twinkling lights. We witness how De La Cruz's celebrity power is as impactful in the Land of the Dead as it remains in the real world. Inside the mansion, a DJ plays music while De La Cruz's movies are projected on giant screens. Synchronized swimmers dive into a guitar shaped pool in the center of the floor. When Miguel stumbles into it and becomes submerged, De La Cruz performatively dives in to "rescue" the boy in front of his partygoers. Upon learning Miguel is his supposed great-great-grandson, De La Cruz places him upon his shoulders to the applause of his guests. The star introduces him to partygoers in his lavish study, on the polo fields of his vast estate, and in the grand hall filled with mountains of gifts which he explains are "from his amazing fans in the Land of the Living who leave more offerings than I know what to do with" (Unkrich 2017).

Figure 10.2. De La Cruz proudly displays the mountains of gifts he receives from the Land of the Living (Unkrich 2017).

Having finally come face to face with his hero and the bounty of his fame, Miguel begins to question if such status is worth the sacrifice of family. Where he expected a sense of resolution, Miguel is troubled by the value De La Cruz places upon wealth and fame, leaving the boy to feel even more lost in resolving his own identity vs. role confusion conflict. Filled with ambivalence, he turns to his idol and says, "I've been looking up to you my whole life—you're the guy who actually did it—did you ever regret it, choosing music over everything else? . . . your family?" Without hesitation, De La Cruz assures him, "We cannot belong to one family, the world is our family! Ooo! Look! The fireworks have begun! (Unkrich 2017). The celebration of his own celebrity outweighs all of De La Cruz's thoughts of family and home.

Miguel begins to question the decision to pursue a connection to De La Cruz and the singer's music over love of the Rivera family. At this key moment, Hector enters the great hall and reveals the truth—he not only performed with De La Cruz but wrote the songs for which De La Cruz is celebrated. "You're crazy!" Miguel counters, desperate to cling to his idealized version of the star. He insists, "De La Cruz wrote all his own songs!" When Miguel eventually accepts this truth and pieces together that De La Cruz poisoned Hector for the songbook, the star has his security guards remove and imprison his former partner. Sensing Miguel's growing suspicion, the singer shares, "My reputation is very important to me. . . . Success doesn't come for free, Miguel. You have to be willing to do whatever it takes to seize your moment. I know you understand," as he has his supposed great-great-grandson imprisoned alongside Hector (Unkrich 2017). The word "understand" here is meaningful: when Miguel stole the guitar, he was certain De La Cruz would "understand" his psychological crisis and bring him a sense of resolution. He repeatedly tells family members that they do not and cannot "understand" him. It becomes clear to Miguel that all the star understands is the value he places on celebrity, and that he will maintain it at all costs. Comprehending this, Miguel's illusions are broken, both about his hero and the idea that being like him will resolve his identity crisis.

The prisoners are tossed into a pit, where Hector explains his only desire is to return to the Land of the Living and see his daughter Coco one more time before being forgotten. He laments that he will never be reunited with her in the Land of the Dead to "give her the biggest hug," and reveals he wrote "Remember Me" for her when she was a young child. Miguel exclaims, "You should be the one the world remembers!" But Hector rejects Miguel's assertion that the purpose of writing music is linked to the goal of achieving mass celebrity. "I didn't write 'Remember Me' for the world, I wrote it for Coco" (Unkrich 2017). Hector, Miguel's true great-great-grandfather, briefly left his family in pursuit of musical fame, but then regretted his decision and attempted to return home before being murdered by De La Cruz. He presents Miguel with a new hybrid identity—one based both on a love of music and the love of family, without sacrificing one for the other.

Dante leads Mama Imelda's griffin-like spirit guide to rescue Miguel and Hector from the pit. Upon landing alongside the extended Rivera family, Imelda accuses her long-lost husband of being heartless in his abandonment of his family, and then putting the life of his great-great-grandson in danger. Miguel recounts how Hector attempted to return to his family, his murder at the hands of De La Cruz, and what he has learned from Hector: "[He died when] he was trying to get home. I didn't want to listen, but Hector was right. Nothing is more important than family. I am ready to accept your blessing and your conditions, but first . . . Hector should be on our ofrenda" (Unkrich 2017). Miguel accepts the role of family in the construction of his values and identity; he is even willing to sacrifice music in order to return to his parents and prevent Hector's ultimate demise. In her examination of the identity vs. role confusion stage, Knight explains psychologists' contention that handling it effectively leads to a stronger sense of personal identity (2017, 1049–1050). By choosing family and a moral value system over the relentless pursuit of celebrity, Miguel finds resolution as he moves toward ultimately discovering a balance between his identity as a musician and a Rivera.

The Riveras confront De La Cruz backstage at his Sunrise Spectacular concert. While they use a video camera to expose his murderous admissions to a stadium full of dead fans, they lose the photograph of Hector that Miguel must take back to the Land of the Living. Imelda and Hector grant the boy their blessing to go home, with no conditions, knowing Hector will soon fade to nothingness. Upon his return, Miguel grabs what is in fact Hector's guitar from the mausoleum, dashes home, and plays "Remember Me" for Coco in her room. The song triggers memories of her father and pulls her back through her dementia-like haze. Coco shares photographs (including the torn photo of Hector which Miguel ultimately restores to the ofrenda) and letters with the family that prove her father composed De La Cruz's songbook and his love for his family never faltered. The film ends with a scene of the following year: a sign on De La Cruz's tomb reads "Forget Me," and all of the dead Riveras (now including Coco and Hector) cross the bridge to join the Day of the Dead Celebration at the Riveras' home where Miguel, in a traditional Mariachi outfit, sings a song about family— "Our love for each other will live on forever in every beat of my proud corazon"—symbolizing the harmonious balance he has struck between family and music (Unkrich 2017). His relatives have accepted his talent and passion, just as he has accepted his heritage and sense of familial belonging. Miguel's social development crisis is successfully resolved— he no longer relies on an outside celebrity figure to support him in his construction of his own identity.

THE CONSTRUCTION OF THE CELEBRITY FIGURE

Coco holds important truths about the benefits and dangers of adolescent attachments to celebrities and reminds us that in the transition from childhood to adulthood, youths must navigate toward a sense of self rooted both in their connection to family and what defines them as individuals. A final truth the film offers to viewers is a glimpse into the mythos surrounding celebrity icons. *Coco* illustrates how these mythic figures are the result of deliberate conflations of their professional performances and crafted reflections of their personal lives, for as scholar Graeme Turner contends, "The star's work . . . has that inevitably self-referential potential as each successive performance contributes to the story of their career" (2014, 21).

The iconic De La Cruz's character is rooted in the Golden Age of Hollywood (1915–1960s) and the Golden Age of Mexican Cinema (1933–1960s) that sprung from it. Stars of this era projected seemingly unattainable images of beauty and opulent lifestyles. Turner argues the modern celebrity was created when film star Mary Pickford "signed a million-dollar contract in 1916." He adds that studios began their art of manipulating public opinion in 1910, when filmmaker Carl Laemmle planted a false news story that actress Florence Lawrence had been "killed in a trolley-car accident" so she could be mobbed by a relieved public when she appeared unharmed (Turner 2014, 12). Viewers often forget that the actors and musicians on screens reflect an image carefully crafted by writers, directors, makeup artists, lighting experts, and public relation agents. Schumaker notes we moved away from cultural or political heroes in favor of those on the screen as "all this formed part of a wider consciousness shift from character to personality, substance to image, and community to narcissism" (2003, 34).

Especially during the Golden Age of Hollywood, studios manipulated and covered up aspects of actors' private lives to maintain this lucrative melding between beloved celebrities and the string of popular characters they played. Actress Lorretta Young was 22 in 1935 when she became pregnant with the married Clark Gable's child; she protected both of their reputations and careers by hiding her pregnancy and then publicly adopting a baby girl who was in actuality her own child. In 1950, Rock Hudson, famous for his roles as a heterosexual leading man, was coaxed into marrying his agent's female secretary to quell rumors of his homosexuality and maintain his image. Joan Crawford famously posed in an apron while holding a mop in order to soften her reputation as being "brash, tough, [and] independent" and instead paint herself as a "devoted mother whose sex appeal and glamour did not prevent her from doing her own housework" (Coontz 1993, 28). Even in death, De La Cruz knows his reputation will shatter if the world (both living and dead) knows he not only stole Hector's songs but also murdered him. Miguel is horrified by his supposed great-great-grandfather's decision to imprison him. The star Miguel so idolized is not heroic or virtuous; his carefully crafted persona is built by studio magic and De La Cruz's own twisted machinations.

Throughout *Coco*, moments and characters effectively poke holes in this constructed version of De La Cruz. Hector inquires why Miguel wants to be a musician; the boy responds it is simply because his supposed relative, De La Cruz, was one, to which Hector adds, "Who spent his life performing like a monkey for complete strangers!" When Miguel insists De La Cruz was the "greatest musician of all time," Hector laughs and offers, "Maybe the greatest eyebrows of all time! But his music, eh, not so much" (Unkrich 2017). Though not yet knowing his former partner was his killer, Hector (and Frida Kahlo) slowly unveil De La Cruz's vanity, superficiality, and lack of true creative talent. Hector's songs launch a career which film studios refine, marketing De La Cruz as a blended action hero, romantic lead, singer, and composer, and this celebrated persona fools generations of Mexican fans until Miguel exposes him at the end of the film. Even De La Cruz is somewhat a victim of this celebrity machine, which brings psychologically vulnerable stars to "look into the mirror of public adoration and media applause and see the reflection of an untouchable human being" (Rojek 2012, 141). Throughout the film, his most devoted fans, and De La Cruz himself, are so enamored by his star power that his human fallacies seem inconsequential. De La Cruz ultimately reaches the level of delusion where he feels any action, even the murder of a child, is defendable in his effort to maintain his legacy as a Mexican film icon.

Ernesto De La Cruz's constructed persona originally benefits Miguel when he feels isolated and stigmatized as an adolescent in a family that forbids music. But this idealization turns into a dangerous level of psychological absorption with the icon that almost costs the boy not only his future, but his life. By crafting a film that introduces us to the power of celebrity, the pitfalls of celebrity worship, and the manipulation that often takes place in constructing the celebrity image, *Coco* sparks critical thinking in a generation of children who will soon reach for celebrity guides as they navigate their own psychological paths toward adulthood.

REFERENCES

Coontz, Stephanie. 1993. *The Way We Never Were: American Families and the Nostalgia Trap*. New York: Basic Books.

Derrick, Jaye L., Shira Gabriel, and Brooke Tippin. 2008. "Parasocial Relationships and Self-Discrepancies: Faux Relationships Have Benefits for Low Self-Esteem Individuals." *Personal Relationships* 15: 261–80.

Gaba, Sherry. 2013. Is Celebrity Worship an Actual Addiction?" *Everyday Health*, September 3. https://www.everydayhealth.com/columns/sherry-gaba-addiction-out-in-the-open/is-celebrity-worship-an-actual-addiction/.

Gleason, Tracy R., Sally A. Theran, and Emily M. Newberg. 2017. "Parasocial Interactions and Relationships in Early Adolescence." *Frontiers in Psychology* 8, no. 255: 1–11.

Hollander, Paul. 2010. "Why the Celebrity Cult?" *Society* 47, no. 5: 388–91. doi:10.1007/s12115-010-9348-9.

King, Barry. 2016. "Stardom, Celebrity, and the Moral Economy of Pretending." In *A Companion to Celebrity*, 315–32. West Sussex: Wiley Blackwell.

Knight, Zelda Gillian. 2017. "A Proposed Model of Psychodynamic Psychotherapy Linked to Erik Erikson's Eight Stages of Psychosocial Development." *Clinical Psychology & Psychotherapy* 24, no. 5: 1047–58. doi:10.1002/cpp.2066.

Maltby, John, Liza Day, Lynn E. McCutcheon, Rapheal Gillett, James Houran, and Diane Ashe. 2004. "Personality and Coping: A Context for Examining Celebrity Worship and Mental Health." *British Journal of Psychology* 95: 411–28.

Marshall, P. David. 2016. *A Companion to Celebrity*. West Sussex: Wiley Blackwell.

Reeves, Robert A., Gary A. Baker, and Chris S. Truluck. 2012. "Celebrity Worship, Materialism, Compulsive Buying, and the Empty Self." *Psychology & Marketing* 29, no. 9: 674–79. doi:10.1002/mar.20553.

Rojek, C. 2012. *Fame Attack: The Inflation of Celebrity and Its Consequences*. London: Bloomsbury.

Schumaker, John F. 2003. "Star Struck." *New Internationalist* 363 (December): 34–35.

Stever, Gayle. 2011. "Celebrity Worship: Critiquing a Construct." *Journal of Applied Social Psychology* 1341: 1356–70.

Stevenson, Nick. 2009. "Talking to Bowie Fans: Masculinity, Ambivalence, and Cultural Citizenship." *European Journal of Cultural Studies* 12, no. 1: 79–88.

Turner, Graeme. 2014. *Understanding Celebrity*. London: Sage.

Unkrich, Lee, dir. *Coco*. 2017; Hollywood, CA: Pixar.

INDEX

ability spectrum, 5–6, 139–40, 143, 145, 149–51
Abuelita (*Coco*), 194, 198
Academy Awards, 29
actual-ideal self-discrepancy, 195
Addison, 55–70, 71n6, 71n9
adventure, 44, 46, 94, 99–101, 103–5, 107, 185
  fiction, 177
  film, 175
  story, 175, 177–78, 185
The Adventures of Pinocchio, 121
agency:
  act freely, 4, 19, 75–76, 89, 90n8, 90n10, 99, 104, 182
  See also National Security Agency (NSA); National Supers Agency (NSA)
Agrabah, 35
Aladdin, 17, 25, 33, 35–36, 42–43
Alice, 93, 95, 98–103, 105–7, 109, 110n6

Alice in Wonderland, 4, 93, 95, 97–102, 105–9, 109n1
Am (*Lady and the Tramp*), 27, 33
American-Arab Anti-Discrimination Committee (ADC), 35
American Dream, 18, 95
American identity, 2, 9, 19, 53–56, 69, 97
  Asian American identity, 27–28, 30, 32–35, 37–38, 41–42, 46–47
Americanize, 18–19, 31
Andersen, Hans Christian, 75
Anderson, Benedict, 53–54
Anna, 75–79, 81–88, 89n1, 89n4, 89–90n6, 90n8, 90n10
anxiety, 140, 144–45, 147–48, 189, 198–200, 203
  adult anxiety about children, 94, 106
apartheid, 56
Apple, 177, 189–90
"Arabian Nights," 35

Arendelle, 75, 83–87, 90n8
Ariel, 55, 87, 110n6
Asian American Citizens for Justice (AACJ), 35
Asian American Political Alliance (AAPA), 32–33
assimilation, 29, 33, 37–38, 56–57, 62, 64, 69–70, 71n8–9
Atlantis: The Lost Empire, 178
Auden, W. H., 126
Audience Research Institute (ARI), 102–3
Austin, J. L., 118–19, 121, 128, 132
Auto, 177, 181–83, 185
autonomy, 144, 158, 161, 165, 168–70, 183, 197
The Avengers, 141, 152, 164–65
Axiom, 179–84, 188

Bagheera, 30–32
"The Ballad of Mulan," 36–39
Baloo, 30–32
Bambi, 87, 91n11, 133n6
"BAMM," 62, 68
Bane, 150
Barrie, J. M., 103
Barthes, Roland, 53
   See also "Myth Today"
Batman, 168
the Beast, 10–15, 17, 20–22, 22n3
The Beatles, 31
Beauty and the Beast (1991), 2–3, 9–18, 20–22, 23n4
Beauty and the Beast (2017), 22n2, 42
Beck, Ulrich, 158, 165–70
Belle, 12–14, 20–21, 22n3, 23n4, 110n6
Bentham, Jeremy, 64, 180
Biden, Joe, 22

Black-Asian cooperation, 28–31, 48
Black Panthers, 30
Black Student Union, 33
the Blue Fairy, 117, 124–27
Bob Parr, 145, 157, 164, 166, 168
   See also Mr. Incredible
Bomb Voyage, 149, 158, 162
Bombardment of Taku Forts by the Allied Fleets, 26
Bonetti, David, 131
Bowie, David, 196
The Boys, 164
Brave, 55
Brody, Michael, 122
Bruhm, Steven and Natasha Hurley, 123
Bucky, 57, 59–60, 63–64, 67–68, 70
Buddy Pine, 149, 158, 162
   See also IncrediBoy; Syndrome
A Bug's Life, 176
Burroughs, Edgar Rice, 58
Buy-N-Large, 177, 179–82

Cabot, Sebastian, 31
Captain America, 165, 168
Captain America: Civil War, 165
Captain Hook, 110nn10–11, 141, 150
Captain McCrea, 180, 182–83, 187
Captain Nemo, 185
Carl Fredricksen, 184–89
Carroll, Lewis, 93
Cars, 176
celebrity worship, 5, 198–206
Celebrity Worship Syndrome, 199
Chaplin, Charlie, 181
Charles F. Muntz, 184–89
Chase, Daveigh, 42
Cheech, 202–3
Cherry Grove, 126
Cheshire Cat, 101

INDEX

children's film genre, 94, 99, 108–9
Chin, Vincent, 34
Chinese Massacring Christians, 26
Chloe the goldfish, 124
Cinderella, 87, 109n1, 110n8, 110n10
Civil Rights Movement, 4, 29–32, 34, 48, 53, 55, 70n5
Classical Era (of Disney), 10
The Coachman (*Pinocchio*), 125–27
Coco, 5, 87, 189, 193–209
Coco, 194–95, 198–99, 205–6
Cold War, 140
Collodi, Carlo (Carlo Lorenzini), 116, 120–21, 124, 130–32
colonialism, 30, 64, 69
commercialism, 180
compensable loss, 159
consumption, 175–76, 179–81, 189
Cooper, James Fenimore, 58
Cornell, Julian, 94, 99, 101, 107–8
Cotter, Holland, 130
Cruise, Tom, 35

Daredevil, 140
Darwinism, 180
Dash Parr, 146–47
Day of the Dead. *See* Dia De Los Muertos
DC Comics, 139, 150
Debating Disney, 1
de Certeau, Michel, 181
deconstruction, 117–20, 125, 130, 132–33
  Kakutani's critique of, 120, 122, 125
Department of Homeland Security, 176
Derrida, Jacques, 115–16, 118–20, 123, 127, 130, 132–33
  "Signature Event Context," 123, 132–33

Descendants, 55
desegregation, 29, 57, 64
The Deuce, 115–16
The Deuce (HBO Series), 116
DeVito, Danny, 25
Dia De Los Muertos, 196–97, 199, 200, 206
disability, 5, 11–13, 16, 21, 139–53, 154n3
  See also ability spectrum; Persons with Disability (PWDs)
disability studies, 2
Disney+, 1–3, 6, 25, 28
The Disney Story Trust, 42–43
Diversity in Disney Films, 1
"Do You Want to Build a Snowman?," 79–82
docile bodies, 65, 70
Doctor Moreau, 185
Doctor Strange, 140–41
dogs (*Up*), 186–88
domesticity, 95, 97, 145
Donoghue v. Stevenson, 160
Dory, 143
Doyle, Arthur Conan, 178
Dr. Doom, 150
Dr. Facilier. *See* Shadow Man
Dug, 184–85, 187–88
Duke of Weselton, 75
Dumbo (1941), 87
Dumbo (2019), 25
duty of care, 159–60
duty to rescue, 160–61, 169, 171n1
dystopia, 169, 179–82, 184, 186–87, 189

ecofeminism, 2
Edna Mode, 148
eight stages of psychosocial development, 197, 199–200, 203, 206

Elastigirl, 143, 146–48, 157
  See also Helen Parr
Ellie Frederickson, 184–86
Elsa, 4, 55, 75–89, 89nn1–2, 89nn4–10
Emperor (*Mulan*), 39–40
Enchanted Objects, 20–21
environmental destruction (perils of), 5, 175, 178–79, 187–88
environmentalism, 5, 178–79, 188–90
Erikson, Erik, 197
  See also eight stages of psychosocial development
Ernesto De La Cruz, 193–209
The Erotic Adventures of Pinocchio: A Bedtime Story for Adults, 116, 120, 128–30, 133
  Allen, Corey, director, 116
  the Fairy Godmother, 128–29
  Gepetta, 116, 129
  Jo-Jo the Pimp, 128–29
  Mabel, 128
Errand into the Wilderness, 55–56, 58, 60–61, 64, 70n3
Esmeralda, 13, 16, 21
ethnocentrism, 26, 28, 33, 49
EuroAmerican, 3, 26–27, 29, 31–34, 37, 40, 45–49
EVE, 179, 182–84, 187–88
Evil Queen (*Snow White and the Seven Dwarfs*), 10, 17, 23n5
Exotic Conquest stereotype, 46

fairy tales, 18, 102, 104, 130
family values, 94, 96–98
fandom, 193, 196, 199
Fantasia, 102
fantasy, 34, 94, 109n1, 116, 196
  constraint of, 4, 93, 95, 101–2, 105–8

genre of, 175
imaginative worlds of, 4, 95, 99–100, 103, 105, 108, 122, 203
restrictive fantasy worlds, 4, 33, 38, 47–48, 95, 97, 99–104
Feast of Fools, 13, 15–16, 21
Federal Theatre Project, 121
femininity, 13, 95, 97–98, 102–6, 110n6
Figaro the cat, 124, 126
Finding Nemo, 139, 142–43, 153, 154n2
Fire Island, 123, 126, 132
Flaherty, Robert J., 43–44
floodgate effect, 159–61
Flower Drum Song, 29
"For the First Time in Forever," 81–82
"For the First Time in Forever (Reprise)," 83–84
42nd Street, 115
Foucault, Michel, 63–65, 180, 187
  Discipline and Punish, 63–65, 179–81, 186–87
  See also docile bodies; panopticon
Frank, Yasha, 121
Frollo, 13, 15–17, 21
From Mouse to Mermaid, 1
frontier, 54–55, 58, 64, 69–70
frontier myth, 55
Frozen, 2, 4, 55, 75–89, 89–90nn1–10
Frozen II, 1, 90n8
Frozen Fever, 89n4
Frozone, 145, 152
Fruzinska, Justyna, 14, 19, 55–56

Gabby Gabby, 177
Gallup, George, 102
Gaston, 13–15, 17, 20, 22nn2–3
Gee, Emma, 32

INDEX

gender, 1–2, 4, 6, 22n3, 36, 39, 61, 94–95, 97–99, 104–6, 109, 110n6, 110n8, 167
   gendered, 4, 46, 95, 97, 99, 102–3, 105–8
   gendering, 98
   gender studies, 106
genetics, 57, 59–61
genocide, 16–17
Genovese, Kitty, 161
Geppetto, 116–17, 122, 124–27, 131–32
Gideon the cat, 125–27
Gil, 143
Gilbert Huph (*The Incredibles*), 166
Giuliani, Mayor Rudy, 116
Golden Age of Hollywood, 203, 207
Golden Age of Marvel, 140
Golden Age of Mexican Cinema, 195, 207
Golden Globe Awards, 29
Good Samaritan, 160–61
Grand Duke, 110n8
Grand Pabbie, 76–78, 84–87, 90nn9–10
Green Book, 54
groupthink, 3, 10, 17–20, 187
"Gypsies." *See* Roma

HAL 9000, 181, 182
Hans, 75, 78, 79, 82, 84, 85–88, 89–90n6
Harris, Philip, 31
Hawai'i, 41, 46
   Hawai'ian, 42, 45
heart of Te Fiti, 43, 46
   See also Te Fiti
Hector, 194, 201–6, 208
Helen Parr, 146, 157
   See also Elastigirl

Hello, Dolly!, 182
The Help, 54
hero(ine), 10–11, 13–14, 17–22, 38, 41–43, 48–49, 55–56, 58, 60, 68–70, 94, 107, 140–41, 152, 163, 184–86, 188, 196, 200–201, 204–5, 207–8
heroism, 13, 33, 36, 40, 47, 90n8, 140–41, 161, 183–84, 188, 208
heteronormative, 4, 36, 123, 130
heteropatriarchal, 98, 106
hierarchy of ability, 148, 150, 153
hierarchy of difference, 151, 153
High School Musical, 53, 55, 57
Honest John, 125, 127
"Honor to Us All," 38
Hook, 110n9
horror, 10–11, 13–14, 17, 44
House Un-American Activities Committee (HUAC), 98
Hsiao, Rita, 37, 41
Hughes, Howard, 185–86
Hugo, Victor, 13, 21, 142
The Hulk, 140–41
The Hunchback of Notre Dame, 3, 9, 10–11, 13, 15–18, 20–22, 22n1, 142

Iago, 17
Ichioka, Yuji, 32
Identity versus Role Confusion, 197, 199, 204, 206
imagination, 13, 26–27, 38, 93, 99–103, 107, 128, 144
imagined communities, 53
Imelda Rivera, 194, 200, 203, 205–6
"In a World of My Own," 93
The Incredibles, 5, 139–41, 143–53, 154nn1–2, 157–70
Incredibles 2, 148, 154n3, 157, 177

IncrediBoy, 149, 158, 162
individualism, 3, 5, 9–11, 18–20
Inside Out, 3
insurance, 163–64, 166–67, 170
Insuricare, 164, 166
invisibility, 147–48
Iron Man, 140–41, 152
    See also Tony Stark
Isherwood, Christopher, 126
"It's a Small World," 45, 122–23

Jack-Jack Parr, 148–49, 154n3
Jackson, Michael, 62
Jafar, 17
January 6 Insurrection, 9–10, 22
Jasmine, 35, 110n6
Jim Crow, 39
Jiminy Cricket, 124–27
Jobs, Steve, 177
John Darling, 103, 105
Journey to the Center of the Earth, 178
The Joy Luck Club, 41
The Jungle Book (1910), 30–31
The Jungle Book (1967), 26, 28, 30–32

Kahlo, Frida, 201–2, 208
Kakamora, 44–45
Kakutani, Michiko, 120, 122, 125
    The Death of Truth, 120
Kevin, 184–85, 187–88
    See also Monster of Paradise Falls
KIKI Art Gallery, 130–31
"Kill the Beast," 14–15
King Agnarr, 4, 75–88, 89nn2–3, 90nn8–10
The King and I, 29
King Louie, 31, 39–40
Kipling, Rudyard, 30–31, 40

Kristeva, Julia, 58–59, 67
Kristoff, 79, 84, 86

Lacan, Jacques, 117, 122, 123
Lady and the Tramp (1955), 27–28, 33
Lampwick, 123, 125–28
Land of the Dead, 200, 203, 205
Land of the Living, 200–206
Lasseter, John, 176, 178
Latin American Student Organization, 33
Launchpad, 5
Law of the Father. *See* Lacan
Lefou, 13, 22n2
Lester (*Incredibles*), 145–46
"Let it Go," 83, 90n7
Lilo and Stitch, 33, 41–42
Lilo Pelekai, 41–42
Lindberg, Charles, 185
The Lion King, 17, 87, 141, 150
litigation, 157–67, 170
The Little Mermaid, 10, 55, 87
The Long Pause, 44
Lost Boys, 29, 103–5
The Lost World, 178
Lots-O'-Huggin' Bear, 177
"Love is an Open Door," 79, 89–90n6
Loving v. Virginia, 32
Lyotard, Jean-François, 130

The Magic Island, 55
Magneto, 165
Mair, Victor H., 36, 38
"Make a Man Out of You," 38
Maleficent, 141
Maltby's Celebrity Attitude Scale, 199
Marlin (*Finding Nemo*), 152

INDEX

Marshmallow (*Frozen*), 79
Marvel, 139–41, 143, 150, 152–53, 154n1
Mary Darling, 110n9
masculinity, 13–14, 22n3, 46, 133n6, 148, 168, 176–77, 185
Māui, 43, 45–47
Maurice, 12, 14, 23n4
Max Medici, 25
Mayerson, Keith, 117, 130–32
McCarran-Walter Act, 29
McCarthyism, 98
"melting pot," 37, 58
Melville, Herman, 58
Merida, 55
Meyer, Richard, 133n5
Michael Darling, 103, 105
middle-class, 36, 40, 42, 45–46, 96–97, 168
Miguel Rivera, 5, 87, 193–206, 208–9
miscegenation, 32, 48
  See also Loving v. Virginia
Moana (1926), 43–44
Moana (2016), 26, 33, 41–49
Moana, 43–49
mob mentality, 3, 9, 11, 15–16, 21, 23n4
model minority stereotype, 29–30, 32, 35–41, 48
modernity, 165, 168, 170
  first modernity, 165–66, 168
  second modernity, 158, 165–66, 168, 170
Monster of Paradise Falls, 184
  See also Kevin
Monsters, Inc., 3, 177, 187
Monstro the Whale, 127
motherhood, 97, 102–5, 107
Motunui, 43–44, 47

The Mouse that Roared, 2
Mowgli, 30–32, 40
Mr. Darling, 103–5
Mr. Incredible, 140, 143–46, 148–52, 157–65, 167–69
  See also Bob Parr
Mr. Waternoose, 177
Mufasa, 17
Mulan (1998), 26, 33, 35–41,43, 45, 47–49
Mulan, 36–41, 47, 110n6
Murphy, Eddie, 40
Murray, Mary Alice, 121
Mushu, 40–41, 45
myth, 4, 19, 34, 53–54, 56, 60, 69
  of American identity, 2, 19, 53, 58, 69
  assimilation myth, 37
  frontier myth, 55
  "Myth Today," 53
  See also Barthes, Roland

National Security Agency (NSA), 176
National Supers Agency (NSA), 157, 162–63, 169
Natty Bumppo, 58
negligence, 159–62
neighbor principle, 160
Nemo, 142–43, 152
Neverland, 102–6, 110n9
Newton, Esther, 126
New York World's Fair, 122, 133
Nietzsche, 61, 69
Norden, Martin F., 11, 13, 142
normate, 20, 139, 143–46, 149, 152–53
Northern Lion Dance, 39–40
Northern Wei Dynasty, 36–37, 39

Oceania, 42–48
Oceanic Story Trust (OST), 42–43, 46, 48
ofrenda, 196, 200–2, 206
Ohmer, Susan, 110nn10–11
Olaf, 84
Olaf's Frozen Adventure, 89n4
Oliver Sansweet, 158–59, 161–62
Omnidroid, 147, 149, 151–52, 166
Orientalism, 26–28
  See also Said, Edward
Orwell, George, 179
other, 17, 21–22, 55–56, 69, 107, 144
othering, 3, 6, 11–17, 20, 21
otherness, 27, 37, 57, 66–67
"Our Year," 68

Pacific Asian, 26, 41–48
panopticon, 63–65, 179–81, 186
  See also Foucault; *Discipline and Punish*
Paradise Falls, 179, 184, 186–87, 189
parasocial relationship, 193–98
Payne Fund Studies (PFS), 96, 109n3
Pelosi, Nancy, 9
Pence, Mike, 9, 22
Persons with Disability (PWDs), 11, 13, 15, 17, 21–22
Peter Pan, 4, 29, 93, 94–95, 97–98, 102–8, 109n1, 110nn9–11, 141
Peter Pan, 103–5, 110n9, 110n11
The Phantom Menace, 178
Phoebus, 17, 21
Pinocchio (Disney film), 4, 115, 117, 120–21, 123–24, 126, 130, 133n1, 133n4
Pinocchio (Disney), 4, 116–17, 121–22, 124–27, 131–32, 133n6

Pinocchio Goes Postmodern: Perils of a Puppet in the United States, 121–22
Pinocchio the Big Fag, 117, 120, 130–33
  Hegemony Cricket, 131–32
  Lamp-Wick, 131–33
  Pinocchio, 130–33
Pleasure Island, 117, 122, 125–27, 133n6
post-9/11, 176–77, 189
post-WWII, 27, 29, 46, 95–98, 109n2, 109n4
The Princess and the Frog, 10, 42
"Problems in American History," 54
prosthesis, 148
prosthetics, 5, 140, 149–53
The Psychoses. See Lacan
Pushing Hands, 41

Quasimodo (Quasi), 10–11, 13, 15–17, 20–22, 142
Queen Iduna, 4, 75–76, 78–81, 83–89, 89nn2–3, 90nn8–10
Queen of Hearts, 101, 109

Rand, Ayn, 168–69
Raya and The Last Dragon, 49
"Raya Southeast Asia Story Trust," 49
Relyea, Lane, 131
"Remember Me," 195, 205–6
Renaissance Era (of Disney), 10, 35, 48, 110n6
Return to Never Land, 110n9
Revivalist Era (of Disney), 10
Rhodey. See War Machine
Rick Dicker, 157, 163, 167
risk, 5, 157–58, 165–66, 170
  individuation of risk, 170

risk analysis, 168
risk of liability, 161
risk of litigation, 157, 161
risk management, 164–67, 169
risk society, 158, 165–67
Roma, 13, 16, 22n1
Roth, Matt, 125
Rothschild, Sarah, 106, 110n7
Russell, 184–85, 188–89

Said, Edward, 26–28, 56
   See also Orientalism
"savage," 44–45, 56, 58, 65–66, 69
Scar, 17, 141–42, 150
science fiction (SF), 5, 175, 177–82, 185, 189–90
Screenslaver (Evelyn Deavor), 177
Seabrook, 4, 53, 55–70, 70n5
Seabrook, William, 55
second modernity. *See* modernity
segregation, 4, 6, 21, 64
self-concept clarity, 203
Shadow Man, 10
Shady Oaks Retirement Home, 185, 189
Shanyu, 39–40
Shere Khan, 30–31
Si (*Lady and the Tramp*), 27, 33
Silver Age of Disney, 28–29, 48
Silver Age of Marvel, 140–41, 143, 145, 153
Simba, 17, 91n11
The Simpsons, 181
Sleeping Beauty, 141
Snowden, Edward, 176–77
Snow White, 116
Snow White and the Seven Dwarfs, 10, 17–18, 23n5, 87, 178
social development crisis, 206

Spider-Man, 145
Star Wars, 178
Stitch, 41–42
"Stop the Steal," 9
superhero, 5, 139–41, 143–45, 147, 149, 152–53, 157, 159, 161, 163–70
Superhero Relocation Program, 157, 163
surveillance, 5–6, 61, 63, 65, 175–83, 185, 187–89
Syndrome, 140, 147, 149–53, 158, 166, 169

Tala, 43
Tarzan, 58
Taylor, Frederick Winslow, 181
Te Fiti, 43
   See also heart of Te Fiti
"That's What Friends Are For," 31
Third World Liberation Front (twLF), 33
Thor, 140
"Thriller," 62
Tiger Lily, 110n10
Tinker Bell, 110n10
Titan: A.E., 178
Tony Stark, 141, 152, 165
   See also Iron Man
tort, 157, 159–62, 169–70
Toy Story, 176
Toy Story 3, 177, 187
Toy Story 4, 177
transhumanism, 152
trauma, 4, 84
Treasure Planet, 178
Trump, Donald, 9
Turner, Frederick Jackson, 54–55
2001: A Space Odyssey, 178, 181

Up, 5, 175–76, 178–79, 184–90
Ursula, 10
Us Again, 189
Valley of the Living Rock, 76–77
Verne, Jules, 177–78, 185
villain, 10, 13–15 17, 21–22, 34–35, 88, 94, 107, 125, 139, 141, 149, 151, 154n3, 158, 178, 185, 187
  supervillain, 140, 151
  villainous, 28, 87, 150
  villainy, 12, 27, 150–52
Violet Parr, 139–40, 147–49, 153
voluntaristic, 19–20
vultures: Buzzie, Flaps, Ziggy, Dizzy (*Jungle Book*), 31

WALL-E, 5, 175–84, 186–89
WALL-E, 179, 181–84, 188
War Machine, 141, 152
Warfield, Chris, 116–17
Warhol, Andy, 123, 133n5
Wasko, Janet, 95, 107
Watchmen, 164
The Wedding Banquet, 41
Weinger, Scott, 35
Wells, H. G., 177, 179, 185
Wendy Darling, 94–95, 98–99, 102–7, 110n6, 110nn9–11
"What Makes the Red Man Red?," 110n10
"When You Wish Upon a Star," 124
"Where You Are," 47
"White Man's Burden," 30, 40
White Rabbit, 99–100
Winthrop, John, 58, 70n4

Wojcik-Andrews, Ian, 96
World Values Survey and the International Social Survey Programme (ISSP), 19
Wunderlich, Richard and Thomas J. Morrissey, 121–22

Xianbei, 36–38
X-Men, 164
X-Men: First Class, 165

yellowface, 36
Yellow Peril, 26, 29, 39
Yellow Power, 4, 26, 30–31, 33–35, 48
"Your Mother and Mine," 104

z-band, 57, 60–61, 63–69
Zed, 55–58, 60–67, 69, 71nn7–9
Zombie Patrol, 57, 62–64, 66
Zombies, 2, 4, 53–70, 70n2, 70–71nn5–9
  Addison, 55–70, 71n6, 71n9
  Bree, 71n6
  Bucky, 57, 59–60, 63–64, 67–68, 70
  Dale, 57, 63
  Eliza, 62, 69, 71nn7–8
  Gonzo, 62–63, 71n8
  Missy, 57, 63
  Principal Lee, 62–64, 66, 70
  Zed, 55–58, 60–67, 69, 71nn7–9
  Zevon, 57
  Zoey, 57, 60
Zombietown, 56, 59, 62, 64, 67–68

ABOUT THE EDITORS

Kellie Deys is an associate professor of English at Nichols College where she chairs the English Department and the Honors program. She received her doctorate in English from Binghamton University. Kellie has published on Margaret Atwood's *The Handmaid's Tale* (in *The Margaret Atwood Studies Journal*), Amazon's *Forever* (in *Gen X at Middle Age in Popular Culture*), and practical applications of Freire's problem-posing method (in *The Journal on Excellence in College Teaching*).

Denise F. Parrillo is an associate professor of English at the Community College of Rhode Island. Her areas of interest include women's and working-class literature/studies and critical theory. Previously, her focus on ecocriticism and ecofeminism led her to work as a campaign organizer for a national nonprofit environmental organization where she helped develop grassroots and grasstops solutions to address climate change and diesel pollution.

ABOUT THE CONTRIBUTORS

Denise A. Ayo received her PhD in English from the University of Notre Dame in 2013 and has since worked in student advising, program management, and curriculum development. In 2019, she began pursuing an MSEd in clinical mental health counseling. She has taught and published on literary modernism, gender issues, and popular culture. More recently, she has turned her attention to the intersection of Disney films and mental health as a way to bring together her training as a cultural critic and interest in the practice of psychotherapy. Her most important pursuit, however, is raising her young daughter.

Aaron Clayton is a professor of English at Frederick Community College. He authored the forthcoming monograph *National Identity and the Zombie*.

Ethan Faust, a writer from Wellesley, MA, is a graduate of Davidson College and the University of Pennsylvania GSE. Ethan has worked as a middle school teacher and as a sports journalist. He has published on the representation of disability in *Toy Story*, and he now writes books for children.

Joseph V. Giunta is a PhD candidate at Rutgers University-Camden's Department of Childhood Studies who hails from Queens, New York. After earning his MA from the cinema studies program at NYU's Graduate School of Arts & Science, his academic interests took an interdisciplinary turn. Chiefly focusing on the children's film genre, he explores fantasy circumscription, childhood subjectivity, and pedagogical functions within popular culture characterizations of youth. Paired with the new sociology of childhood, he investigates ideologies of childhood and constructions of young people in multimedia narratives, specifically considering the oscillating representations of their moral agencies, unique peer cultures, and interactions with play. His research has appeared in online academic journals and paginated collections of scholarly works and has been presented at various academic conferences across North America. He plans on continuing his career in academia and ultimately teaching cinema, media, and childhood studies at the university level.

Farisa Khalid graduated with a PhD in English from George Washington University in May 2021. She has an MA in art history from New York University. She specializes in modern and contemporary British and global Anglophone literature, modern drama, film, and animation. Her work has appeared in *Animation, Journal of Popular Film and Television, The Journal of Popular Culture, Modern Fiction Studies, Journal of Modern Literature*, and *South Asian Review*.

Vincent A. Lankewish teaches humanities and AP English at the Professional Performing Arts High School in Manhattan. His articles have appeared in *Victorian Literature and Culture, Nineteenth-Century Studies, Religion and the Arts, Dickens Studies Annual, College Literature, Pedagogy*, and *English Journal*. He is completing a book manuscript entitled *Seeing through the Marriage Plot: Same-Sex Marriage, Queer Vision, and the Rise of Ophthalmology in Victorian Britain*.

Christopher Maiytt is a history instructor at Glen Oaks Community College and an EFL teacher for 学而思网校 (Xueersi). His research in propaganda film history and Asian American experience was presented at Lawrence University's Film and History conference (Madison, 2019). His most recent published research also includes a historiography of World War II propaganda, which explores early animated Disney films, among others.

Susan Ray is an associate professor of English at Delaware County Community College outside Philadelphia. She received her doctorate in English from Binghamton University, where she specialized in nineteenth-century British literature. Her work has been published in *Victorians: A Journal of Culture and Literature, George Eliot-George Henry Lewes Studies, Proposia: A Journal of Creative Writing*, and Gale Cengage's *Literary Criticism of Hard Boiled Detective Fiction*. She is currently writing a guidebook on William Makepeace Thackeray for undergraduate readers. In addition to nineteenth-century literature, she's involved in the fields of composition theory and pop culture studies.

Associate professor **Dr. Francine Rochford** works in the School of Law of La Trobe University, Australia. She gained her doctorate from the University of Melbourne, completing her dissertation on institutional liability in negligence, and prior to that completed a masters of law, focusing on the sociology of law. She has researched and written extensively on civil law matters, particularly in relation to the law of torts, and recently co-authored a textbook, *Contemporary Australian Tort Law* (2020). She publishes regularly in areas of law and literature and law and popular culture. She has contributed interdisciplinary papers to *The Palgrave Handbook of Incarceration in Popular Culture, The Language of Law and Food*, and the *Entertainment and Sports Law Journal*, as well as more traditional legal publications such as the highly regarded *Griffith Law Review*. Rochford also publishes extensively in relation to the law of education and water law and policy. She has been a visiting researcher at the Centre for Water Law, Policy and Science at the University of Dundee, Scotland; a visiting scholar at University of Limerick School of Law; and an international visiting environmental law scholar at Lewis and Clark Law School in Portland, Oregon.

www.ingramcontent.com/pod-product-compliance
Lightning Source LLC
Chambersburg PA
CBHW061712300426
44115CB00014B/2656